BETWEEN THE SWORD AND THE WALL

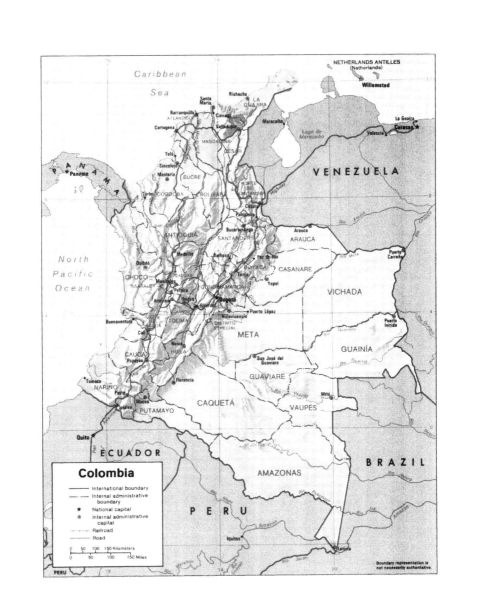

Colombia

International boundary
Internal administrative
boundary
★ National capital
⊛ Internal administrative
capital
Railroad
Road

0   50   100   150 Kilometers
0   50   100   150 Miles

Caribbean
Sea

NETHERLANDS ANTILLES
(Netherlands)
Willemstad

PANAMA
Panamá

North
Pacific
Ocean

VENEZUELA

Lago de
Maracaibo

La Guaira
Caracas ★
Valencia

Santa
Marta
Riohacha
LA
GUAJIRA
Barranquilla
ATLÁNTICO
Ciénaga
Cartagena
Valledupar
Maracaibo
MAGDALENA
CESAR
Tolú
Sincelejo
Montería
SUCRE
Turbo
CÓRDOBA
BOLÍVAR
NORTE
SANTANDER
Cúcuta
Pamplona
ANTIOQUIA
Bucaramanga
SANTANDER
Arauca
ARAUCA
Medellín
Barranca
Puerto Carreño
Quibdó
CHOCÓ
BOYACÁ
CASANARE
VICHADA
Manizales
RISARALDA
CALDAS
Pereira
Tunja
Yopal
Armenia
QUINDÍO
Ibagué
CUNDINAMARCA
Bogotá ★
Buenaventura
VALLE
TOLIMA
Girardot
Puerto López
DISTRITO
ESPECIAL
Cali
Villavicencio
Puerto
Inírida
CAUCA
Neiva
HUILA
META
Popayán
GUAINÍA
Tumaco
NARIÑO
Pasto
Florencia
San José del
Guaviare
GUAVIARE
Ipiales
Mocoa
PUTAMAYO
CAQUETÁ
VAUPÉS
Mitú
Quito
ECUADOR
AMAZONAS
BRAZIL
PERU
Iquitos
Leticia

Boundary representation is
not necessarily authoritative.

PERU

BETWEEN THE SWORD AND THE WALL

The Santos Peace Negotiations with the Revolutionary Armed Forces of Colombia

HARVEY F. KLINE

THE UNIVERSITY OF ALABAMA PRESS TUSCALOOSA

The University of Alabama Press
Tuscaloosa, Alabama 35487-0380
uapress.ua.edu

Typeface: Scala and Scala Sans

Cover image: Colombian president Juan Manuel Santos signing
the peace agreement with FARC leader Rodrigo Londoño Echeverri
(Timochenko), 2016; courtesy of the Government of Chile
Cover design: Todd Lape / Lape Designs

Cataloging-in-Publication data is available from the Library of Congress.
ISBN: 978-0-8173-5991-1
E-ISBN: 978-0-8173-9311-3

Dedicated to the memory of the thousands of Colombians who died during this war and in the hope that the millions who survived it will now live peacefully in their beautiful country

Before reaching the final line, however, he had already understood that he would never leave that room, for it was foreseen that the city of mirrors (or mirages) would be wiped out by the wind and exiled from the memory of men at the precise moment when Aureliano Babilonia would finish deciphering the parchments, and everything written on them was unrepeatable since time immemorial and forever more, because races condemned to one hundred years of solitude did not have a second opportunity on earth.

—Gabriel García Márquez, *One Hundred Years of Solitude*

Contents

Illustrations

Preface

I BECAME INTERESTED IN COLOMBIA in 1964 when I was an exchange student at the Universidad de Antioquia in Medellín. As the violence was ending between the Liberal and Conservative Parties, I wondered why, in such a beautiful country with so many nice people, Colombians were killing each other. As time would show, almost simultaneously with the end of the partisan conflict, new patterns of violence began appearing—first from Marxist guerrilla groups, followed quickly by government-sponsored "self-defense" or paramilitary groups, and later the illicit drug trade.

As a result, Colombia has given me more than enough to study for more than fifty years. I returned there in 1968 to write my doctoral thesis and since have made eighteen trips to Colombia, three times funded by the Fulbright-Hays Program, twice teaching at the Universidad de los Andes in Bogotá, and on five other occasions conducting research in the political science department of that university.

This book is the fifth that I have written on the attempts of Colombian presidents to end the endemic violence in their country. *State Building and Conflict Resolution in Colombia, 1986–1994* covers the presidencies of Virgilio Barco and César Gaviria. *Chronicle of a Failure Foretold: The Peace Process of Colombian President Andrés Pastrana* deals with the Andrés Pastrana administration. The third is *Showing Teeth to the Dragons: State-Building by Colombian President Álvaro Uribe Vélez, 2002–2006*. The fourth is *Fighting Monsters in the Abyss: The Second Administration of Colombian President Álvaro Uribe Vélez, 2006–2010*.

Acknowledgments

Although I am completely responsible for the contents of this book, I have many individuals to thank for their help in the project. Special thanks for this book go to Francisco Leal, Magdalena León, and Armando Borrero, friends since 1968 when Pacho and Armando were among my colleagues and coauthors at the Universidad de los Andes. These three friends helped me make contacts with many of the experts interviewed for this book. Another sincere thank-you goes to the Departamento de Ciencia Política at the Universidad de los Andes for the reasons already stated. The departmental director in 1968, Fernando Cepeda, has been a valuable contributor to all my research and more recently many other faculty members have been generous in their sharing of information and thoughts with me.

My special appreciation goes to Cynthia McClintock of George Washington University. She was a reviewer of the manuscript I sent to the University of Alabama Press and made many suggestions for improvement. This is a better book because of her suggestions.

I also thank hundreds of people who gave me time for interviews over the years, in many cases continuing to give information and viewpoints by email and Skype. I assure them, whether or not they agree with what I have written in this book, that I did consider their views seriously.

As in all my scholarship, I thank my wife, Dottie. I have explicitly thanked her in five books before this one and have dedicated two to her. She has always been the best critic of my manuscripts, as well as my excellent in-house copyeditor and translator. On numerous occasions, she has selflessly gone with me to Bogotá, including one time when our first child was born there and another for a year with all three of our children. She makes so many things possible by being with me.

Soli Deo Gloria.

Abbreviations

AUC	Autodefensas Unidas de Colombia (United Self-Defense Forces of Colombia)
BACRIM	Bandas Criminales (Criminal Bands)
CD	Centro Democrático (Democratic Center)
CGSB	Coordinadora Guerrillera Simón Bolívar (Simón Bolívar Guerrilla Coordinator)
DAS	Departamento Administrativo de Seguridad (Administrative Department of Security)
Ecomún	Economías del Común (Cooperative Solidarity Economies)
ELN	Ejército de Liberación Nacional (Army of National Liberation)
EPL	Ejército Popular de Liberación (People's Liberation Army)
FARC	Fuerza Alternativa Revolucionaria del Común (Common Alternative Revolutionary Force, 2017–)
FARC	Fuerzas Armadas Revolucionarias de Colombia (Revolutionary Armed Forces of Colombia, 1964–2017)
JEP	Jurisdicción Especial para la Paz (Special Jurisdiction for Peace)
MAS	Muerte a Secuestradores (Death to Kidnappers)
M-19	Movimiento 19 de Abril (19th of April Movement)
PTN	Puntos Transitorios de Normalización (Transitional Normalization Spots)
SAC	Sociedad de Agricultores de Colombia (Agricultural Association of Colombia)
ZVTN	Zonas Veredales Transitorias de Normalización (Transitional Local Normalization Zones)

BETWEEN THE SWORD AND THE WALL

Introduction

THE STORY THAT FOLLOWS ANALYZES in detail the peace negotiations between the Colombian government under President Juan Manuel Santos (2010–2018) and the Revolutionary Armed Forces of Colombia (Fuerzas Armadas Revolucionarias de Colombia, FARC), a Marxist guerrilla group whose insurgency began in 1964. The efforts of five previous presidents to negotiate peace with the FARC all failed. The Santos period marked the first successful set of negotiations between the government and the FARC. This feat was possible for two reasons. First, a new balance of power existed between the two sides at the start of the Santos administration, in large part because of the changes in the Colombian military made possible by the massive military aide program from the United States through Plan Colombia. Second, although conditions favorable to peace existed, success was not guaranteed. President Santos succeeded where others before him had failed because he established a set of able negotiators with a clear strategy.

At the same time, this is the story of President Santos's negotiations with his immediate predecessor, Álvaro Uribe Vélez, who firmly opposed the peace process. Personal differences between Santos and Uribe largely drove the conflict between these two figures. However, the two leaders also represented very different Colombian constituencies, political and social. Almost all Colombians wanted an end to the conflict, but some in the Uribe faction demanded an unmitigated military defeat of the insurgents. Other Uribe supporters favored a peace agreement, but only if it included the imprisonment of the FARC leadership. Other supporters of the peace agreement, realizing that government forces had not defeated the FARC militarily (and very likely never would), favored a compromise.

The FARC, the Santos administration, and the Uribe opposition never met face-to-face during these negotiations, yet President Santos strove to find a peace agreement acceptable to both the FARC and Uribe. He was, to use the Spanish metaphor *entre la espada y la pared*, between the sword and the wall.

While formal negotiations with the FARC ensued in Cuba, the Colombian government's discussions with its own citizens occurred in two contexts. Traditionally, Colombia's rule has been democratic in the sense of having an elective president and congress. While in many other Latin American countries the president governs with few checks from other branches of government, in Colombia the national legislature and judiciary do actually temper the power of the executive. However, the central government in Bogotá has been weak since it never has had the ability to enforce the laws in many parts of the country.

The demobilization of paramilitary forces under the first Uribe administration exemplifies this multiactor bargaining in a democratic context. To combat guerrilla insurgents during the presidency of Guillermo León Valencia (1962–1966), the government avidly supported the establishment of "self-defense groups." In the following years those groups grew in number and size, especially after the drug dealers started some of them. As they became independent from the government, increasingly they were called "paramilitary groups." After bargaining with both the paramilitary forces and Congress, President Uribe successfully disbanded those paramilitary groups through the establishment of the Law of Justice and Peace, which provided a framework for the demobilization of thirty thousand paramilitary troops.[1] Likewise, the Santos peace agreement also depended on equally complex diplomacy among the three principal forces: the FARC, the president, and Congress.

Upon leaving office on August 7, 2010, Uribe enjoyed an approval rating of over 70 percent. Unlike his predecessors, however, he remained active in politics. From when he first learned of the peace process in 2012 until it was completed in 2016, the former president used Twitter to openly and publicly communicate his differences with President Santos. The diverse Uribe constituency included the thousands who had suffered, from assassinations, kidnappings, and forced displacement, under the guerrilla violence as well as many who would benefit from a continuation of it. For Uribe and his constituency, the only acceptable solutions to the guerrilla violence required the complete defeat of the insurgents or a negotiated settlement that included their imprisonment.

Marxist insurgencies had erupted in many Latin American countries in the wake of the Cuban Revolution of 1959. Guerrilla warfare in Peru ended by military means and in Nicaragua, Guatemala, and El Salvador through diplomacy. In the latter three instances, the negotiations succeeded in part because financial support from the Soviet Union, largely funneled through Cuba, abruptly evaporated. But in Colombia the FARC conflict persisted when Soviet funding dried up because of the income derived from drug trafficking.

Many experts believe the conflict in Colombia would have ended far earlier if the insurgents had been deprived of this illicit source of revenue.[2]

At the start of the Uribe presidency, the Colombian government was incapable of enforcing the rule of law in large swaths of the nation. The diverse topography of the land, with three ranges of the Andes, portions of the Amazon rainforest, and the Orinoco grasslands, led Colombian historian Eduardo Pizarro to conclude that Colombia is the third most geographically challenged country in the world. As Pizarro reported, "According to the Index of Geographical Fragmentation constructed by the Center for International Development of Harvard University, Colombia was in third place of the 155 nations studied."[3] As I highlight in chapter 1, Colombia reached a low point in the 1980s when it led the world in homicides per capita. At that time, the nation consisted roughly of three parts: the Andean interior, largely controlled by the government; the southern part of the country, including the Amazon rainforest, under the de facto government of the FARC; and the remainder of the country, controlled by paramilitary groups.

All Colombian presidents since the emergence of the Marxist guerrilla groups made efforts to increase the ability of the government to enforce laws in the entire country. So too did national governments in Western Europe in the seventeenth and eighteenth centuries as they absorbed regions and city-states. In the introduction to *The Formation of National States in Western Europe*, Charles Tilly discusses the variables in the process when he reports what he and his contributors decided to compare: "The organization of armed forces, taxation, policing, the control of food supply, and the formation of technical personnel . . . activities which were difficult, costly, and often unwanted by large parts of the population. All were essential to the creation of strong states; all are therefore likely to tell us something important about the conditions under which strong or weak, centralized or decentralized, stable or unstable, states came into being."[4] Applicable to the Colombian case is Francis Fukuyama's observation that "the essence of stateness is, in other words, enforcement: the ultimate ability to send someone with a uniform and a gun to force people to comply with the state's laws."[5] Simply put, when Álvaro Uribe assumed the presidency, a large part of Colombia operated outside the law.

During the presidency of César Gaviria (1990–1994), the Colombian state grew stronger because of the end of the violence between the Medellín and Cali drug cartels, as well as some demobilization of paramilitary groups. During the presidency of Álvaro Uribe (2002–2010), additional progress took place when the national organization of paramilitary groups disbanded and some thirty thousand of its members demobilized.

[handwritten margin note right: Geography]

[handwritten note at bottom: Wasn't this process largely unsuccessful on the ground?]

Until Santos, no Colombian president had ever succeeded in negotiating with the FARC. Even the most ambitious effort, that of President Andrés Pastrana (1998–2002), failed to arrive at a "mutually hurting stalemate." I. William Zartman defines this as a situation in which "either by their own conviction or through the influence of others, leaders can perceive themselves to have reached a hurting stalemate, where violence takes too great a levy without bringing sufficient gain." The situation becomes "ripe," however, only if both sides reach this conclusion.[6] In other words, both sides concede that the costs of continued warfare exceed the benefits. Throughout this book and in chapter 8 in particular, I show how multiple factors transformed the Santos presidency into such a "ripe" moment, including the balance of military power, the perception of leaders on both sides, skillful negotiators on all sides, and support from international actors.

ORGANIZATION OF THE BOOK

This book considers the Colombian peace process, which is itself a long story that features many significant actors and spans seven years. I stress the importance of individual leaders, from all three sides of the negotiation debate, who made the decisions that influenced the course of the peace process, its end result, and its aftermath. While many participants were important, the ones listed in appendix 1 contributed the most. This is to stress that, while certain matters were "givens" in the Colombian case, all the results came from decisions made by human beings. Appendix 2 provides a chronological list of the major agreements.

The chapters of this book are organized in four parts. Part 1 provides the historical background of Colombia before 2010, analyzing the possibilities and constraints that Santos had to contend with in his quest for a peace accord with the FARC. There I first examine the context of Colombian politics before 2002, including the lack of an effective central government; a history of violence and the complications that came with the introduction of Marxist guerrilla groups, paramilitary squads, and drug cartels; and how the balance of power changed during the administration of President Álvaro Uribe.

Part 2 analyzes the peace process negotiations from their secret beginning in 2010 until their completion in 2016. Each chapter begins with the bargaining between the government and the FARC and ends with the bargaining between then president Santos and former president Uribe. That latter bargaining increased over time as the results of the largely secret negotiations in Havana, Cuba, became more widely known.

Part 3 of the book deals with the plebiscite of October 2016 in which the Colombian people rejected the Santos peace agreement and with the new final agreement that the government negotiated with the FARC. The part concludes with a comparison of the second final agreement with the first one.

In part 4, I present two sets of conclusions, one dealing with the agreement and the other with its implementation. I consider two major questions: First, why did Santos's negotiations with the FARC lead to an agreement when those of his predecessors all failed? Second, given evidence from the first two years after the approval of the agreement, will the peace agreement lead to changes in the country, in addition to the end of the counterinsurgency war?

The Colombian case includes lessons for negotiations in other countries, even though the situations in countries with internal conflict may not be exactly like that of Colombia. On the one hand, this book shows how individuals—in the Colombian government, the democratic opposition to the peace agreement, and members of the Marxist guerrilla group—made decisions that led to the signing of a peace agreement that ended one of the longest conflicts in Latin America. On the other, it also shows how opposition rights in a democracy might make peace agreements more difficult.

PART ONE

Historical Background of Colombia before 2010

WHEN JUAN MANUEL SANTOS BECAME president on August 7, 2010, Colombia was a country in which changes in the preceding eight years, during the presidency of Álvaro Uribe Vélez, had resulted to a certain degree in a new balance of power, thus altering the established patterns of political behavior that had persisted for more than two hundred years. The purpose of this first part is to analyze the possibilities and constraints that Santos encountered. The two chapters of this part analyze those two themes: the context of Colombian politics before 2002 and how the balance of power changed during the administration of President Álvaro Uribe. The result was the framework in which President Santos could consider negotiations with the Revolutionary Armed Forces of Colombia.

CHAPTER ONE

Political Patterns before 2002

The Context of Government Decision Making before the Administration of President Álvaro Uribe

THE PEACE PROCESS OF PRESIDENT Juan Manuel Santos with the Revolutionary Armed Forces of Colombia (Fuerzas Armadas Revolucionarias de Colombia, FARC) took place in different circumstances from that of previous governments. In this chapter I consider the decision-making constraints of presidents before 2002 in two ways: through the history of violence in the country and through the cases of earlier presidents who had unsuccessful negotiations with the FARC.

THE GENERAL CONTEXT

Colombia always had a central government with little ability to enforce its laws in much of the country. Three key patterns of political behavior in the first years of independent Colombia came from the weak state and produced an even weaker one.[1] Although no specific individuals can receive credit or be assigned blame, these are the patterns from which the weak state was conceived and persisted. In the absence of a central authority, the most powerful regional individuals and groups ruled. Large landowners were dominant at first but were later joined by emergent economic groups. Those who ruled often used violence to do so. This situation was the result of a weak legal system, the use of violence in partisan conflict, and domination by elites, who often governed together even though they urged their followers to fight each other.

The Legal System

Although there was a central government in Colombia after 1830, it never constructed a strong law enforcement presence in much of the country. The situation was in part the result of choices made by governing elites who feared that a strong military or police force might be a threat to civilian government, as had happened in other Latin American countries. Instead the decision was

[handwritten margin note: So the paramilitares were always tied to colonial capital]

[handwritten margin note: Private law enforcement became paramilitares]

made to allow private groups to take the place of official law enforcement. These privatized police forces began with the landowners of the nineteenth century and over time extended to include the paramilitary groups of the late 1960s through the late 1990s who were enlisted to assist the military in the fight against the guerrillas.

[handwritten margin note: feudalism]

Since the national government never attempted to construct a police force large enough to enforce its decisions, real power in such a geographically diverse nation rested with local and regional elites. In some cases, the departmental governments set up police forces to take care of egregious crimes. However, neither the national armed forces nor the national police were allowed to have much power. As former president Alfonso López Michelsen pointed out in 1991, private landowners in the nineteenth century made the rules for the areas of their landholdings, chose some of their employees to enforce them, and imprisoned workers who misbehaved. López argued that the leaders of the country had made a trade-off: unlike other Latin American countries, violence did not originate from the government but from the lack of government.[2]

It is probable that a strong national police force was not feasible in nineteenth-century Colombia because of the geographical barriers of the country. However, another reason for this decision included the fear, on the part of Colombian leaders, of the institutions of a strong state, especially the armed forces and the police. Many other Latin American countries had seen such institutions end elective governments. In addition, Colombian leaders, primarily from the upper economic groups, did not want to pay the taxes sufficient to create a strong military and national police force. They thought it better to let those who needed rule enforcement (the large landowners) to enforce it themselves. Not constructing a national police force left real power in local hands, instead of delegating it to some distant national government. Finally, it was counterintuitive for a regionally based power elite to construct a centralized constabulary.

The central government had even less ability to make and enforce laws during the federalist period of nineteenth-century Colombia (1853–1886). During this period, law enforcement rights and duties reverted to the states. The period with the most federalism came after the Rionegro Constitution of 1863, which took federalism to its extreme by giving the nine states all powers not expressly delegated to the central authorities. States had the right to establish their own postal systems and were free to establish the requirements for voting in national and local elections.

The Use of Violence in Politics

The second key pattern in the first years of independent Colombia had to do with the use of violence in politics, which often involved members of one po-

litical party killing the opposition in the name of party. Factions of the economic elite formed two political parties in the 1830s. The Liberal Party favored
free international trade, federalism, and a limited role for the Roman Catholic
Church in secular matters. The Conservative Party took the opposite position
on all three issues, favoring economic protectionism, a strong central government, and a role for the Church in secular matters such as education. The pattern of violence between the two parties began in 1838 and lasted until 1965.
The violence intensified when religion became a component of the partisan
conflict, even though nearly all Colombians were Catholic. The Conservative
Party adopted policies that the Roman Catholic Church wanted while the Liberal Party was anti-clerical. Beginning in the early cases of violence, the government initiated the practice of pardoning the instigators of the conflicts.
Thus the consequences of using violence were less serious for individuals.

As a result, political competition in Colombia was never limited to peaceful means. Eight civil wars took place during the nineteenth century, six of
which pitted all or part of one of the two parties against the other party. The
civil wars were in part about the different ideologies of the two parties, but
having power was also important. The civil wars came after national elections,
with the party that lost the election asserting corruption in the vote count and
beginning an armed rebellion. During these civil wars, the masses of poor
people in the countryside knew of the national political system and "participated" in national politics. This participation did not mean that the masses
had influence on the policies of the elites. Instead most of the mass participation was originally because of affiliations with large landowners, who instructed workers dependent on them when and against whom to fight. In
those civil wars, thousands of poor campesinos died.[3]

The tradition continued into the twentieth century, with a short period of
partisan violence in 1930 and a longer period from 1946 to 1965. As Fabio
Zambrano Pantoja interprets this historical trend, "The *real people*, that is to
say, the majority of the population, learned politics through the use of arms
before they did through the exercise of the suffrage. First one learned to fight
and later to vote. This caused the exercise of politics to be conceptualized as a
conflict before it was conceptualized as a place of concord, in this way apply-
ing the generalized idea that *war is the continuation of politics by other means*."[4]

The frequency and intensity of violence in the nineteenth century had effects that lasted at least until the 1960s. The numerous civil wars and the
widespread participation of the campesinos led to a strict and intense partisan socialization of the masses. Many campesino families had martyrs, family
members who had been killed, disabled, or raped by members of the other
political party. While the party identification of campesinos originally might
have come from their patrons or other local political leaders, at some point
these identifications developed lives of their own based on the past. Colom-

bian sociologist Eduardo Santa said that Colombians began to be born "with party identifications attached to their umbilical cords."[5]

In the twentieth century, the two largest outbreaks of partisan violence came when there was a change of political party in the presidency. The first was in 1930 when Liberal Alfonso López Pumarejo won. Under the Constitution of 1887, the president appointed all governors and the governors appointed all mayors. With the López Pumarejo victory, political power in the entire system changed, with Liberals replacing Conservatives as governors and mayors. Campesinos with ties to the Liberal Party took lands from those of the Conservative Party, knowing that the Liberal-dominated government would not punish them. The 1930 conflict was short-lived because of a brief international conflict with Peru over Leticia, a Colombian port on the Amazon River.

Partisan conflict between 1946 and 1965 marked the bloodiest period of Colombian history up to that point. At least two hundred thousand people died in this civil war between the Liberal and Conservative Parties. This period was so intense that, until it was superseded by a more violent period, Colombians referred to it as "La Violencia," even though the word in Spanish refers to any violence. Now many Colombians also refer to the period since the 1960s as "La Violencia."

At the time of the original La Violencia, Colombia was a changing country. During the early and mid-twentieth century, the population was growing rapidly and urbanizing. In the midst of growth and change, there were great inequities. Only 10 percent of children in primary school reached secondary school, over 70 percent did not make it to the third grade, and only 1 percent made it to university.[6]

The midcentury civil war showed the weakness of the Colombian state. Although political leaders measured the legitimacy of the state by the favorable results of its macroeconomic policies, Marco Palacios argues that "the Violencia is best seen as an expression of the chronic deficit of state authority, rather than as a manifestation of the state's collapse. In fact, the state during this period was powerful enough to facilitate an unprecedented accumulation of capital: the plutocracy served itself with a big spoon throughout the 1950s, even as the socioeconomic gap widened."[7] Michael J. LaRosa and Germán R. Mejía, stressing the importance of the maintenance of public order, emphasize the period in this way: "In a nation of regions, a nation that geographically defies unification, La Violencia was a phenomenon that clearly demonstrated the weakness of the Colombian state. The Colombian government, for all intents and purposes, was confined to the Plaza de Bolívar, the main square in Bogotá, and other main plazas at regional capital cities. People in the countryside had no incentive to obey arbitrary laws, radiating out from a distant capital and written by politicians who never understood rural life in Colombia."[8]

Because of this system of violence, other cleavages, such as social class and regionalism, remained secondary to Liberal and Conservative party identification. Third parties were notably unsuccessful until after a constitutional change in the early 1990s. Violence became the normal way to handle disagreements. A Colombian sociologist said in an interview, "We have no ways to channel conflicts. Probably because of the traditional, oligarchic set-up of the Liberal and Conservative Parties, we never developed peaceful ways to resolve conflict. If we have disagreements, we only think of violence as the way to solve them."[9] As LaRosa and Mejía state, "This is one of the fascinating ironies that emerges when considering Colombia's nineteenth- and twentieth-century history: violent conflict has tended to occur within the strictures of constitutional procedure and process."[10]

The Elite Political Game

The final set of key patterns in the first years of independent Colombia was that elite political groups might form coalitions when they were not mobilizing their followers in civil wars. While the members of the parties were allowed and even encouraged to take up arms against the members of the other party, the party leaders generally got along quite well with each other. They came from the same economic groups and belonged to the same exclusive social clubs. Colombians of a radical persuasion often called them *la oligarquía* (the oligarchy). On twelve occasions between 1854 and 1949, one political party at the elite level entered a coalition with all or part of the other political party. These elite coalitions tended to take place when presidents assumed dictatorial powers, when party hegemonies shifted, and, especially in the twentieth century, when elite-instigated violence got out of control.[11]

The only military dictatorship of the twentieth century took place in the context of the systemic breakdown of La Violencia. On June 13, 1953, Lieutenant General Gustavo Rojas Pinilla staged a coup that ended the presidency of Laureano Gómez and disrupted democratic government until 1958. The leaders of the Conservative Party had divided into two groups at that time: the historical Conservatives who supported Gómez and a moderate group that did not support his government. After the coup, members of the elite factions of both political parties welcomed the Rojas dictatorship, with the obvious exception of the deposed historical Conservatives. This bipartisan support was to last for several years, although Rojas, who considered himself a Conservative, received his most active support from the moderates of that party.

Rojas's first measures included a pardon and amnesty for political prisoners and for all who were fighting, as well as restoring the freedom of the press, which Gómez had ended. The amnesty was a success, and deaths from La Violencia fell from 22,000 in 1952–1953 to 1,900 in 1954–1955.[12] However, Rojas was unprepared for his position and seemingly had no true program to offer the country besides a moral agenda.

The partisan elite (except for the moderate Conservatives) became increasingly restive with military government, especially after Rojas called a national convention to draft a new constitution. He began talking about a "third force" (a vague idea about a coalition of all groups of society, also patterned after the Perón experience in Argentina). It became increasingly clear that Rojas was not going to hold the 1958 presidential election.

By early 1957, most organized groups opposed Rojas. Leaders of the parties were planning a coalition government; the Catholic Church had lost interest in the Rojas experiment. Leaders of most of the economic interest groups, representing the upper levels of Colombian economic life, had supported the trade unions in general strikes. On May 10, 1957, the top military leaders asked Rojas to leave the country. After his departure, these leaders formed a caretaker military junta to govern until a new president could assume office.

On August 7, 1958, Alberto Lleras Camargo was inaugurated as the first president in the most notable case of an elite coalition, the National Front. From 1958 to 1974, the two parties constitutionally shared power equally based on a consociational agreement first proposed by leaders of the Liberal and Conservative Parties and later approved by a national referendum and a constitutional amendment.[13] During this period, the presidency alternated between the Liberal and Conservative Parties and no other party was legal. They divided all legislative bodies equally, as they did executive cabinets at all levels, governors, mayors, and non–civil service bureaucrats.

Under the National Front, two Liberals were president (Alberto Lleras Camargo, 1958–1962, and Carlos Lleras Restrepo, 1966–1970) and two Conservatives (Guillermo León Valencia, 1962–66, and Misael Pastrana Borrero, 1970–74). Political competition was primarily between the factions of the two legal parties. In 1968, a constitutional reform ended some of the stipulations for the National Front while extending other requirements. It ended the requirement of a two-thirds vote for congressional approval of legislation and strengthened the rulemaking authority of the president to the detriment of Congress.

Because of its defining characteristic of bipartisanship (to the exclusion of other groups) and because of the Cold War context in which it existed, the National Front repressed political dissidence and sought to co-opt and control both the poor and the emerging middle classes by widening party patronage networks. One might have expected the Colombian state finally to develop a bureaucracy based on merit under the National Front, since the old party hatreds had been discarded. No longer did the concern exist that, if the government under one party constructed a strong state, a later government under the other party would use the constabulary of the strong state in revenge. However, as Francisco Leal Buitrago argues, during the years of the National Front, Colombia lost that opportunity: "Bureaucratization and clientelism substituted for sectarianism as the source of reproduction of the political parties. Nevertheless, in spite of the profundity of this change, the long-lasting political weakness of the state was not significantly altered. The bureaucratization of the dual-party system and the transformation of clientelism into the axis of the political system prevented the widening and modernization of the state from significantly increasing the extent of the state."[14]

The judicial system, marked by corruption and inefficiency, came out of La Violencia even more subservient to the executive branch. The Ministry of Justice was established only in 1945, after a half century in which justice was organizationally subordinated to politics in the Ministry of the Interior.[15] After the National Front, that judiciary faced dramatic new challenges, first from Marxist guerrilla groups, then from drug dealers, and finally from paramilitary groups that the government itself had established.

THE CHANGING VIOLENCE AFTER THE END OF THE NATIONAL FRONT

The National Front ended when Alfonso López Michelsen became president on August 7, 1974. However, new forms of violence had appeared in Colombia even as the National Front was ending the old bipartisan violence. First were Marxist guerrilla groups, followed by state-sanctioned "self-defense" or paramilitary groups and, several decades later, drug dealers.

The Guerrilla Groups

The influence of Marxist revolutionary groups in the countryside went back to the final years of La Violencia. The first such group to emerge was the pro-Castro Army of National Liberation (Ejército de Liberación Nacional, ELN). It arose after a group of Colombian scholarship students went to Cuba at the height of the Cuban missile crisis in 1962. Some in the group asked for and obtained military training and began a series of discussions about a *foco*, or "focus," strategy for Colombia.[16] The idea of this strategy, as used in Cuba by Fidel Castro, was that a dedicated band of revolutionaries can launch very small-scale guerrilla warfare at any time. It could serve as a focus for the rapid growth of more general guerrilla warfare and at some relatively early time a general uprising capable of seizing political power. The ELN was officially born on July 4, 1964, and initially comprised primarily university students.[17]

In 1966 the Communist-dominated Revolutionary Armed Forces of Colombia (Fuerzas Armadas Revolucionarias de Colombia, FARC) was founded, although Communist-oriented peasant defense groups predated the organization by more than fifteen years. As early as 1949, the Communist Party urged the proletariat and others to defend themselves. At times the FARC claimed that its founding was in May 1964 when the Colombian military tried to wipe out a small guerrilla group in the Marquetalia area of Tolima department. The government termed the area an "independent republic," and President Guillermo León Valencia vowed on more than one occasion that "tomorrow we are going to capture Tirofijo [Manuel Marulanda, the leader of the insurgent group]." The effort failed, and the guerrilla fled, officially forming the FARC two years later. Leader Tirofijo continued to head the FARC until he died of a heart attack in 2008.

While originally founded with a campesino perspective and calling for radical social changes, the FARC, Alejandro Reyes argues, had become in the 1980s "true war machines with autonomy from the social causes that originated them." Some FARC fronts, pressured by the leadership of the organization, began "taxing" small and medium drug producers.[18] Later, according to the Colombian and US governments, the FARC became a major exporter of illicit drugs. FARC leaders always denied that they were in the drug trade, saying instead that the guerrilla group only took payment from people who were raising and producing drugs in FARC-controlled areas. The United Nations Development Program in 2003 had estimated the FARC's annual income from the drug trade at US$204 million. A 2012 calculation released by the Colombian prosecutor general's office stated that total profits had increased to around US$1.1 billion a year.[19]

A third guerrilla group appeared in 1967 when the Maoist wing of the Colombian Communist Party founded an armed organization, the People's Liberation Army (Ejército Popular de Liberación, EPL). In the 1960s and 1970s, it was especially active in the Santander department. In the mid-1970s, the guerrilla group began using kidnapping and extortion as a means of financing itself. In the late 1980s, its most active fronts were in the banana-growing areas of Urabá.

A final guerrilla group was the 19th of April Movement (Movimiento 19 de Abril, M-19). The M-19 appeared after the presidential elections of April 19, 1970, in which former general Rojas Pinilla appeared to have won, only to have later government returns show that he had lost. The M-19 was always somewhat of a romantic, Robin Hood–type movement. It carried out a number of urban guerrilla activities: most notably, stealing a sword that belonged to liberator Simón Bolívar in 1974; kidnapping all the guests (including the US ambassador) during a cocktail party at the embassy of the Dominican Republic in 1980; kidnapping and executing a missionary from the United States in 1981; and seizing the Palacio de Justicia in downtown Bogotá on the morning of November 6, 1985. The army reestablished control the following day, but only after more than one hundred deaths, including eleven of the twenty-four Supreme Court justices, and the gutting of the palace by fire.

Paramilitary Groups

Private justice began early in Colombian history; the country has been rife with paramilitary groups since its inception. In the nineteenth century, they first appeared as large landowners established their own justice systems on their lands. Private justice appeared in a different form in the twentieth century during La Violencia. The first self-defense groups to organize themselves then were the peasant self-defense groups in Tolima. In the 1950s, similar groups appeared in other places. The FARC originated in one such group.

In 1965, as Marxist guerrilla groups were appearing, President Guillermo León Valencia issued Decree 3398, and in 1968, during the presidency of Carlos Lleras Restrepo, Congress passed Law 48. The decree and the law gave legal status to private armed groups by stating that the government could use any citizen in activities to reestablish normalcy. In this way, the weak state could enlist the help of private groups to battle the guerrillas. The army was to arm and train private individuals, and close ties developed between many paramilitary groups and the military.

These important decisions during the Valencia and Lleras Restrepo administrations might have made sense in the short run, but in the long run, they caused the state to have even less power. As Philip Mauceri states, "The state response to insurgent groups in Colombia can best be characterized as 'abdication and privatization,' a process in which state actors provide the legal framework, legitimacy, logistical support, and on occasion armaments to private societal actors in order to combat insurgents."[20]

In the 1970s, with the growth of the FARC and other guerrilla groups and their increasing hostility toward the civilian population, especially ranchers and large farmers who could pay protection money, those with traditional political affiliations adopted the "self-defense" structure to repel the guerrilla attacks. Many of the self-defense groups arose in response to the constant demands of the guerrillas because it was clear that the government could not guarantee to protect them.[21]

During the presidency of Virgilio Barco (1986–1990), paramilitary groups experienced dramatic changes. Earlier the groups comprised individuals who produced legal agricultural products. However, as the drug lords became wealthy, they bought more land. While at first they bought land to become gentlemen farmers, later they used the land to grow coca. Soon, drug money began supporting paramilitary squads. Paramilitary groups changed in two other important ways by the end of the Barco presidency. First, according to some sources, the number of deaths attributed to paramilitary activity exceeded those attributed to guerrilla activity. While there is no doubt that the number of deaths from paramilitary activities was increasing, reliable statistics do not exist to substantiate the claim that those deaths were greater than those from guerrilla activities. Second, the Barco administration stated that the government would no longer support paramilitary groups. However, at least to a degree, the relationship continued to exist.

Drug Dealers

The final ingredient in the Colombian violence was the drug trade. Colombia began to take a major role in the international marijuana trade in the 1970s. However, it developed its key function in the illicit drug industry when Medellín drug leaders first decided to diversify to cocaine and then initiated large shipments of the drug. As a result, a new economic group grew up around the illicit drug industry. Later, the cartels of Medellín and Cali became internationally known, but as early as December 1981 the Colombian drug industry held a secret national convention at which 223 drug gang bosses created a death squad called Death to Kidnappers (Muerte a Secuestradores, MAS). The drug leaders pledged US$7.5 million to the squad, whose goal was to kill all kidnappers and to end the guerrilla practice of kidnapping people, including the "honest, hardworking drug gang bosses," for ransom.[22]

The various armed actors were interrelated. The drug dealers had connections with paramilitary groups, as did the government officially until the Barco presidency and in fact even afterwards. In addition, guerrilla groups developed relationships with drug dealers, first by protecting their fields and factories, later by "taxing" them, and in some cases by entering the drug enterprise directly. The only generalization about relations among the different groups, albeit macabre, seemed to be "the enemy of my enemy is my friend."

Criminality reached high levels. To the extent that they had existed before, the norms of coexistence and justice collapsed. The national homicide rate, which had declined from 32 to 23 homicides per 100,000 inhabitants between 1960–1965 and 1970–1975, rose steeply to 32 in 1985, 63 in 1990, and 78 in 1991–1993. The rate did fall to 56 homicides per 100,000 inhabitants in 1998 only to rise again to 63 in 1999–2000. Impunity increased. While the number of deaths by violence increased from 4,000 in 1960 to 30,000 in 1993, the number of individuals charged remained unchanged. Of the reported homicides, 97 percent went unpunished.[23]

Finally, drug groups entered politics. Voters in the Antioquia department elected Medellín drug lord Pablo Escobar as an alternate member of Congress in 1982. Evidence also exists that the drug trade leaders, or narcos, influenced the presidency. The most notable case was of president Ernesto Samper (1994–1998). Soon after his election, cassette tapes appeared that indicated that Cali drug cartel leaders contributed to his campaign. Samper immediately denied the allegation but governed under the shadow of the accusation during his four years.

THE FIRST FIVE ATTEMPTS TO END GUERRILLA CONFLICT THROUGH NEGOTIATION

Before 1998 there were five Colombian presidents who attempted to end guerrilla violence through negotiations. The first three were Belisario Betancur (1982–1986), Virgilio Barco (1986–1990), and César Gaviria (1990–1994). President Ernesto Samper (1994–1998) made fewer attempts in part because of his alleged connection to drug groups. The most ambitious attempt was by President Andrés Pastrana (1998–2002). All these efforts failed.

The Betancur Attempt

In the first six weeks after becoming president on August 7, 1982, Belisario Betancur announced that he would name a peace commission. Law 35 of 1982 granted amnesty to all those in armed conflict with the government before November 20, except for those who had committed non-combat-related homicides, those who had committed homicides including "cruelty," and those whose victims had been in a position of "inferior strength." Guerrillas already imprisoned for the pardoned crimes—whether indicted or convicted— would be released. In the first three months, some four hundred guerrillas accepted the amnesty.[24]

The Betancur administration based its peace initiatives on the assumption that guerrilla violence was the product of objective circumstances of poverty, injustice, and the lack of opportunities for political participation. As a result, the government reached agreements with three guerrilla groups: the M-19, the FARC, and the EPL. In all cases, there were truces, which were to be followed by a national dialogue. The dialogue was never very well defined and did not take place.

After negotiations between the government and the FARC in April 1984, the president announced the Agreement of La Uribe, which included (1) a cease-fire for one year; (2) the creation of a high-level commission to verify compliance with the agreement; (3) the granting of a series of juridical, political, and social guarantees to facilitate the transition of the guerrilla forces back into civilian life; and (4) a rehabilitation program for peasant areas affected by the violence. The accord promised to end extortions, kidnapping, and terrorism. On May 11, 1984, as called for in the agreement, the FARC founded a political party, the Unión Patriótica. In its first year at least 165 of its members were killed.[25]

betrayed

Also in May 1984 the government signed similar truces with the M-19 and the EPL. Only the ELN had not signed a truce. However, by the end of 1985, only the FARC truce continued. Leaders of the other two guerrilla groups accused the government of causing the break, while the government faulted the subversives. Casualties increased, culminating on the morning of November 6, 1985, when the M-19 seized the Palacio de Justicia on the Parque Bolívar in downtown Bogotá, resulting in more than one hundred deaths.

The FARC truce was still formally in place at the end of the Betancur presidency. However, hostilities had also resumed between that group and the government. The military, including consecutive ministers of defense Generals Fernando Landazábal Reyes and Gustavo Matamoros D'Costa, had opposed the process throughout.[26]

[handwritten margin note: military opposition to peace now stage]

The Barco and Gaviria Attempts

President Virgilio Barco announced no new peace initiative at his inauguration on August 7, 1986, despite continued violence. Only during the last two years of the Barco presidency did changing circumstances lead the government and several guerrilla groups to bargain. For the government, the context had changed because the growth of paramilitary attacks gave such a negotiation higher priority. Several guerrilla groups also faced different conditions. This was especially the case for the M-19, which was militarily weak, had less legitimacy after the Palacio de Justicia attack, had never had a coherent revolutionary ideology, and had suffered rapid leadership turnover.[27]

In March 1989, the government and the M-19 signed the Declaration of Cauca, expressing their intentions to begin the process of the reintegration of the guerrilla group. Under the declaration, the members of the subversive group would occupy an area in the mountains of Cauca, where the Colombian military would protect them. Five hundred soon arrived. Working tables were to be set up at once so that the two sides could arrive at agreements to bring the guerrilla group into the political process.[28]

On July 17, 1989, the M-19 and the government signed a pact that would lead to the demobilization and disarming of the guerrillas over the following six months, during which time the working tables would continue. Later there was difficulty in the process when Congress failed to pass a constitutional reform suggested by President Barco; however, in January 1990 a joint declaration of the government and the guerrilla group indicated that, although the disarmament and pardon would not be on the agreed-upon date, they would look for ways to make the peace formula viable.[29]

During the presidency of César Gaviria, there were negotiations with the guerrilla groups who had entered a coalition called the Simón Bolívar Guerrilla Coordinator (Coordinadora Guerrillera Simón Bolívar, CGSB). Gaviria's view was that the dissolution of the Soviet Union in Eastern Europe and the end of the Cold War had taken all viability from guerrilla conflict and converted many of the subversives into common criminals. Nonetheless, representatives of the Colombian government met with ones of the CGSB in Cravo Norte in the department of Arauca in May 1991; in Caracas, Venezuela, from June to November 1991; and in Tlaxcala, Mexico, in March 1992.

Although in the last year of the Gaviria presidency there were some successes with small guerrilla groups, the peace process with the CGSB was a failure. Five basic reasons caused that failure. First, the two sides had different ways of conceptualizing peace. While for the government peace meant the absence of armed conflict, for the guerrilla groups it meant a change in the basic structure of Colombian capitalism. Second, some participants on both sides thought that they could still win the war. There was little or no reason to negotiate since they believed their side could still win militarily. Third, especially in the case of the FARC, the income from the cocaine trade made a continuation of the conflict desirable. Fourth, neither side had viable proposals. While the government could never convince the guerrillas to accept its peace proposal, the subversives did not seem to have more than ideological slogans. Finally, both sides lacked unity. Each side had important splits, including between the civilians and the military on the government's side and between the FARC and the ELN within the CGSB.[30]

The Samper Presidency

The peace process with the guerrillas was far from complete when Ernesto Samper replaced César Gaviria on August 7, 1994. Samper did little in peacekeeping efforts, largely because of his need to defend himself constantly against accusations stemming from the alleged drug money in his campaign. His administration, however, did arrange a plea bargain with the leaders of the Cali drug cartel.

The Samper presidency also faced a new strategy from the FARC. At its eighth national conference in 1993, the guerrilla group decided to construct a guerrilla army capable of defeating the Colombian armed forces in places of clear, strategic value. To that end, the FARC created fronts with blocs and strengthened regional commands. Likewise, the FARC repeated its goal of urbanizing the conflict through its Bolivarian militias. In addition, the FARC announced a platform of ten social and political reforms that the state would have to make to form a government of national reconciliation and reconstruction.

The effect of this change in the FARC strategy became dramatically apparent by 1996. Major attacks from April 1996 to November 1998 led to serious defeats of the Colombian military. In the El Billar case, the FARC attacked an elite group of soldiers with counterinsurgency training and demonstrated that the army was not capable of detecting or preventing the mobilization of nearly eight hundred guerrilla fighters. The Miraflores attack occurred only four days before the inauguration of Andrés Pastrana and after he had begun discussions with the FARC leaders about peace talks. The Mitú attack showed that the FARC was capable of capturing a departmental capital, even if it were one of the smallest and most remote.[31] Clearly, the Samper years (1994–1998) were ones with the FARC at its zenith and the Colombian military at its all-time low.

Also notable in the Samper presidency was the founding of the United Self-Defense Forces of Colombia (Autodefensas Unidas de Colombia, AUC) on April 18, 1997. Led by Carlos Castaño, the AUC claimed that it was not composed of paramilitary groups organized by the government, but rather independent groups. In addition to self-defense, the AUC carried out offensive actions against people it considered guerrillas or sympathizers. Massacres became common and thousands of people fled to cities to escape the crossfire of guerrilla and paramilitary forces.

Earlier, in 1995, Carlos Castaño had begun the work of convincing each one of the regional paramilitary groups of the necessity of a union, with one commander, one insignia, one uniform, and one policy. At the beginning, the acceptance of one policy was not essential. In this way, Castaño's personal paramilitary group became the model in both political and military structure. It began with about three thousand troops but was soon to grow. The importance of the AUC in bargaining was to be seen in later presidencies. In addition, the military importance of the AUC was shown when it had successes. Most notable were the AUC battles in Córdoba and Urabá with guerrillas (both the ELN and the FARC) and the Colombian armed forces. In those two areas of Colombia, more people died than in all of the Central American civil wars combined or in the Cuban insurrection.[32]

The Colombian government was facing a new problem, one of its own creation. As noted above, the governments of Guillermo León Valencia and Carlos Lleras Restrepo had legalized self-defense groups. Yet when the guerrilla threat grew, the drug monies entered the paramilitary groups. When Castaño organized the groups nationally, the putative solution to the guerrilla problem became at least as bad as the original difficulty. Misusing the work of Mary Shelley, leaders began saying "We created a Frankenstein."[33]

The Pastrana Negotiations with the Fuerzas Armadas Revolucionarias de Colombia

In 1998 the Colombian people elected Andrés Pastrana as president after he promised to negotiate with the guerrilla groups. On June 15, 1998, Pastrana sent his campaign manager Víctor G. Ricardo to meet with FARC leader

Manuel Marulanda, and the two agreed that if Pastrana were elected, talks would begin between the government and the FARC on January 7, 1999. On June 16, 1998, Pastrana announced that, if elected, one of his first decisions would be to pull government troops out of five municipalities in southern Colombia, an area of 42,138 square kilometers (16,270 square miles) and some 90,000 inhabitants. The FARC had asked for this territory before as a precondition for bargaining with the government. During the years of the Ernesto Samper presidency, the armed forces had constantly resisted a demilitarized zone. The only way to explain this about-face is that the military could not resist a decision made by a president elected with the establishment of such a zone as a central part of his electoral platform.

On June 21, 1998, Pastrana won the presidential election. On July 9, the president-elect met with Marulanda, and they discussed the FARC proposal to pull all security forces out of the five municipalities to create a temporary "clearance zone" for the holding of peace talks. The government encountered a problem by failing to realize that "the devil was in the details." There were no explicit agreements about how the guerrillas would use this territory. Nor was there a clear definition of the role of the government in the region.

From January 1999 until February 2002, the FARC and the Pastrana administration had a series of meetings in the demilitarized zone. The government did not insist that the FARC enter into a cease-fire before the process began; indeed, the cease-fire was one of the matters for them to negotiate. The government honored its pledge that the insurgents would have complete control of the demilitarized area during the dialogues.

The talks began badly when FARC leader Marulanda failed to appear at the first meeting, a clear indication of the weak position of President Pastrana. FARC leaders claimed that a paramilitary group planned to assassinate Marulanda there. Later there were frequent disagreements over procedures. One side or the other walked away from the negotiations, not ending them but, in the Colombian argot, "freezing" them until the other side did something or stopped doing something. Each side continued military actions, at times doing something that caused the freezing of the talks. The FARC continued to protest the actions of paramilitary groups, activities that the guerrilla group considered the same as government actions.

The negotiations did lead to several procedural agreements, the most important of which was the establishment of a commission of notables on May 11, 2001, to recommend ways to do away with paramilitarism. Each side was to choose two members. This commission was an idea to get past the paralysis of the negotiating table. Since the two sides had failed to reach agreements at the table, the purpose was to let the outside group come in with recommendations. In August and September, the commission emerged as a key player in the process. First, Commissioner Ana María Gómez, one of the two members chosen by the government, resigned after meeting with President Pastrana. She stated that she did not agree with the draft the group had prepared, especially the part that called for the immediate establishment of a constituent assembly. Her opinion was that such an assembly should come after the demobilization of the guerrilla and paramilitary troops and not immediately; otherwise political instability and polarization would increase.[34]

On September 19, the commission (now with two members named by the FARC and only one by the government) issued a report recommending that the talks between the government and the FARC proceed under a six-month cease-fire. The lengthy document included many major points. Most importantly, during the truce, the government and the FARC would respect the norms of international humanitarian law. Both sides would abstain from using unconventional weapons, such as mines, gas cylinders, and dispersion bombs; from recruiting minors; and from attacking civilian populations. The FARC would not carry out attacks against civilians (such as kidnapping), forced collection of contributions, or attacks on either the transportation or the energy and petroleum infrastructure.

The report suggested a number of other measures: The government and the FARC would study mechanisms of financing that would allow subsistence to the combatants during the truce. The government promised to work on crop substitution and manual eradication of drugs, and both sides agreed to the protection of the environment. The negotiation table would arrive at agreements that would include a definite plan of constitutional reform, as well as those points that should be considered by Congress or implemented by the executive. While all of this sounded like a possible way for the two sides to make progress, in the end none of the proposals were accepted.

The peace process ended six months later in February 2002 after FARC troops kidnapped Senator Jorge Gechem Turbay. The only substantive agreement that the two sides reached in nearly three years of talks was for an exchange of military and police personnel that the FARC had captured for guerrilla members that the government had seized and held in jail. In May 1999, the two sides agreed to a common agenda, of little importance because it was a compromise in which each side listed the points it wanted to talk about and because neither side followed it anyway.[35]

In the end, the process was a failure. Three major conclusions come from an analysis of those three years of conversations. First, each side was willing to either participate in or break off the talks depending on what seemed to be in its best interest. The reasons for suspending the dialogues always had to do with something that the other side was doing away from the bargaining table. Second, almost all of the agreements were about the procedures to follow in the conversation, with only one on a substantive matter.[36] Third and most importantly, the power of the guerrilla group was at an all-time high. It was so strong militarily that it had begun a successful war of movements during the Samper administration. It was also strong economically, with the US government in 2004 estimating that FARC income from drug trafficking was US$100 million a month.[37]

Alejandro Reyes argues that the Pastrana peace process gave two lessons to the country. First, the political establishment did not know what social reforms were necessary to prevent the violence. Second, neither did the guerrillas have a political program of reforms that could build the content of a realistic and credible peace negotiation. Reyes concludes that the Pastrana peace process "was the period in which it was demonstrated more clearly that a peace process with the guerrillas is not possible if there is no unity of command in the political and military leadership. The FARC demanded that the government dismantle the paramilitary groups as a condition for progress in the peace negotiations. Implicit in this requirement was the idea that the paramilitary groups existed as an expression of an official policy of dirty warfare and ignored the relative autonomy and self-sufficiency that such groups had at that time."[38]

During the Pastrana presidency, two things happened that were to change the military balance of power between the government and the FARC. One was a restructuring of the military through Plan 10,000. Proposed by Generals Fernando Tapias and Jorge Enrique Mora Rangel, the plan was to increase the membership of the military by replacing 14,355 draftees with 9,996 voluntary soldiers and 4,359 regular soldiers. These new troops would make up twenty-one combat battalions. At the same time, the duration of obligatory military service was extended from eighteen to twenty-four months. As a result, the size of the military increased from 134,137 in 1998 to 160,000 by 2002.[39]

This change coincided with Plan Colombia, a massive military aid program from the US government. While the plan talked about strengthening the economy and making the country more democratic, it also stressed combating the narcotics industry and promoting the peace process. Since to a large degree the FARC was running the narcotics industry, Plan Colombia from its beginning had at least an implicit anti-guerrilla theme. In an interview, a member of the Colombian bargaining team said, "Plan Colombia was a happy coincidence with the structuring of the armed forces."[40]

CONCLUSION: WHY PEACE NEGOTIATIONS FAILED BEFORE 2002

At the beginning of the Pastrana negotiations, Rafael Pardo, former minister of defense during the Gaviria presidency, in a more theoretical fashion analyzed two principal dimensions that past Colombian presidents had combined differently in their respective attempts at peace. The first was whether there were preconditions for bargaining. The second was what bargaining dealt with.

The first dimension Pardo considered was whether the insurgent groups were to enter a cease-fire as a precondition for other negotiations. That was the case in the Betancur and Barco talks. It was successful for the demobilization of the M-19 towards the end of the Barco presidency and for the beginning of the process with the EPL, although that course of action did not end until the early days of the Gaviria administration.

In the Gaviria peace process, there was no such precondition. Hence bargaining took place while armed conflict was ongoing, with all the difficulties that went along with that combination. Each side, from time to time, took military actions with the goal of increasing its power at the bargaining table. However, this carried the possibility that one side would go too far in such an attempt, leading to either a temporary or definite suspension of the negotiations.

The second issue, Pardo argued, was that there were two different assumptions behind the bargaining—the "volunteerism" or "idealism" of Betancur and the "political power" conceptual framework of Barco and Gaviria. The search for peace under Betancur can been seen as a kind of act of contrition by an establishment that recognizes its errors, at least partially embraces the concerns of the insurgents, and is clearly willing to make amends. As Pardo put it, "The peace politics of the Betancur government were guided by goodwill, the creation of mutual trust, and demonstration of a capability to agree on substantive issues. The state acknowledged past behaviors and undesirable conditions that fostered violence—such as inequality, injustice, and poverty— and made clear its desire to remedy the situation."[41]

Barco and Gaviria operated from a different conceptual framework. They assumed that the conflict was about power; therefore, they believed that the negotiations should be about power and not about the socioeconomic issues that might have caused the conflict. Barco used that framework with the M-19 and the EPL, and Gaviria continued with the same framework during the first two rounds of negotiations with the CGSB. However, during the third round in Tlaxcala, Mexico, in 1992, there was an abortive attempt to discuss substantive issues.

Pardo analyzed the consequences of the philosophical differences of the two approaches. Under the first, the government relinquished the defense of a series of beliefs, including those pertaining to the legitimate use of force by the government, in an attempt to get closer to the guerrillas' posture. This action led to more conflict between the president and the armed forces. As Pardo summarized it, "The difference between the two approaches is that one is based on demonstrating the government's ability to rectify, and the other is concerned with creating the conditions to negotiate about peace. One implies that it is necessary to solve everything—or almost everything—before making peace; the other indicates that negotiation—and especially negotiation about political power—is the only necessary element to arrive at peace."[42]

In a less theoretical way, in my studies of these abortive negotiations, I conclude that there are four factors that explain why peace negotiations before 2002 failed: Colombian geography, military conditions, the existence of paramilitary groups, and bargaining mistakes.

Two characteristics of Colombian geography made negotiations difficult. One was the combination of mountains, plains, and rainforest leading some to judge Colombia to be one of the most topographically challenged countries *Geo* in the world. Such terrain made it difficult for the government to launch a successful counterinsurgency war, and in its absence, the FARC had no reason to negotiate. The second was Colombia's porous international borders with Venezuela, Brazil, and Ecuador, which made it easy for insurgent groups to find safe haven.

The second factor was military in nature. Although neither side had been *Military* able to win the war, some leaders on both sides still believed that their side could prevail militarily.

Third was the existence of the paramilitary groups. While the government claimed that it was no longer training or arming the private groups, the FARC leaders refused to believe this and considered the paramilitary groups to be *Para* part of the government. Indeed, the FARC argument had some validity since some regional military commanders continued to have relationships with the paramilitary forces.

The final reason was bad bargaining tactics. Various administrations at times named negotiators based on personal or political reasons rather than *bad* an individual's proven record in bargaining. At times presidents made their *bargaining* place in history dependent on success in bargaining, in effect making themselves weaker negotiators. Often one side, usually the government, gave something to the other without asking for or receiving something in exchange. Both sides at times accepted vague agreements that later caused problems because of the lack of details. Such poor tactics made agreeing on an agenda difficult.

As I show in the next chapter, the context changed from 2002 to 2010, thanks to the strong will of president Álvaro Uribe and money from the US government. Juan Manuel Santos inherited a situation that was more propitious for negotiation with the FARC.

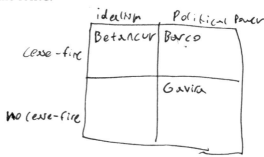

Changes in the Balance of Power during the Administration of President Álvaro Uribe

DISARRAY AND LAWLESSNESS PREVAILED IN Colombia when Álvaro Uribe Vélez assumed the presidency on August 7, 2002. Over twenty thousand FARC troops occupied the countryside, the highest number ever. Several of its fronts were positioned near Bogotá. Paramilitary troops ruled in vast areas of the country, perhaps as much as in one-third of the national territory. People feared travel beyond the major cities due to the danger of kidnapping. Statistics provided by the National Planning Department indicate how dire the situation was. Murders had risen from a yearly average of 25,039 during the last two years of the Ernesto Samper presidency (1996–1998) to 26,891 during the four years of the Pastrana administration (1998–2002). In the same time period, yearly averages for kidnappings rose from 2,068 to 3,106; terrorist attacks from 744 to 944; attacks on towns from 90 to 130; massacres from 114 to 176, massacre victims from 607 to 1,013; and, most dramatically, internal refugees from 3,907 to 41,355.[1] In addition, by the end of the Pastrana presidency, mayors of 420 of the 1,120 municipalities had been forced to flee because of the violence,[2] and 157 municipalities had no police officers because guerrillas had expelled them.[3]

That was the immediate context that Álvaro Uribe, former governor of the economically important Antioquia department, faced when he became president. Appendix 1 lists a number of key persons in the Santos-FARC-Uribe negotiations in chronological order. The first is Álvaro Uribe Vélez. Elected as an independent candidate with 53 percent of the vote in the first round of the presidential election in 2002, he had presented a platform of one hundred points, the second of which might be considered the theme of his first term: "I dream of a Colombia in which we can all live in peace."[4] The FARC set off bombs near the Plaza de Bolívar during his inauguration.

Uribe began his presidency with two major policies to end violence. The first was to negotiate with groups that were willing to declare a cease-fire. The second was to strengthen the Colombian military. The United Self-Defense Forces of Colombia (Autodefensas Unidas de Colombia, AUC) soon took steps to begin a cease-fire, but the FARC was never willing to declare an end of hostilities.

NEGOTIATIONS

In his inaugural speech, Uribe announced that his administration would search for "useful dialogue" with groups outside of the law, but only if they first entered into cease-fires. That made his position similar to those of Betancur and Barco but different from that of Pastrana. Later the policy had much greater specificity. There would be a program of stimuli for the demobilization and disarming of guerrilla and paramilitary troops through a decree of internal disturbance, ready for the president and his ministers to sign. Certain individuals, such as those who had carried out kidnappings, genocide, acts of ferocity, and homicides outside of combat, were not eligible to receive the benefits. That is, the incentives were not for the higher-level officials of the guerrilla and paramilitary groups who had judicial processes already started against them, but instead for lower-level members of the groups.

The Autodefensas Unidas de Colombia

The Uribe administration had success with the Autodefensas Unidas de Colombia but had no comparable accomplishments with the FARC. By the end of 2002, the government had signed a cease-fire with the AUC, and by the end of 2006, over thirty thousand paramilitary troops had demobilized. Critiques of Uribe stated that the president had personal connections with the paramilitary groups.

Important in this process with the AUC was the mid-2005 congressional approval of the Law of Justice and Peace. Colombia's democratic government meant that after President Uribe proposed a law, Congress had to approve it and the Constitutional Court had to find that the process was within the guidelines of the constitution. Some members of Congress had connections with the paramilitary groups. Since Congress chooses the Constitutional Court, it was possible that paramilitary groups had influence in its selection. On December 23, 2002, the government formed the Exploratory Commission of Peace and charged it with making contacts with the paramilitary groups that had publicly proclaimed a cease-fire and indicated that they wanted to enter a peace process. During the first months of 2003, paramilitary leaders met with the commission, as well as congressional representatives and members of the Catholic Church.[5]

In May 2003, President Uribe announced that he would submit a bill to Congress that would not punish members of paramilitary groups, even if they had committed atrocious crimes.[6] The top AUC leaders Carlos Castaño and Salvatore Mancuso had already made it clear that there could be no progress in the process unless extradition was eliminated.[7] The multifaceted bargaining of President Uribe with the paramilitary groups and Congress had begun, as well as the debates between those whose first priority was to end the violence and those who were most concerned with the rights of victims.[8]

In August 2003, Minister of Interior and Justice Sabas Pretelt de la Vega presented a bill of "penal alternatives" in the Senate to cover the two groups. He stated that this was not to be a law of "pardon and amnesty"; rather it was a plan of investigation and sanctions for crimes that could not be pardoned and was directed to both the guerrilla and paramilitary groups. Under the proposal, individuals would receive the benefits of the law under six conditions: a cease-fire by the group to which the individual belonged; turning in of arms; promising not to take up arms again; accepting a punishment other than jail; making reparations to victims; and promising not to commit an "intentional crime" in the future.[9]

Members of Congress made great objections to the bill and opponents made seven counterproposals. The administration also presented a revised proposal in April 2004. Debates about the law took place during the rest of that year and the first half of 2005. The multifaceted arguments were between the government and the paramilitary groups, within Uribe's Partido de la U, in Congress, and with the government of the United States. Members of the judicial branch made a few statements, even though the Constitutional Court delayed its final ruling for many months.

Congress approved a revised version of the proposal in mid-2005. The major clauses of the law were that alternative punishment would consist of suspending traditional imprisonment and replacing it with lighter sentences in exchange for contributing to peace and making reparation to the victims. The confinement of persons convicted of atrocious crimes like massacres would be between five and eight years, in a place designated by the governmental prison authority, which could be an agricultural colony. To be eligible, one had to surrender goods, minors recruited, and victims of kidnapping; further, the group must not have been organized with the specific goal of drug trafficking or of illegal enrichment. After a hearing and during the following sixty days, the office of the prosecutor general would investigate and verify the acts confessed by the accused. Members of an armed group that demobilized would state the circumstances of time, method, and place in which the crimes were committed. If new crimes were discovered after sentencing, the same alternative punishment would apply if the person collaborated in the clarification of the crime, admitted to having participated in it, or if the omission was unintentional. Members of armed groups who benefited from the law would have the obligation of repaying the victims of the actions of which they were guilty. If no victims were found, the payment would go to the national reparation fund.[10]

Failure with the FARC

Some political analysts suggest that Uribe was stubborn about the FARC because the guerrilla group had assassinated his father in 1983.[11] Most of the discussion between his administration and the FARC had to do with devising an exchange of hostages held by the FARC for captured FARC guerrillas, or a "humanitarian exchange" as Colombians commonly called it. The idea was to exchange around five hundred FARC members in Colombian prisons for forty-five hostages in the hands of the insurgent group, including politicians, soldiers, and police officers, as well as three US military contractors.

As mentioned in chapter 1, during the Pastrana peace process the government granted a demilitarized zone to the FARC, removing all military and police forces. The FARC became the government, making and enforcing its decisions on all inhabitants of the area. Because of the failure of the Pastrana process, in the 2002 presidential election Uribe took a position against such a concession, and during his first administration refused to grant it. When, toward the end of his first term, the president gave in a bit on his original policy, the disagreement then became about which areas of the country would be demilitarized.

The peace process between the Colombian government under President Uribe and the FARC went through various stages. It began with each side stating its conditions for the process while at the same time issuing belligerent statements about the other side. The second stage came in mid-2003 when the FARC seemed to be more willing to use an intermediary, first approaching the Rio Group (a permanent association of political consultation of Latin American and Caribbean countries, created in Rio de Janeiro, Brazil, on December 18, 1986), then the Colombian Roman Catholic Church, and finally the United Nations. The Colombian government, FARC leaders, and representatives of the United Nations and the government of Brazil discussed plans to have FARC leaders meet UN representatives in Brazil. In the end, the meetings never occurred. After that abortive attempt, the third stage, from October 2003 until April 2005, was more like the first: posturing, belligerence, and blaming the other. Then there was a fourth period, beginning in July 2005, during which more optimism was possible. Momentum for an exchange seemed to exist as the first term of Álvaro Uribe ended on August 7, 2006. However, that progress ended on October 19, 2006, when the FARC set off a car bomb outside of the Escuela Superior de Guerra in Bogotá.

Strengthening of the Military

The policies of President Uribe also led to changes in the Colombian military. Additional troops, new weapons and communications equipment, and a change in strategy were all made possible by Plan Colombia, a massive military aid program. As a result, Colombia became third in the world in the amount of US military assistance received, only behind Egypt and Israel. Begun in 1998 during the Andrés Pastrana administration, the program was originally directed against the drug trade. During his first administration, Uribe skillfully identified the guerrillas as terrorists, hence making his policies similar to those of President George W. Bush. After the terrorist attacks on the United States on September 11, 2001, the US government began its fight against terrorism in Iraq and Afghanistan. The United States also changed the goal of Plan Colombia to ending terrorism—and as Uribe defined the term, that objective included the FARC and the ELN.

The Uribe policy assumed that the origin of violence was in the historic weakness of the state and its inability to exercise its authority. Security was the responsibility not only of the army and the police but also of all three branches of the government, of the international community, and of the citizens.

With that logic, the policy was centered on two axes. The first was to recover control of the national territory through a stronger military. The second was a legal offensive. The former included the creation of high mountain battalions, of patrols of "soldiers from our town" to assist the police, and of networks of cooperating individuals, based on rewards to informers. The high mountain battalions were professional soldiers trained in special skills and able to work at very high altitudes. Before that time, guerrilla troops had been able to elude the military by fleeing to great heights. The "soldiers from our town" were an addition to the armed forces, numbering as many as fifteen thousand volunteers recruited by regional commanders in small towns. They were considered soldiers and hence were under the same professional code of conduct. They were uniformed but unlike regular soldiers lived in their homes and combined their military duties with other activities such as study or work. After three months of training, they received rifles that they were not allowed to take home. They guarded bridges or other infrastructure of their region and reported on strange movements within it. They also assisted the regular army, and a patrol of armed forces made up of regular and professional soldiers and police agents always accompanied them.

In his efforts to make the military stronger, President Uribe also added to the number of troops and had the majority as volunteers, as opposed to conscripts. The qualitative changes were impressive, leading Colonel Germán Giraldo Restrepo and Gabriel Marcella to conclude, "The armed forces have been totally restructured. The impact of the restructuring is tangible, not only operationally, but also in the form of support by the Colombian people, who have more confidence in their government and armed forces." Giraldo and Marcella summed it up this way: "In conclusion, the army underwent a remarkable restructuring while fighting, in a period of seven years. The fact that the government and people supported the process facilitated this great achievement. The army responded as an institution to the challenge of the new warfare and has gained credibility and legitimacy nationally and internationally. The army has taken on an enormous challenge, and there is much work left to do in order to triumph. The support of the international community, particularly the United States, and the will of senior civilian leaders and in the army helped achieve goals thought impossible in 1998."[12]

Overall, the results of the first Uribe administration (2002–2006) were impressive. Military expenditures went from 2.8 to 3.3 percent of the GDP in five years. Seven high mountain battalions were created, as well as fifteen mobile brigades, fourteen groups of urban anti-terrorist forces, thirty-two anti-kidnapping groups, and fifty-four mobile squads of mounted police. "Soldiers from my town" entered 754 municipalities. There were 4,355 new marines, 20,000 new mounted police, 14,000 new regular police aids, and 13,000 new regular soldiers. All in all, a total of 96,000 new members were added to the police and armed forces.[13]

Another initiative was to get citizens more involved in counterinsurgency activities. The Uribe policy did this in three related ways: having a network of citizen cooperation, using informers, and giving rewards for useful information. The network of citizen cooperation had the goal for Colombians "to stop feeling afraid of cooperating with each other and to cooperate permanently with the authorities." In addition to furnishing information confidentially to help the armed forces, citizens would cooperate in civic duties through organizations set up by the national police.[14]

The idea of rewards was to compensate anyone who gave information about insurgent groups to the government. Rewards were given on Mondays. Some went to members of the network of citizen cooperation, and others to individuals who were not members of that organization. In 2005, for example, the government paid a total of COL$7.716 billion to individuals who gave information that led to successful operations against terrorist groups and drug dealers.[15]

The result of the security policy was that the armed forces took the offensive against the guerrillas. With massive investments in the forces, Uribe launched

Plan Patriota, the military component of Plan Colombia begun in 2003 with the goal of removing guerrilla forces from all parts of Colombia.[16] The first phase was Operation Liberty I in Cundinamarca, the department around Bogotá, through which the army achieved the destruction of many FARC fronts. The second stage of the plan took place in the south of the country, the heart of FARC military operations and coca growing.

The second part of the Uribe security policy was a legal offensive with a declaration of internal disturbance under which the government decreed a property tax, falling most heavily on businesses, and created two rehabilitation zones, in the Montes de María area of the department of Norte de Santander and the entire department of Arauca. The Constitutional Court approved the first declaration of internal disturbance but found its prolongation unconstitutional.

The security policy led to important qualitative achievements, giving renewed hopes of security to Colombian citizens. They were able to travel between cities during holidays through military-guarded caravans. The armed forces captured important leaders of the FARC. As early as July 2004, the Ministry of National Defense reported on several favorable trends in lower levels of violence. The results of the Uribe administration, using the funds of Plan Colombia, were impressive. Homicides at the end of the Uribe presidency in 2010 were 51 percent of what they were at the start of his presidency in 2002 while kidnappings in 2010 were only 9 percent of what they were in 2002. The number of displaced people in 2010 was 23 percent of what it was in 2002.[17] These dramatic changes meant that kidnappings, terrorist attacks, and displacements were less than 20 percent of what they had been eight years before.

Yet not all agree that President Uribe was the reason for the success. One sociologist, for example, preferred to give credit for these improvements to the US military aid that made more troops possible, brought better weapons and communications equipment, and led to better counterinsurgency tactics. He also thought that Juan Manuel Santos, during his tenure as Uribe's minister of defense, deserved more credit than the president himself.[18] There were also negative characteristics of the Uribe administration, especially during his second term. Enforcement of the Law of Justice and Peace resulted in few convictions because of the weaknesses of the judicial system. This result was close to impunity for most of the thirty thousand demobilized paramilitary troops. Three factors explain this failure: the chronic weakness of the Colombian judicial system, the text of the law itself, and the infiltration of the justice system by individuals with connections to drug groups, paramilitary groups, or both. In 2013, leaders who had been imprisoned began to be freed after having served eight years in jail. The state had never tried and convicted them, but they had served the maximum sentence they could have received as punishment.

Some benefits came from the Law of Justice and Peace, including the information gathered about the connections between seemingly legitimate politicians and the paramilitary groups. In these *parapolítica* relationships, politicians received financial support from the paramilitary groups. In exchange, the groups benefited from lax enforcement of laws. The connections of many elected and appointed politicians to the paramilitary groups showed that any division between the "legitimate" and the "illegitimate" systems of Colombian politics was misleading, semantic, artificial, and simply wrong. At the end of 2006 and beginning of 2007, investigations showed that the paramilitary-political connections included both large landowners and members of Congress, departmental assemblies, the office of the national prosecutor, the armed forces, the national police, and perhaps even the Supreme Court.

During the second Uribe administration, groups continued to operate outside the law. While the paramilitary groups of the AUC no longer existed, emerging criminal gangs, known as the Criminal Bands (Bandas Criminales, BACRIM), became more important. In this incarnation, they were especially connected to the drug trade but were still killing, causing the homicide index to be high. The Uribe policies did have some positive effects, but the data indicate clearly that the BACRIM phenomenon was serious at the end of his presidency. Two years after Uribe left office, the Integrated Intelligence Center estimated that one group, the Urabeños, had 1,970 combatants and another, the Rastrojos, had 1,656, although military actions against the groups had decreased their numbers.[19] The Urabeños had more troops than the ELN, were beginning to dominate FARC drug routes, and were absorbing FARC deserters.

Also during the second Uribe administration, members of the Colombian government made decisions based on the belief that the end justified the means. One case was when military officers killed poor people, dressed them as guerrilla fighters, and included them in the body counts (called "false positives" in Colombia). Some officers received punishment for this, but there was no evidence that President Uribe had any responsibility. It does indicate, nevertheless, a weakness of the Colombian government, one that preceded the Uribe administration and went at least as far back as 1990.[20] In two other cases, illegal wiretaps (*chuzadas*) and surveillance took place. The major targets of the wiretaps were Uribe opponents, including one member of the Supreme Court. Several officials of the Administrative Department of Security (Departamento Administrativo de Seguridad, DAS) were punished. Even though it has not been proved, some Colombians still believe that President

Uribe either ordered the wiretaps or knew about them and should be (or will be) punished someday.

There is no evidence that President Uribe was personally responsible for either the *falsos positivos* or the *chuzadas*. This does beg the question, however, of how much responsibility Uribe should have had for the people under him in the military and in the DAS that did participate in these actions. How accountable should a leader be for illegal activities carried out by his or her subordinates?

CONCLUSION

President Álvaro Uribe Vélez, a product of a Colombian political system that had existed for almost two centuries, wanted to change it. He was successful in extending the military power of the state to some parts of the country where guerrilla forces had enjoyed de facto power. That accomplishment was possible because of funds, arms, communications equipment, and advisors that came from outside of the country through Plan Colombia. With the exception of a small number of individuals in the power establishment with alliances with the FARC or the ELN, that accomplishment took nothing away from anyone with vested interests in Colombian politics. Hence, removing the guerrilla forces from the central parts of the country was the easy part of state-building.

Yet it was that very same anti-FARC military strategy that made it impossible to negotiate with guerrilla groups successfully. Uribe's assumption was that, if the strategy were continued, the military would some day be able to defeat the FARC. Whether that would have been possible is the kind of question that might be debated for decades. Some would point out that there was no guarantee that Plan Colombia would continue, while others would add that, as long as it had drug money, the FARC would continue to be strong. Finally, some would note that geographical difficulties made it impossible for the state to have all of the national territory under control. Nevertheless, the actions of Álvaro Uribe Vélez, when he was president and afterward, suggest that some still thought that the possibility existed that either the FARC could be defeated militarily or that the guerrilla groups would surrender unconditionally.

As the Santos negotiations would show, it was extremely important that thirty thousand paramilitary troops demobilized during the Uribe administration. However, the economic and political power of the paramilitary groups was untouched. Therefore, it is not surprising that the *parapolítica* problem existed or that the Law of Justice and Peace was not enforced rigorously.

As I show in the chapters that follow, the Uribe administration established an essential precondition for the peace process by changing the military balance of power between the government and the FARC. As Sergio Jaramillo, high commissioner for peace during the Santos administration, stated, "The change that is most often mentioned—the change in the military balance—was undoubtedly a necessary condition for the negotiations to take place, but not enough."[21] Political scientist and journalist María Jimena Duzán had more specificity in her analysis, arguing that after the death of Tirofijo in 2008, FARC leaders Alfonso Cano and Pablo Catatumbo realized that the balance of forces had changed, largely because of Plan Colombia. Cano often said to Catatumbo, "If it is not possible to have an equilibrium of force, it is very difficult to win the war." Duzán also noted that neither Cano nor Catatumbo had fought for fifty years to end up in a war of resistance. After Juan Manuel Santos won the presidency, Catatumbo was among the first contacts that the Santos administration made about the peace agreement.[22]

Many of the experts whom I interviewed in 2017 had reached the same conclusion that the military balance of power changed during the Uribe administration. A sociologist used slightly different terms: "The most important reason that the process was a success was because the FARC leaders were tired, knew that they were not going to win, and could not imagine another fifty years." When I asked whether this was because of Plan Colombia, he replied affirmatively and added, "Yes, and they had lost so many leaders, not only Reyes and Jojoy, but others in the middle ranks."[23]

Another sociologist, an expert in asymmetrical warfare, went into considerable detail: "The FARC, no matter how headstrong, could not fail to see that after fifty years they were at an impasse. When a guerrilla group retreats and weakens, the possibility of staying together diminishes. It is said that, just by enduring, the guerrilla group wins while the state loses. But with declining size and capabilities, after so much time of struggle, they could not keep up morale."[24]

Nearly all the interviewees mentioned this change in the military balance of power as an important factor. A political scientist said, "The military balance was the key factor. So many of the older FARC leaders had been killed. The younger generation did not have the same intensity. In addition, the marginal gains for the Colombian military were going down. Militarily a stalemate had been reached; both sides realized they could not win."[25] An economist added that the most important part of Plan Colombia was the improvement of the military's technology.[26] A sociologist suggested that the FARC leadership, as early as 2008, had decided that it would have to negotiate because of the military defeats and leaders killed as a result of Plan Colombia.[27] In his book, Francisco Barbosa stated simply that the FARC were worn out.[28]

An interviewee who is a sociologist and journalist reached the same conclusion when he said that "the reason this peace process worked when earlier ones didn't was because the leaders of the FARC knew that there was no chance they would win. They were weakened by changes in the technology of the military, Plan Patriota, and the development of mobile units."[29] A member of the negotiating team of the government also saw Plan Patriota as the key beginning. He said, "Without a doubt, the change of the military balance of power was the most important reason that negotiations were successful this time. In the 1990s the FARC changed to a war of movements and had many important victories. They wanted to surround Bogotá, and in 1999 the FARC had sixteen fronts close to Bogotá. They were carrying out kidnappings in the streets of the city and in the offices of important business owners. The gradual change in the military balance began in 2003 with Plan Patriota. That began the weakening of FARC that led to its negotiation because they realized they couldn't win by force of arms."[30]

President Santos was also precise in giving his reason for the success of the negotiations: The change in military balance of power was shown in Operation Jaque, which came on July 22, 2008, when a military/intelligence maneuver liberated Colombian politician Íngrid Betancourt, three US citizens, and eleven military officers.[31] According to Santos, "Operation Jaque had two diametrically opposed effects. For our military, for our army, it was an injection of morale, enthusiasm, optimism, self-confidence. On the other hand, for the FARC it was a mortal blow to their morale, to their enthusiasm, to their ability to continue that war they had waged for so many years. In other words, it was decisive as an additional factor in the search for peace, because it was about taking away from the FARC that capacity and that desire to continue the war."[32] Juan Manuel Santos was minister of defense at that time.

The first major conclusion of this book is that Plan Colombia during the Uribe administration made it possible for President Santos to lead a peace process that resulted in an agreement with the FARC. That the military balance of power had changed was a necessary precondition. The new troops, weapons, and communications equipment that came from Plan Colombia had lessened the importance of the geographic barriers. The Colombian armed forces were stronger than ever, and the FARC was weaker. The FARC leaders no longer had safe havens within Colombia or in neighboring countries; they were not as secure as before. As a result, their rhetoric notwithstanding, FARC leaders saw little possibility of their winning the war someday.

Statistics back up this argument. During the Uribe years the total number of troops in the armed forces and police increased from 291,316 to 431,900, a rise of 48 percent. At the same time, the estimated number of FARC combatants fell from 24,000 to 8,000, a loss of two-thirds.[33] The armed forces also improved because of better weapons and communications equipment. Yet the military was not able to defeat the FARC, and, in its much weaker position, the guerrilla group had no realistic chance of winning.

Because of this development, as will be shown in the following chapters, there was a change in the nature of the negotiations. No longer, as in earlier negotiations, did one side "freeze" the negotiations. Now both sides demonstrated that they wanted the negotiations to succeed. Both sides feared failure for which they would be held responsible. They took actions, issued positive statements, and made goodwill gestures.

As presented in chapter 1, the analysis of peace processes before 2002 points to four factors that prevented successful peace negotiations: geography, military conditions, paramilitary opposition, and bargaining mistakes. The study of the Uribe years shows that the actions during those eight years gave Juan Manuel Santos certain bargaining advantages when he became president. Colombian geography had not changed, but the weapons, training, and communications equipment that came with Plan Colombia made pockets of de facto guerrilla control more difficult. Likewise, the March 2008 Colombian military attack that killed FARC leader Raúl Reyes in his camp about a kilometer inside of Ecuador showed that safe refuge was no longer guaranteed.

These were seminal events. Alejandro Reyes argues that the important events of 2007 and 2008 were the death of Raúl Reyes, the seizure of three of his computers, and Operación Jaque in which Colombian politician Íngrid Betancourt, three US citizens, and eleven military officers were liberated. Reyes argues that the three events signaled "the beginning of the end of the FARC, overwhelmed by the voluntary surrender of hundreds of their troops and the dismantling of their lines of command and control."[34]

In addition, the Uribe negotiations with the AUC and its demobilization removed one of the perennial problems of past negotiations. No longer could the guerrilla group argue that the government was using its paramilitary allies against it. It also led to increased power for groups representing victims,[35] which would be important in the Santos negotiations, as shown below.

The question then remained of whether the Santos administration would be able to avoid other difficulties. Would leaders on either side oppose the negotiations because they thought their side could still win? Could the two sides reach an agenda at the beginning of the process? Would able negotiators be appointed? Would Santos avoid putting too much of his prestige on the success of the bargaining? Would agreements have the necessary specificity? And would the delicate matters be negotiated only after ones more amenable to compromise?

PART TWO

The Santos Negotiations

In this part of the book, I turn to the negotiations between the Colombian government under Santos and the FARC in Havana and to the opposition to the agreement in Colombia. In chapter 3, I analyze the beginning of the negotiations in rural areas of Colombia and in Venezuela and the first three agreements achieved in Havana, Cuba. Chapters 4 and 5 continue the analysis of the other agreements. Each chapter concludes with a summary of the major accomplishments and the reasons why they were possible. The chapters also include the criticisms of the peace process, especially those from Álvaro Uribe and other members of the Centro Democrático.

CHAPTER THREE

The Beginning of the Negotiations and the First Three Agreements

August 2010 to March 2014

Pʀᴇsɪᴅᴇɴᴛ Jᴜᴀɴ Mᴀɴᴜᴇʟ Sᴀɴᴛᴏs ᴇɴᴛᴇʀᴇᴅ the presidency with a different concept of how to solve the problem of the FARC insurgency than that of his predecessor Álvaro Uribe Vélez. The Santos administration soon began secret meetings with representatives of the FARC, meetings that led to an agreement to an agenda for a secret meeting in Havana, Cuba. Negotiations there led to three agreements in this time period.

Before August 2010 Juan Manuel Santos seemingly had a close relationship with Álvaro Uribe. He founded the Social Party of National Unity (Partido de la U) to support Uribe in August 2005 and served as the minister of defense during Uribe's second term.

The constitution allowed a president to have two terms, but some Uribe followers attempted unsuccessfully to change that.[1] Santos waited until Uribe was unable to seek a third term before announcing his presidential candidacy, saying as he waited that if he did become a candidate, he would continue Uribe's policy of "democratic security."[2]

When the people of Colombia elected Santos president in 2010 as the candidate of the Partido de la U, he promised to lead a government of national unity that would carry out the transition from "democratic security" to "democratic prosperity." He formed a national unity coalition, which added the Conservative, Cambio Radical, and Liberal parties to his party. That coalition held 76 of the 102 Senate seats and 137 of the 164 seats in the lower house of Congress elected in 2010. Therefore, Santos enjoyed greater support in the legislative branch than any other Colombian president who attempted negotiations.

As mentioned in chapter 2, Santos inherited a different military balance of power with the FARC than presidents had encountered in previous negotiations. During the Uribe years, the total number of troops in the armed forces and police increased from 291,316 to 431,900, a rise of 48 percent. At the same time, the estimated number of FARC combatants fell from 24,000 to 8,000, a loss of two-thirds.[3] In addition, the Colombian military was better armed, had better weapons and communications equipment, and was better trained for counterinsurgency warfare, all thanks to Plan Colombia. It changed the military balance of power. While the FARC had momentum at the beginning of the Pastrana negotiations, the government had the impetus as the Santos administration began talking with FARC leaders.

Santos also had ideas different from those of Álvaro Uribe. In 2010 when president-elect, he met Sergio Jaramillo, who had been his assistant in the Ministry of Defense and would serve as high commissioner for peace during his presidency, and said, "I want to reopen a channel with the FARC guerrillas in order to explore the possibility of making a peace agreement that will end the war."[4] Many consider Sergio Jaramillo to be the architect of the peace process. In an interview, a sociologist characterized Jaramillo's importance in this way: "The genius of the Santos process was Sergio Jaramillo. He was the one who came up with the idea of the agenda. After some time in the Fundación Ideas para la Paz think tank . . . he had been in the ministry of defense during the Uribe years, working especially on human rights. It is very possible that he helped Santos in the early attempts at a peace process then. He also wrote a professional code for the armed forces."[5]

As mentioned, although President Santos enjoyed a different military balance of power and had different ideas, he was negotiating with the FARC in the context of a political system in which he did not have complete power. In addition to the legislative and judicial constraints, potential opposition to a Santos peace agreement with the FARC came from the military (which had opposed previous peace processes) and regional elites (some of whom were much more affected by the FARC than others).

Álvaro Uribe turned out to be the principal opponent to the Santos peace process. The two men were very different in regional background (Medellín and Antioquia for Uribe, Bogotá and Cundinamarca for Santos) and social status (son of a rancher and son of the *El Tiempo* newspaper dynasty). Most importantly, during his presidency Uribe refused to state that Colombia had an internal conflict; rather his position was that the guerrilla groups were terrorists.

In his inaugural address, Juan Manuel Santos made it clear that his government's approach to negotiating with the FARC would be different from his predecessor's. He said, "The door to dialogue is not locked. I aspire, during my government, to lay the groundwork for a true reconciliation among Colombians. Of a true spiritual disarmament, built on lasting foundations."[6] This was a dramatic change from Álvaro Uribe who called the guerrilla groups "terrorists," a term that he successfully used to get military aid from the United States in Plan Colombia. When Santos used the term "internal conflict," he indicated that he would be willing to talk with the FARC when it freed its hostages, halted "terrorist acts," and stopped recruiting child soldiers and planting land mines.[7] According to Sergio Jaramillo, this statement was the first of ten steps that made the peace process successful: "The first step was, simply, to recognize that there was a window of opportunity for peace, and above all, to recognize the conflict."[8]

This Uribe-Santos disagreement dominated Colombian politics throughout the FARC negotiations and afterwards. As one interviewee said, "This disagreement about whether we have terrorists or internal conflict is the basic reason for the conflict between the two."[9] Historian and priest Fernán González González used stronger terms when he contrasted the thinking of Uribe and Santos: "Uribe saw the conflict as between absolute evil and good, without the possibility of dialogue. This was opposed to an idea of politics as the collective construction of the social order through dialogue between adversaries, who are relative and not absolute enemies, to seek a negotiated solution to social conflicts and tensions."[10]

A member of a human rights organization in an interview reported that his group immediately saw promise in the Santos inaugural address: "Our group had supported the idea of a peace process during many years, going back to the 1970s. We were very pleased when, in his first inaugural address, President Santos mentioned armed conflict instead of terrorism."[11]

NEGOTIATIONS WITH THE FARC

The negotiations of the Santos administration with the FARC went through four stages between his inauguration and the signing of the peace agreement in August 2016. The first two were secret, one through intermediaries within Colombia and Venezuela and the other an exploratory encounter in Havana, Cuba, between February 23 and August 26, 2012. The third was a two-day table of conversations in Oslo, Norway, in October 2012. The fourth was the dialogue table that began in Havana on November 15, 2012.

In addition to a significant change in terminology in the Santos inaugural speech, other signs of better possibilities of negotiations with the FARC arose from the beginning. There was a difference of international context. Presidents George W. Bush and Álvaro Uribe conflicted with socialist leaders Hugo Chávez of Venezuela and Evo Morales of Bolivia while Presidents Barack Obama and Juan Manuel Santos were more pragmatic. In November 2010, Santos called President Chávez his "new best friend."[12] When I asked a Colombian sociologist if he had been surprised that Santos was able to reach an agreement with the FARC when his predecessors had failed, he replied, "Since the Santos-Chávez meeting, in the first week of the Santos administration, I knew that something was going on regarding peace. Chávez, consistent with his model, always wanted to be a front-line actor in a possible peace for Colombia. Uribe put him in charge of mediating and then, because Chávez broke the regular channel of communication between the governments, took him out of the game. In addition, Santos himself had already tried a rapprochement with the FARC, with a view to a peace agreement, during the Samper administration."[13]

The Preliminary Talks

Since the first two stages were secret, at the time there was little information about them. Later, observers described the beginning of the contacts between the government and the FARC. Enrique Santos, brother of Juan Manuel Santos, and journalist María Jimena Duzán published books in 2014 and 2018, respectively. High Commissioner for Peace Sergio Jaramillo wrote an article for *El Tiempo* in July 2018. The government's chief negotiator, Humberto de la Calle, published his "revelations" about the peace process in March 2019.

Brother of the president, Enrique Santos participated actively in the negotiation drama. In his book, he reported that in September 2010, one month after the inauguration, the president told him that exploratory talks with the FARC had already started and that these came from the unsuccessful talks during the Uribe administration. Furthermore, Juan Manuel Santos told him that he could play a key role and that Santos would propose he serve as the president's personal delegate for the first formal meeting. Later, the president told his brother that the FARC had interpreted his choice as a positive sign of the government's trust and commitment. The president also informed him that contact had been made with FARC leader Pablo Catatumbo through Henry Acosta, an economist from the Valle del Cauca department who had served as a link between the government and FARC leaders from 2004 to 2006.[14]

At about the same time, the government set up a committee to study the lessons learned in previous peace processes. Advisor for national security Sergio Jaramillo and the rector of the Universidad Militar Nueva Granada, General Eduardo Herrera, directed the initial group.[15] Called the Sanhedrin (a reference to the ancient Jewish supreme council and tribunal), it met monthly in Bogotá or Cartagena. The group increased its membership to include Jonathan Powell, chief negotiator under Tony Blair on Northern Ireland; Joaquin Villalobos, ex-commander of Farabundo Martí National Liberation Front in El Salvador; Enrique Santos; and Dudley Ankerson, an Irish intelligence expert.[16]

The group met during the eight months of the secret negotiations with the FARC. Harvard professor Bill Ury also attended a February 2011 meeting. Ury had developed a strategy of negotiation based on the cycle of mourning. Co-founder of Harvard's Program on Negotiation, he is one of the world's leading experts on negotiation and mediation. The basis of negotiation, according to Ury and his Harvard colleagues, is that the process is much like grieving the death of someone. When one side makes a new proposal, the other side goes through a four-step process that begins with denial, then moves on to rage and sadness, and ends with acceptance of the new reality.[17]

Jonathan Powell presented an agenda that had the end of the conflict as its principal goal. That is to say, if an agreement were reached with the FARC, it would have to disarm.[18] When the Sanhedrin met again in Cartagena in April 2012, after the first two exploratory meetings between government and FARC representatives had taken place, President Santos also participated in this three-day meeting, and the experts agreed that the agenda would have to go beyond disarmament to include social changes and political participation. Since the FARC had based its struggle on the need for land, the Sanhedrin decided to make the agrarian point first on the agenda. They did not present this as a concession to the FARC but as an opportunity for the state to modernize the countryside. They also made the victims a central theme, as well as illicit drugs. Since the FARC did not recognize the legitimacy of the state, they included in the proposal the creation of a transitional justice system and a truth commission, both of which would be in accord with the Rome Statute of the International Criminal Court. Finally, they divided the agenda into three phases: the exploratory that was already taking place; a secret phase, during which an agreement would be made about the bases to begin the negotiation; and public negotiations.[19]

The Sanhedrin established the negotiation model that is shown in figure 3.1. As Sergio Jaramillo said, "We were therefore obliged to follow a 'prudent strategy,' which is nothing more than going step by step and doing things incrementally, building on concrete results. It is well known that the best way to ensure cooperation between adversaries is to build results gradually over time, which in turn builds confidence, because it shows seriousness."[20]

The establishment of the plan was essential. As President Santos later said in a forum in Oslo, "We prepared well for these negotiations, and we have worked in parallel to create the momentum necessary to allow us to end this conflict. . . . We have learned from earlier experiences in order to avoid repeating the mistakes of the past and, in that sense, every step we have taken has a logic and a reason."[21]

During the same time, government and FARC representatives had begun their secret talks. By the middle of 2010, both sides had indicated their willingness to sit at the negotiation table with no discussion of who the winners or losers were. In January 2011, the first direct contacts of the two sides

---

Exploratory phase

Two subphases

Recognition of the mutual will to negotiate

Determination of guidelines for agenda, rules of operation, participants, place, and the role of the international community

Negotiation phase

General agreement on previously decided issues

Implementation phase

Implementation of the agreements

Endorsement of the agreements

Demobilization, disarmament, and reinstatement

Implementation of substantial agreements

Transition from arms to politics

Creation of a model of transitional justice

Source: Information from Eduardo Pizarro, *Cambiar el futuro: Historia de los procesos de paz en Colombia (1981–2016)* (Bogotá: Penguin Random House Grupo Editorial, 2017), 375.

Figure 3.1. Government's negotiation model

began in the Cesar department near the Venezuelan border. For the government, the delegates were Jaime Avedaño and Alejandro Eder; for the FARC, they were Rodrigo Granda and Andrés París. The Venezuelan government of Hugo Chávez was active from the beginning.

The objectives of the first meeting were to decide which countries would be the guarantors, where the dialogues would take place, and how the guerrillas would get to the zones where they would disarm and be reincorporated into society. The parties decided that Cuba and Norway would be the guarantors, that Cuba would be the place for the dialogues, and that the International Red Cross would take care of the guerrilla transfer.

As a Colombian sociologist pointed out, it was essential that the negotiations were in Cuba because FARC delegates felt safe there. At the same time, Cuba was trying to improve relations with the United States.[22] Sergio Jaramillo considered the choice of Cuba to be very important. As he wrote, "We thought that Cuba had an interest in helping to end the armed conflict, and that was exactly what happened. It gave the FARC the necessary security guarantees, offered us a place where we could negotiate peacefully, and generously provided us all the human and material resources to make a success of the negotiation. Norway, for its part, provided all its known professionalism and accompanied the negotiation with great intelligence (for example, bringing in groups of experts in transitional justice to speak with the FARC), from beginning to end."[23]

The government and the FARC met secretly for the second time on La Orchila, a Venezuelan island. The FARC still wanted the dialogues to take place in Venezuela. For Sergio Jaramillo, Cuba was better because confidentiality would be easier and because internal conflict in Venezuela might affect the process. The two sides met for the third time on a farm in Barinas, Venezuela. Representatives of the guarantee countries attended. The meeting took place two weeks after FARC commander Alfonso Cano had been killed in a government attack. Although personal relations were cooler, the fact that the FARC delegates were present was a sign that they wanted the process to continue.[24] Alfonso Cano had viewed the interactions favorably.[25] There was concern that the new leader Rodrigo Londoño (a.k.a. "Timoleón Jiménez" or "Timochenko") might not favor negotiations as much as Cano had. However, in his public statements and letters to President Santos and the public, Timochenko showed that he was cognizant of the bad political standing of the FARC. That encouraged him to have additional interchanges with Santos and the Colombian people.[26]

These three meetings and the second round in Havana were secret. As Sergio Jaramillo argued, "The third step—and perhaps the critical step—was to insist on holding secret talks first and reaching a framework agreement before initiating any public peace process." Secrecy was necessary for three reasons:

> First, it allowed both sides to talk seriously and to test the other without the pressure of public opinion, and without the temptation to use the media to please their own audience. . . .
>
> Second, the framework agreement that we signed on August 26, 2012— the General Agreement—not only established the agenda, but the terms and vision of the peace process. It was a kind of "contract," so that the government, the FARC, and especially the Colombian people, knew exactly what we

were getting into and what the negotiation agenda included (and no less important, what not). And it made clear, as we will see, that this time the end of the conflict would actually be discussed.

Third, the secret conversations conferred the necessary dignity to the peace process and developed the methods that later guided the process. We treated each other as interlocutors at a negotiating table and spoke to each other with respect. This is something that, even now, some do not accept. They argue that the government "made itself equal" to the FARC.[27]

From then on, the process continued seriously. The government established a working team, made up of five members of the administration: Jaramillo; Frank Pearl, minister of the environment; Alejandro Eders, counselor for reinsertion; and presidential advisors Jaime Avedaño and Lucía Jaramillo, both of whom were experienced in negotiations. These early discussions required maximum secrecy. While the talks were going on, every three days or so President Santos warned that there could be no dialogue with the FARC "until they show their willingness to lay down their arms."[28]

During that time, the government team had dozens of meetings in Bogotá to discuss the agenda that Sergio Jaramillo had drafted. For the government team, the clear matter to negotiate was the end of armed conflict. In addition, there would be no discussion of the objective and subjective causes of the conflict. Nor would the government negotiate the economic model of the state or the status of the armed forces. There would be no bilateral cease-fire until the two sides had agreed to the essential points.

Very importantly, the government team agreed that the agenda would include the phrase "nothing is decided until everything is decided." While one Colombian sociologist who is a conflict expert said that such was common in labor negotiations,[29] this was the first time that it was stated explicitly in the negotiations between the Colombian government and guerrilla groups. It gave additional flexibility in bargaining because every agreement was just a draft until the final agreement was complete. As the conflict expert put it, "No one is partially obligated because the agreement must be organic and because a concession made may be conditional on another reciprocal one."[30] Sergio Jaramillo interpreted this phrase: "That is, the government was not going to commit to doing any of this if the end of the armed conflict were not also agreed to."[31] Humberto de la Calle added, "The purpose of this rule was to avoid, in the event of a breakdown, it being alleged that the already provisionally agreed upon had a life of its own. This rule, agreed to by both parties, sought to allow the completion of pre-agreed texts without the fear that they would then become irreversible traps. Without that rule, the talks would not progress."[32]

Enrique Santos summarized the plan of the government: "It is a matter, of course, of not repeating the mistakes made by the Colombian state in its negotiations over the past thirty years with the guerrillas, and of having very much in mind the lessons of Caguán [where the Andrés Pastrana negotiations had taken place]."[33] A Colombian sociologist had similar conclusions: "The position of Juan Manuel Santos seemed to say that the FARC could not win in a negotiation the revolution that they did not achieve by armed force. Not discussing the country's economic and social development model was a success. The issue remains for them to promote through the channel of electoral and parliamentary political struggle."[34]

According to the British newspaper *The Guardian*, a key breakthrough after almost four years of secret talks between the two sides came during a visit by President Santos to Cuba, where he met both Fidel Castro and Hugo Chávez. Officially, President Santos went to Cuba to discuss the Americas summit, but the principal purpose of that trip was to discuss the peace initiative. That meeting, in which they agreed on a detailed agenda, was the first of many in Havana between the two sides, facilitated primarily by Cuba and Norway with the backing of Venezuela.[35]

Sergio Jaramillo maintained that constructing the international environment was one of the steps that led to success: "One of President Santos' first acts of government was—beyond all differences—to sit down with President Chávez as responsible neighbors to lower the tension. . . . That's what dialogue achieves. After speaking with President Santos, Chávez radically changed his position with Colombia and instead of supporting the guerrillas he decided to support the peace process."[36]

The Exploratory Meetings in Havana

On February 24, 2012, exploratory meetings began in Havana. They lasted for six months and included sixty-nine encounters at the table in ten sessions. President Santos had previously chosen Humberto de la Calle to be the principal negotiator, knowing that he needed a politician who knew how to navigate in rough waters. Sergio Jaramillo was not that person. Between the two men, de la Calle had held the higher position in government, that of vice president. Naming a former vice president as the spokesperson showed the FARC that the president was serious. In addition, de la Calle was the one who knew FARC leaders. During the Gaviria administration, as minister of government he was the head of the negotiations.[37]

The combination of Humberto de la Calle and Sergio Jaramillo proved to be advantageous in the negotiations. María Jimena Duzán described Jaramillo as the inflexible man at the negotiating table and de la Calle the one who "would come in to smooth over the rough places and look for consensus."[38]

With the selection of de la Calle and Jaramillo, the government organized a negotiating team with credibility for Colombians and with negotiating ability. This combination presented a clear departure from previous negotiations. In comparison, the Santos negotiators were better prepared. Many of the experts whom I interviewed made this argument. A sociologist compared the two administrations in the following way: "In the Pastrana negotiations the chief negotiator, Victor G., was a friend of the president. He was a disaster. The genius of the Santos process was Sergio Jaramillo."[39] Two other social scientists gave credit to chief negotiator Humberto de la Calle. A sociologist rated de la Calle as an excellent negotiator, liberal not only in political party but also in his vision of the world. He was the chief negotiator during the entire negotiations.[40] A political scientist was even stronger in his praise, saying, "Humberto de la Calle was so indispensable that I think that if he had not been the negotiator, the process would have failed. He, unlike others, was able to listen to the other side calmly, even when they made ridiculous demands."[41]

In the opinion of a historian, it was the complementary nature of the two that was crucial. He said, "The de la Calle-Jaramillo team was important. Jaramillo was more like the university professor but did not have a compromising personality. De la Calle was calm, a good negotiator, and a good spokesperson for the public. He also had very good relations with President Santos."[42] A sociologist expressed similar views differently: "The combination of de la Calle and Jaramillo was like a 'good cop, bad cop' situation. Jaramillo was the brains of the negotiation; de la Calle was the patient negotiator."[43]

During the first day of secret talks in Havana, Enrique Santos spoke first for the government. Reading from a document approved by Sergio Jaramillo, the president's brother advised the FARC that this was its last opportunity to transform its armed struggle into a political one and, if it let this opportunity pass, the future that waited for it was as a criminal band co-opted by drug trafficking. FARC negotiator Mauricio Jaramillo countered, saying that the government delegates represented a mafioso state that had lived with paramilitarism and had imposed policies of social inequity, accommodating the warlike policy of Alvaro Uribe.[44]

Later in the first day, the FARC delegates refused to accept that they were perpetrators of violence, arguing instead that they were victims. The day ended badly when the two sides discussed the topic of disarmament. Sergio Jaramillo wanted the agenda to say that, if they arrived at an agreement, the first thing that the FARC would have to do would be to turn in its weapons. The FARC would not agree to turning in its arms before the implementation of the agreement because it did not trust the government. Mauricio Jaramillo protested, "Our struggle is tied to arms, and we are not the only ones who combine the forms of struggle. The oppressive paramilitary state also does it. And now it turns out that that state is the one that is going to tell us that before they make the reforms we have to disarm?"[45]

Sergio Jaramillo insisted, "This issue of weapons delivery must go into the agreement. If it does not go in, I do not agree, and we will return tomorrow to Bogotá because here we are, my dear sirs." Before Sergio Jaramillo got up from the table, Mauricio Jaramillo contended, "All the dead people in Colombia from now on will be because of you." Sergio Jaramillo replied, "Think what you want, but if that does not go in, we have nothing to do, and we leave tomorrow to go back to Bogotá."[46]

This was the first crucial moment in the peace process, a time when the negotiations could have terminated. The exchange was similar to the arguments in previous negotiations that generally led to one side or the other leaving the table. It appeared that the negotiations were going to end just as they began. The government negotiators decided to return to Colombia. They needed to ask the Cuban government for permission for their airplane to depart. Later in the day when Sergio Jaramillo and Frank Pearl were going to the airport, they were advised that the Norwegians and Cubans wanted to talk to them. The Cuban facilitator suggested semantic changes, that they use the wording "laying down of arms" instead of "surrender of arms" and "reincorporation" instead of "demobilization."[47] The two sides approved this change and continued the talks.

For eight months, these talks remained secret. On August 26, the two sides signed the General Agreement of Havana for the End of Armed Conflict in Colombia. They made it public on August 27. From the first day of the exploratory meetings, the government had made it clear that it would not cease military operations and that what happened in the conflict in Colombia would not interfere in the conversations in Havana.[48] The two sides successfully worked out an agenda under those conditions.

The General Agreement was ambitious and contained six items. Each of these topics had various subheadings. The agenda outlined in the agreement was as follows:[49]

1. Comprehensive agricultural development policy

> (1) Access and use of land, wastelands, formalization of property, agricultural borders, and protection of reserve zones.

> (2) Programs of development with a territorial focus.

> (3) Infrastructure and land improvement.

> (4) Social development: health, education, housing, and eradication of poverty.

(5) Stimulus to agricultural production and the economy of solidarity and cooperation, technical assistance, subsidies, credit, generation of income, marketing, and labor formalization.

(6) Food security system.

2. Political participation

(1) Rights and guarantees for the exercise of political opposition . . . and access to the media.

(2) Democratic mechanisms of citizen participation.

(3) Effective measures to promote greater participation in the national, regional, and local policy of all sectors, including the most vulnerable population, equality of conditions, and guarantees of security.

3. End of the conflict

Comprehensive and simultaneous processes to bring about

(1) A bilateral and definitive cease-fire and an end to hostilities.

(2) Abandonment of arms and reincorporation of the FARC into civil life economically, socially, and politically.

(3) Government review of the status of individuals charged or convicted of belonging to or collaborating with the FARC.

(4) Government intensification of the fight to end criminal organizations and their support networks, including the fight against corruption and impunity, in particular against any organization responsible for homicides and massacres or that undermines human rights defenders, social movements, or political movements.

(5) Government evaluation of and adjustment to institutions to address the challenges of the construction of peace.

(6) Guarantees of security.

(7) Clarification of the phenomenon of paramilitarism within the framework of what is established in Point 5 (Victims) of this agreement.

4. Solution to the problem of illicit drugs

(1) Illicit crop substitution programs and development plans with

community participation in programs of substitution and environmental recovery of the areas affected by illicit crops.

(2) Programs for prevention of consumption and for public health.

(3) Solutions to the matter of production and marketing of narcotics.

5. Victims

Compensation of victims is at the core of the agreement. To that end the subjects will be

(1) Human rights of the victims.

(2) Truth.

6. Implementation, verification, and endorsement

The signing of the Final Agreement begins the implementation of all of the agreed points.

(1) Mechanisms of implementation and verification: implementation systems, giving special importance to the regions; monitoring and verification commissions; and procedures for resolution of conflicts.

(2) International accompaniment.

(3) Schedule.

(4) Budget.

(5) Tools of dissemination and communication.

(6) Mechanism of endorsement of the agreements.

The General Agreement ended with ten operating rules:

1. In the sessions of the Table up to 10 people will participate per delegation, of which up to 5 will be plenipotentiaries who will carry the respective voice. Every delegation will have up to 30 representatives.

2. To contribute to the development of the process experts can be consulted about the themes of the Agenda once the corresponding procedure is clarified.

3. To guarantee the transparency of the process, the Table will prepare periodic reports.

4. A mechanism will be established to make public the progress of the Table. The discussions of the Table will not be made public.

5. An effective communication strategy will be implemented.

6. To guarantee the broadest participation possible, there will be established a mechanism to receive proposals about the points of the agenda from citizens and organizations, by physical or electronic means. By mutual agreement and at a specific time, the Table can make direct consultations and receive proposals about the points mentioned, or delegate to a third party the organization of participation spaces.

7. The government will guarantee the necessary resources for the Table to work, which will be administered in an efficient and transparent manner.

8. The Table will have the necessary technology for the process to advance.

9. The conversations will begin with the topic of agricultural development policy and will continue in the order the Table agrees on.

10. The conversations will be held under the principle that nothing is decided until everything is decided.

The very last operating rule—the principle that nothing is decided until everything is decided—turned out to be very important. At a time of stalemate between the two sides, one or both might accept the inclusion of a point, knowing that it was not necessarily part of the final agreement. The rule also reflected the history of previous agreements when one side or the other would come back to something that already had been agreed upon, although this principle had not been accepted officially until now.

Although the items still lacked specificity, with this agenda the Santos administration had already done something that earlier administrations had not been able to do. In the case of the Pastrana peace process, years passed before an agenda was established—and then it was largely ignored. The Uribe administration had never agreed to negotiations, much less to an agenda for them. Of course, at this point it was not clear that the two sides would follow the agenda.

President Santos insisted that the two sides should avoid the errors of past negotiations. Although he was dedicated to peace, it would not be a peace at any price. Santos appeared to be attempting to avoid the previous problem of presidents, especially Andrés Pastrana, who lost bargaining power by link-ing their prestige to the success of the peace process. The president also received the support of the political parties in his coalition, the Roman Catholic Church, and business leaders. In a public opinion poll, 74.2 percent of the respondents supported a dialogue with the FARC.[50]

Oslo

The third phase of exploratory meetings took place in Oslo, Norway. As the formal installation of the dialogue table, its purpose was to reach agreement on the agenda. At the two-day Norway meeting, the parties decided on details such as the time for the Havana meetings to begin, secretarial support, and the use of computers. On October 17, in the news conference after the talks, FARC secretariat member Iván Márquez launched a fiery critique of the free trade policy of the government and called for its transformation. This was the first time that the FARC delegates violated the agreed-upon agenda. As time would show, each side would ignore the rhetorical outbursts of the other. This was different from prior negotiations when one side or the other threatened to end the negotiations because of such statements. Something had changed.

The Havana Negotiations Begin

On November 15, 2012, the two sides began negotiations in Havana. Although President Santos anticipated that the table would not last long, in the end the talks lasted nearly four years. In his opening statement, Enrique Santos said to the FARC delegates, "You can play a role in all this because it has to do with the essence of your agrarian struggle. You should understand the possible connections between the historical agenda of the FARC and what the government is proposing regarding the development of the countryside." The FARC replied, saying that it had always wanted peace. Rodrigo Granda, international spokesman of the guerrilla organization, charged that the FARC had not begun the violence; the state had. This was not the last opportunity; the FARC had heard that before. The FARC was neither tired nor defeated. Its goal was to achieve power, but armed struggle was not the only way to do it.[51]

Comprehensive Agricultural Development Policy

The two sides began negotiations in Havana by considering the first topic, a comprehensive agricultural development policy. Since the FARC originated as a campesino movement calling for better conditions in the countryside, the placement of the land issue first was at least symbolically a victory for the guerrilla group. There were two other reasons that land transformation was a logical way to begin. First, at a general level, because of the conflicts of the state with guerrilla and paramilitary groups, Colombia had become a country of victims and victimizers, making any social reform difficult. Second, the armed conflict and the drug trade had led to a greater concentration of land-holdings in a few hands, had caused internal displacement, and had made the poor campesinos even poorer.[52]

Furthermore, as two interviewees pointed out, the context was promising. One said, "The land issue was dominant throughout the twentieth century. In the end, the peace agreement plans to distribute ten times more land in ten years than had been distributed during the entire century."[53] Another placed the negotiations in context of recent governmental actions: "It was advantageous that the Law of Victims and the land restitution laws had been passed before the negotiations began."[54] At the end of 2010 Santos had proposed a law of victims and restitution of lands. Congress approved Law 1448 in June 2011. Between 2011 and 2016 the government established twenty-two regional offices in the most affected areas.[55]

President Santos signed Law 1448 under pressure from domestic and international human rights groups as well as from the Colombian Constitutional Court. The law aimed to facilitate truth, justice, and comprehensive reparations for victims, with a guarantee of no repetition. It granted all victims the rights to damages, restitution of prior living conditions, a range of social services, and special protections in legal proceedings. Those who had been displaced were entitled to the return of their land or to an equivalent plot of land or monetary compensation. The law also included symbolic reparations measures, such as the creation of a national day of memory and the collection of oral testimonies to preserve historical memory.[56]

Although Congress passed the law before the negotiations began in Havana, it can be considered the first step in the resolution of the conflict with the FARC. However, the FARC thought at first that it was a trick of the government to take land away from campesinos.[57]

At the beginning of the Havana talks, the FARC created the first potential disruption when it tried to leave the approved agenda by proposing a bilateral cease-fire for the Christmas season. President Santos defused this promptly, assuring the FARC that there would be no bilateral cease-fire. As pointed out in the previous chapter, the government had made it clear that a cease-fire would come when all other matters had been resolved. Nonetheless, on November 18 Iván Márquez announced that the FARC was declaring a unilateral two-month cease-fire to last until January 20. This posture was very different from that of the FARC in previous negotiations—the guerrilla group wanted a cease-fire more than the government did and was willing to declare one even if it were not reciprocal. This was another indication that the FARC was bargaining from a weaker position and the government from a stronger one.

As soon as negotiations began, the FARC immediately violated the agreed-upon rules by making public statements. Chief negotiator Humberto de la Calle said that "confidentiality exploded like a soap bubble" when the FARC "used the media without restraint. Every day they went to the microphones with their preaching, proposals, and rants, in an exercise that was extremely damaging. The strategy of the FARC was to flood the media."[58] Very soon another problem arose when the FARC delegates began raising issues that were not on the agreed-upon agenda by bringing up criticisms of the political system in general. That, along with their public statements, gave the impression that the agenda had been set aside and that in Havana the two sides were negotiating a revolution. De la Calle maintained that he made statements "a thousand times" to correct that false impression. He also reported, "At the table, after the morning rhetorical flood, in truth we focused on the specific aspects of the agenda. In the outside world, the torrent of the FARC was unstoppable, but, in my view, quite harmless in real terms of the negotiation, although harmful to public opinion."[59] The government, however, limited its public statements to general ones, only being specific when agreements were reached.

By November and December, the government saw that the negotiations were advancing in a positive direction by allowing FARC leaders to issue rhetorical statements which it then ignored. While perhaps these statements had importance to the guerrillas back in Colombia or to their foreign allies, they had little practical importance.[60] As it was obvious at many points during and after the negotiations, the FARC was not a homogenous organization. One important difference was that some of its fronts were more involved in the cocaine trade than others.

A positive change came when the two sides agreed to open the process for contributions from Colombians in general. Three mechanisms were established for the transition of their ideas to the table: a forum about the agrarian theme to be held in Bogotá from December 17 to 19; regional meetings; and a website that was to serve for communications in both directions. The negotiators would post joint communiqués while citizens would have virtual participation by communicating their ideas to the negotiators.

These three mechanisms were at least symbolically valuable as critics had seen many earlier peace processes as closed (i.e., with little input from individuals outside of the president's inner circle). As I show in chapters 4 and 5, input did come from victims and women, among others. However, criticism of Santos and the peace process had already begun in Colombia.

Several negative events also happened during November and December 2012, but none so serious that either side considered ending or "freezing" the dialogues. The first was that the FARC repeated its earlier request for the release of Simón Trinidad, a FARC leader who was serving a sixty-year jail sentence in the United States for drug trafficking and money laundering. President Barack Obama refused that request and the FARC accepted that.

The second happened in early December when FARC representatives seemed to contradict each other in what they reported about kidnapping victims. Rodrigo Granda claimed that the guerrilla forces had released them all, as President Santos had set as a precondition for the negotiations. However, in an interview with the Cuban newspaper *Juventud Rebelde*, Sandra Ramírez, the widow of FARC founder Manuel Marulanda, disclosed, "Yes, we have prisoners of war, and we are going to turn them over but the state should turn over our people who are there in the prisons."[61] This was a problem of semantics that took place because the FARC leaders had pledged not to kidnap more civilians but had never promised not to capture more "prisoners of war," as they called the military and police. This was a case of the "devil being in the details," but in the end it caused no major problems.

The third damaging occurrence came in the first week of December 2012 when the FARC termed the changes in the justice system for military officers just passed by the Senate a "terrible step toward impunity." The new law stated that the military courts would adjudicate all crimes except genocide, forced disappearances, extrajudicial executions, sexual violence, torture, and forced displacement, all of which were crimes against humanity.[62] As time would tell, the first final agreement would call for military officers to be subjected to the same adjudication for their counterinsurgency actions as FARC members.

During all of this, the two sides had begun their negotiations with the first item of rural reform. In addition to an inequitable distribution of land, more than 40 percent of rural properties lacked a legal title. That situation existed not only in areas on the periphery but also in the coffee-producing parts of the country in which 36 percent of the land had no legal title.[63]

In mid-January 2013 the FARC made a new proposal about the agrarian issue that included fifteen points. The first was noteworthy: since the first negotiations began with the Betancur administration in the 1980s, the FARC had called for expropriation of all large estates. This time the guerrilla group wanted the end of such holdings only if they were unproductive, inadequately exploited, or idle. There are two possible reasons for this change: first, fewer Colombians lived outside of cities. In 1970, soon after the FARC began, 43 percent of the people lived in rural areas. In 2010, only 22 percent lived in rural areas.[64] Second, the FARC leaders were no longer from campesino backgrounds; rather, many had a university education.

In a similar fashion, instead of an absolute prohibition of foreign ownership of land, the FARC softened its position to the establishment of strict limits to foreign ownership. A third modification had to do with free trade agreements. While previously the FARC had called for their termination, now it asked for their revision to protect food sovereignty. These three changes showed that the guerrilla group had dramatically changed its demands. The FARC also proposed that the government carry out an agricultural registry to define the uses of the land, something the country had not done for more than forty years. Perhaps the FARC's most controversial proposal was for tax penalties for lands that were idle, unproductive, or inadequately utilized, as determined by that land registry. Previously the FARC (and even some political leaders) had demanded the expropriation of inadequately used lands. These significant changes from the past showed that the FARC had modified its demands and gave hope that the guerrilla group would be more flexible in other points.

Away from the table, a FARC front captured two police officers in the Valle department in late January 2013, giving rise once again to a controversy over whether the FARC had continued its kidnapping activities. The guerrilla group tried to justify its actions, saying, "We reserve the right to capture as prisoners, members of the security forces who have surrendered in combat. They are called prisoners of war, and this phenomenon occurs in any conflict there is in the world."[65] In a tough statement, the government asked the FARC if it really wanted to end the armed conflict. If not, the two sides were wasting their time. Chief negotiator Humberto de la Calle asserted, "You have to call things by their name. A kidnapping is a kidnapping, no matter who the victim is."[66] Yet there was no suspension of the negotiations.

Tension was high as the meetings resumed in February 2013. The FARC had kidnapped three petroleum contractors, certainly not individuals who qualified under its definition of "prisoners of war," and guerrilla leaders were dying in battles. In previous negotiations one side or the other had "frozen" the process, meaning that it left the bargaining table but did not definitively end the bargaining. Neither side did that in this case or at any other time during the Santos-FARC negotiations. Nevertheless, FARC commander Timochenko reminded the government that it was the government's idea to negotiate without a cease-fire. He did not explain why the FARC had violated its pledge not to kidnap.

The first week of February, in a news conference, FARC delegate Iván Márquez read a document called "Eight Minimum Proposals for the Reorganization and Use of the Land." The proposal called for 39.5 million acres (16 million hectares) of land to be distributed to campesinos, of which a minimum of 22.2 million acres (9 million hectares) would be for individual or collective ownership, and the other 17.3 million acres (7 million hectares) would be for "areas of campesino food production." The proposed rural zones would have political, administrative, economic, social, environmental, and cultural autonomy, and even "the administration of justice through the mechanisms of community justice."[67]

The FARC also proposed an end to the policy of criminalization and persecution of small drug producers, and the suspension of aerial herbicide spraying and other forms of eradication, which in its opinion generated negative socioenvironmental and economic impacts. Márquez said that the use of the land should be redirected toward sustainable agricultural production, and that, in his view, plans should be considered "for legalizing some marijuana, poppy and coca leaf crops for therapeutic and medicinal purposes, for industrial use, or for cultural reasons."[68] While clearly related to the agrarian questions, the drug issue was another item on the agenda.

By mid-February the tone, language, and temperament of FARC leader Márquez had changed, possibly because former president Álvaro Uribe had recently voiced opposition to the peace process, meaning that each side had less room to maneuver. For the Santos administration, this opposition made it more important that the negotiations show progress, even if doing so meant compromise, so that President Santos would be reelected in 2014. As for the FARC, since Uribe's opposition to the peace process raised the possibility that the next president might not be so favorable to negotiating, the guerrilla group's leaders were more willing to compromise with the government. The positive tone of the negotiations increased even more when the FARC liberated three police officers that it had held as prisoners of war.

Despite all of this, two difficult items remained at this time in the negotiations on the topic of rural development policy. One was about the campesino reserve zones. The FARC proposed giving the zones autonomy, converting them into collective territories, and designating the campesinos as a group with their own political rights in the manner of some ethnic minorities. The proposal of the guerrillas included at least fifty such zones. De la Calle noted that the government strongly opposed those conditions but agreed to assist the zones with economic development.[69] The other item of contention, once again not really part of the first point of the negotiations, dealt with victims. The FARC believed that not only was the state responsible for the victims but it should be held accountable for them also.

Yet in spite of the acrimonious environment created by irrelevant statements and public rhetoric, the negotiators in Havana continued discussing the first item of the agenda. They considered the estimated 250,000 campesinos who had no land who would benefit from the land bank and the updating of the land registry. These were especially difficult issues since the possession of land was a source of power for large landowners, paramilitary squads, and drug dealers. President Santos talked about the unclaimed lands as well as those seized from the drug dealers and the paramilitary groups. Having those lands in the land bank was not too controversial. However, it became much more contentious when Santos mentioned 321,237 acres (130,000 hectares) in the eastern plains that he said FARC leader "El Mono Jojoy" had seized. Also complicated were the estimated 247,105 acres (100,000 hectares) that individuals who were neither guerrillas nor paramilitaries had seized. In addition, the land bank would also presumably include those lands that individuals occupied through corruption of the government's land reform institution.[70]

With all these complications, towards the end of February the negotiations seemed to be making little progress. Juan Manuel Santos, demonstrating his ability as a negotiator, warned the FARC that if there were no progress in the peace talks in Havana, the government would have no choice but to leave the table. Iván Márquez encouraged the president not to do so.[71] Once again this showed the shift of power from previous peace processes. The government, as the stronger power, said that it was willing to leave the negotiations, a strong bargaining move even if it were just a bluff. In addition, it also showed for the first time that neither side wanted the blame for the failure of the talks.

Yet, as time would tell, the two sides had devised an efficient way of negotiating—that is, through working groups. Sergio Jaramillo described the method in this way: the table with all the plenipotentiaries, where visions were exchanged and proposals were made; the editorial commission, where specific proposals were exchanged and the text of the agreement was agreed upon; the gender commission, where the text was examined and proposals were made to ensure that the agreement reflected a gender perspective; the commission for the point concerning the end of the conflict, where the terms of the bilateral and final cease-fire and cessation of hostilities were agreed upon, with the participation of active officers of the military forces and the national police; and the jurists, who dealt with the point of criminal justice. Jaramillo added, "The formal procedures of negotiation were important as well. The fact that we worked for three days, stopped one day, and continued for three more, no matter what day of the week it was, gave a strange sense of structure to the negotiation. As did, in contrast to all that formality, the informal meetings we organized between the heads of delegations known as the '3 x 3s,' where we explored proposals and solved problems."[72]

As March 2013 began, the two sides had reached preliminary agreements on the first item of their agenda, including on the access to and use of unproductive land, the formalization of property rights, the agricultural frontier, and the protection of reserve areas. The FARC delayed progress with statements that did not deal directly with the land issue. For example, in late March it declared in a communiqué that it was not realistic to think that its members would go to jail; they would not spend several years in prison so that they could later participate in politics. The FARC also insisted that a constituent assembly should consider the peace accords. As made clear in the agenda agreed to during the second-stage conversations in Havana, the parties would consider these topics at later times.

At the end of March, both sides had a sense of the need to move more quickly, in part because two former presidents—Andrés Pastrana and Álvaro Uribe—seemed ready to make the peace process an issue in the 2014 presidential election. During the Andrés Pastrana negotiations, political opposition to the peace process had made success less likely. However, political opposition had the opposite effect on the Juan Manuel Santos bargaining at least until that presidential election. The Uribe opposition encouraged both sides to bargain more rapidly. The FARC feared that a new administration might be against negotiations, leading the group to be more compromising, while President Santos feared that if the negotiations did not have positive results before the March 2014 congressional and May 2014 presidential elections, he and his coalition were more likely not to be reelected.

When the negotiations resumed on April 22, the FARC named new negotiators who represented the military and drug trade factions of the guerrilla group. They were from the Bloque Sur, which operated in Putumayo and now publicly stated that it supported negotiations and was in total subordination to FARC leader Timochenko. This was an effort to strengthen the unity of the guerrillas.

The guerrilla group also arrived with a new proposal for a "profound agrarian reform." Its four new major points contained a hundred "minimum proposals" and seemed to go further than previous statements with terms such as "end of large land ownings," "slowing down of foreign ownership of land," "return of sovereignty to the people," and "stable and lasting peace."[73] The FARC negotiators were going in circles and coming back to matters that they had previously agreed to, although in this case it was going back to a proposal instead of an agreement.

In April two things detracted from reaching an agreement. First, Centro Democrático presidential candidate Óscar Iván Zuluaga criticized the peace process, arguing that a legitimate state should not negotiate with a guerrilla movement that engaged in drug trafficking and other criminal activities. Second, the FARC once again strayed from the agenda, insisting that the negotiations needed to consider the victims of the conflict. The guerrilla group also contended that all the victims came from actions of forces of the state, with the possible exception of errors the FARC might have committed during the conflict. The government, on the other hand, claimed that the FARC should publicly acknowledge that it was responsible for thousands of victims.

Despite these challenges, on May 26, 2013, the two sides announced their first agreement on an item of the agenda, calling it "Towards a New Colombian Countryside: Comprehensive Rural Reform."[74] Under this agreement, the state would distribute 7 million acres (3 million hectares) of land to 250,000 campesinos, an amount far lower than the 39.5 million acres proposed by the FARC. It also would give campesinos the same guarantees that city dwellers had to health benefits, work, education, infrastructure, and housing. All of this would take place in a period of ten years. The two sides had agreed on this in a document with three major themes—people, territory, and means— and based on the premise that through the timely and effective distribution of land the conflict could be lessened. The people were the campesinos who would receive land. The territory was the badly distributed land that was a major cause of the conflict. The means would be a land bank made up of un-occupied lands and those in the control of illegal groups. Other methods in-cluded a land registry; investments in health, education, housing, and infra-structure; and reserve zones.

While the original FARC position gave administrative autonomy to the re-serve zones, the final agreement read, "The parties agree that the campesino reserve areas, provided by law since 1994, may be one of the instruments of rural development, where warranted."[75] There was no stipulation that they would have administrative autonomy. This should be considered an issue on which the FARC accepted the government's position.

This agreement about rural reform was the first one between the Colom-bian government and the FARC since the Betancur administration thirty years before. Although the published document was not the complete confiden-tial agreement, it was a multipage text. As mentioned before, it was tenta-tive since the two sides had resolved that no agreement on one of the points was final until all the points of the agenda had been decided. Hence it was not in its final form.

The two sides had clearly compromised on their original positions. When *El Tiempo* reporter Marisol Gómez Giraldo interviewed FARC leaders Pablo Catatumbo and Iván Márquez, the latter said, "We are not asking for im-possible things." He added that the guerrilla group was not asking for "radi-cal changes" but instead for regulations in agreement with the constitu-tion. In the opinion of reporter Gómez, Catatumbo and Márquez were de-termined to clear up any doubts that the country might have about their will for peace, since there had been no agreements in the six months since the beginning of the negotiations. Catatumbo said, "We are speaking truth-fully, but we are talking about sensitive issues that have not been resolved for fifty years, and that cannot be fixed in months. If it were so easy, we would have already found a solution." For Márquez, it was notable that many Co-lombians doubted the FARC. "But we are working here with everything," he observed.[76]

On Twitter, President Santos proclaimed, "We truly celebrate this funda-mental step in Havana towards a full agreement to end a half century of conflict." He added, "We will continue the process with prudence and responsibility." Chief negotiator Humberto de la Calle noted that the agreement included "an ambitious program of land allocation to peasants" that would revitalize the peasant reserve areas and, in his opinion, lead to a "rebirth of the Colombian countryside that could happen in the context of the end of the armed conflict." He did mention, however, that some points were still pending.[77]

This first tentative agreement was remarkable for at least five reasons. First, it appealed to the FARC ideology since the movement was originally a campesino movement calling for land reform. Second, it was a relatively easy issue. Vast amounts of land were in the hands of the government because of the paramilitary demobilization, hence giving land to campesinos did not mean taking it away from large landowners. Third, it demonstrated that in principle the two sides could reach agreements, making it easier for subsequent accords. Fourth, even the potentially most contentious issue—taking unproductive land from owners—had a tradition in the country going back to the 1930s. Finally, it showed that each side was making realistic demands, unlike the more radical ones of the past by the FARC.

Negotiations on the Topic of Political Participation

The second agenda topic, political participation, had the potential to be more controversial than rural development. The complicated task was to come up with ways that members of the FARC could legally participate in politics. With the exception of several years after the Betancur peace process in the 1980s, the group had continually been in arms, fighting the government for nearly fifty years. Humberto de la Calle said that FARC political participation had always been a potentially controversial topic. He reported that public opinion polls were showing that around 70 percent of the people opposed it.[78] At the same time, however, the chief negotiator stressed the dual importance of the topic: "From the beginning, it was clear to us that one of the objectives and, at the same time, one of the incentives in a process of talks with a guerrilla organization, was to get them to lay down their arms and enter into politics."[79]

The political participation theme had three topics: the rights and guarantees for the exercise of opposition and for new movements that might appear after the signing of the final agreement; democratic mechanisms for citizen participation; and the means to promote greater political participation at all levels with guarantees of security. These matters included access to the means of communication, institutional reform, a law to guarantee political opposition, a special electoral district for campesinos, media monopolies, and something called "popular power," among others.

Humberto de la Calle outlined the government's position as follows: The negotiators could discuss state-managed new and alternative forces in the media. They could take a close look at the procedures that give parties and movements access to electronic media. They could allow temporary use of small stations in the regions where the reintegration of combatants would be carried out to educate about peace and the end of the conflict. They could expand the range of state support for campaigns within a framework of greater equity. However, the idea of modifying the ownership of the media was buried.[80]

While many people assumed that a central discussion would be assigning seats in Congress for demobilized FARC members for a limited period, it soon became clear that instead at this point the priority of the FARC was the right to offer candidates at the local, regional, and national levels. Some politicians suggested the idea of a transitory electoral system, which would allow the FARC to take part in the 2015 regional elections. However, Congress would have to approve that system. Others raised the possibility of the renewal of the legal standing of the Unión Patriótica so that it could participate in the 2014 national elections.

The guerrilla group made a ten-point proposal,[81] including the following items, some of which strayed from the agreed-upon agenda:

1. Democratic restructuring of the state and political reform.

2. Full guarantees for the exercise of the opposition and for the right to win the presidential election and be in the government.

3. Full guarantees to the guerrilla organizations in rebellion and their fighters for the exercise of politics in case of a final agreement.

4. Democratization of information, communication, and the mass media.

5. Encouragement of participation of regions, local authorities, and territories.

6. Social and popular participation in public policy and planning and, in particular, economic policy.

7. Guarantees of political and social participation of peasant, indigenous, and Afro-descendant communities, and other excluded social sectors.

8. Encouragement of social and popular participation in integration of America.

9. A political culture for participation, peace, and national reconciliation, and the right to protest and to social and popular mobilization.

10. A call for a national constituent assembly.

The electoral reform that the FARC proposed would guarantee equity for all parties; would eliminate clientelism, corruption and criminal practices; and would end the requirement of a minimum number of votes in previous elections for political parties to present candidates. The approval of a "statute of opposition" would give political guarantees as well as assurances of personal safety. The state would make reparations to the members of the Unión Patriótica who had been subjected to violence, and the party would recover its judicial standing. As mentioned in chapter 1, the FARC had the Unión Patriótica as its legal political party, under the terms of the Betancur peace plan. Paramilitary groups then assassinated many of its members.

The following day in Havana, the FARC delegates gave more information about their demands, saying that the Chamber of Representatives should be changed. Instead of the current arrangement in which each department had representation based on its population, the FARC proposed a territorial chamber in which each department would have at least three members. In addition, campesinos, indigenous, and Afro-Colombian communities would have representation.[82]

On August 22 President Santos responded to the ten-point FARC proposal, calling the themes "profound reforms to the structure of the state," initiatives that went, in the opinion of the government and other observers, much beyond what had been contemplated in the agenda approved at the beginning of the peace process. The president argued that the FARC proposal was "a decalogue of reforms of the state, which are not negotiable" and said that these "leaders of the FARC must stop asking for the impossible because it will not be granted to them." The president was emphatic, stating, "We said that we were not going to discuss any public policy, any fundamental reform of the state; that we were going to discuss some rules of the game so that the FARC, and I hope the ELN, will exchange bullets for votes, weapons for arguments."[83] Santos showed strong bargaining ability in this instance.

The FARC clearly wanted to add to the agenda. As the language within its communiqué demonstrated, in addition to a constituent assembly, it now proposed the restructuring of the state; the redefinition of public powers; the elimination of the presidential system; the constitutional redesign of the judicial-economic order; the renovation of the armed forces; the popular election of the inspector general, the comptroller, the prosecutor general, and the defender of the people; and the automatic recognition of political parties. This move sounded more like the problems that had happened in the Gaviria and Pastrana negotiations—straying away from the agenda and demanding changes in the state.

The government first responded to the idea of the constituent assembly when Minister of the Interior Fernando Carrillo replied that in principle there was no possibility of such an assembly. As time would tell, he was probably correct when he said, "If we continue in that line, we will create a counter-revolutionary constituent assembly, in the sense that what we will achieve is to delay all our accomplishments and go back in time." He added that "the 'no' is very clear in the case of a constituent assembly."[84] As shown below, late in the negotiations the FARC delegates dropped the idea of such a body to rewrite the constitution.

However, rather than demands that might end or dramatically change the bargaining process, these FARC demands were first positions in the negotiations. The possibility of compromises existed and later did take place. During the debate about guarantees of the FARC becoming an opposition party, the guerrilla group proposed that campesinos have three seats in the Senate and five in the lower house. The guerrilla delegates also suggested the establishment of a truth commission. It would be an independent group that would investigate the causes of the conflict. This last idea did not fit in the agenda topic at the time but would come up later, and the two sides agreed to the establishment of a truth commission.

During the third week of September, FARC leader Timochenko announced that his group would break the agreement of confidentiality in the negotiations. Although this was a change of the procedural agreement, government representative Humberto de la Calle said that he did not consider this a serious threat. Several days later the FARC leader said it had not been a threat and announced that the talks would remain confidential even though, as he added, President Santos had made public statements about the negotiations. On October 3 Iván Márquez read the "First Report on the Status of the Peace Talks." Instead of revealing previously unknown details about the negotiations, it repeated things that the FARC had already stated in communiqués and declarations.

The delegates discussed these topics as October 12, 2013, drew near, the anniversary of the formal installation of the dialogue table in Oslo in 2012. Since the 2014 elections were imminent, President Santos considered three possibilities of the best way to proceed: continuing negotiations, suspending them until the elections were over, or completely ending them. In a theme seen in earlier negotiations between the government and the FARC, each side blamed the other for the slow progress of the talks. In the end, Santos decided to continue the talks.

The government and the FARC succeeded in reaching an agreement on political participation, the second item of their agenda. On November 6, they released a joint communiqué to announce it. For Humberto de la Calle, the government was participating in a game of "three-cushion billiards." First, the government and the guerrillas would agree on a mechanism for the elaboration of a statute for the opposition and discuss general guidelines for this purpose. Second the political parties would be convened, and social organizations would present their ideas to finalize the content of this statute. Third, the government, within the framework of the end of the conflict, would promote the issuance of the relevant regulations.[85] The agreement on political rights can be summarized as follows:[86]

> Rights and guarantees in general for the exercise of political opposition and in particular for new political movements that emerge upon signing of the Final Agreement. Access to media.

> Democratic mechanisms for citizen participation, including direct participation at different levels and on various themes.

> Effective measures to promote wider participation in national, regional, and local politics from all sectors, including those that are most vulnerable, on a level playing field and with security guarantees.

A number of more specific items described the establishment of structures to facilitate these measures. While it might have seemed unnecessary, previous negotiations demonstrated difficulties afterwards when agreements had lacked sufficient detail. First, a national event would bring together the spokespersons of political parties and movements to create a commission in charge of defining the guidelines for the statute of guarantees for the parties that declared themselves in opposition (the proposed Statue of Opposition). The timeline would be agreed upon in the sixth item of the agenda (that is, under implementation, verification, and endorsement). This commission would submit its proposals regarding the Statute of Opposition, and based on these guidelines, the corresponding legal framework would be prepared.

Second, another national event would take place, during which spokespersons of social movements would make proposals for legislation related to guarantees, the promotion of democratic citizen participation, and other activities that social organizations might carry out. Citizen participation would empower citizens.

In addition, the two sides agreed on measures to guarantee and promote a culture of reconciliation, coexistence, tolerance, and nonstigmatization, requiring that they direct language and behaviors towards respect for the ideas of both political opponents and social and human rights organizations. For that purpose, the agreement included the establishment of councils on reconciliation and coexistence, at the national and territorial levels, to give advice and accompany authorities in the implementation of the agreement.

Without doubt, the agreement on political participation was the most significant document signed by the Colombian government and the FARC in the fifty years that the guerrilla group had existed. However, the document that the two sides released to the public lacked specificity, and some details remained confidential, which led to surprises later. The major surprise was that no seats had been assigned to the FARC in national, regional, or local legislative bodies. Instead, seats in the lower house of Congress were given to the areas of the country most affected by the violence. Apparently, the government had proposed, and the FARC accepted, that the guerrilla group would get no seats until it demobilized, a justice system was in place for it, and it made reparations to victims. It is not clear why this issue did not come up in 2013 but, as chapter 5 will show, the number of seats for the FARC later changed because "nothing was decided until everything was decided."

Negotiations on the Topic of Illicit Drugs

The FARC provoked one of the largest crises of the negotiations to that point in November 2013 when it tried to bring up matters that were not on the agenda, arguing that the preliminary agreement had opened the door to other themes. In this second incident when the peace process could have ended, the government seriously thought of leaving the table. The crisis ended because of the firmness of President Santos and the flexibility of both sides.[87] In an interview in *El Tiempo*, economist Henry Acosta (who had been instrumental in the early talks) said, "The government delegation met in Bogotá to discuss the possibility of leaving the table. Dr. Sergio Jaramillo, as a great facilitator, called me to see if I could help. I spoke for about forty minutes with the president, and he thanked me for being the first person in his office to tell him not to leave the table. Finally, the parties reached an agreement."[88]

When the two sides met again at the beginning of December to begin to discuss the agenda's illicit drugs topic, the FARC presented a document with ten major points, summarized below, that sounded more like a wish list than a serious proposal:[89]

1. A comprehensive, sovereign, democratic, and participatory anti-drug policy aimed at the rural poor and consumers.

2. Structural conditions for overcoming illicit uses of coca, marijuana, and poppy crops.

3. Recognition and encouragement of nutritional, medicinal, therapeutic, artisanal, industrial, and cultural uses of coca leaf, marijuana, and poppy crops.

4. Substitution of illicit uses of coca, marijuana, and poppy crops, and alternative development programs.

5. Immediate suspension of aerial spraying with glyphosate and comprehensive reparation for its victims.

6. Demilitarization of the anti-drug policy, elimination of imperialist interventionism, and decriminalization for the rural poor.

7. Treatment of psychoactive drug use as a public health problem and decriminalization for consumers.

8. An anti-drug policy focused on the dismantling of narco-paramilitary, criminal, and mafia structures preserved by the state.

9. An anti-drug policy focused on the pursuit of capital involved in the economic process of drug trafficking.

10. Responsibility of states for central capitalism, regional commitments, and requirements for the implementation of a global anti-drug policy.

The goal of the guerrilla group, as stated later in a communiqué, was "to contribute to the solution of the economic and social problems of the peasants in rural communities, who have been forced to grow coca, poppy or marijuana. In order to advance in the creation of material and non-material conditions for good living conditions for peasant families and communities, the FARC-EP present the following basic guidelines for a 'National Program for the Substitution of the Illicit Use of Coca, Poppy or Marijuana Crops.'"[90] That is to say, the position of the FARC was that campesinos had to grow illicit drugs because of the inequalities of the legitimate economic system. Later in the month, the guerrilla group, once again drifting from the agenda item, called for a constituent assembly.

The FARC delegates refused to accept that they were drug dealers and said that their only connection to the drug trade was a "tax" that they received from the growers, processors, and dealers who operated in the areas in which the guerrilla group had importance. Those funds were used for the FARC's revolutionary activities. The government, on the other hand, wanted the FARC to make a clear statement that it would end all relationships with the drug trade and would assist the government in its anti-drug programs. At one point when it was clear that no agreement was possible, de la Calle announced, "Gentlemen, this point is essential. In view of the impossibility of reaching an agreement, the government delegation is withdrawing at this time."[91]

In this third incident of near failure of the peace negotiations, de la Calle reported that the delegation left chagrined and that he personally thought that the peace process had ended. He requested that the airplane be made available for the delegation to return to Colombia. However, at about 11:00 p.m. Dag Nylander and Rodolfo Benítez, the representatives of Norway and Cuba respectively, visited the delegation, informing them that the FARC delegates wanted to make another effort to resolve this problem.

The government delegates had made a clear threat that they were ready to end the negotiations when for a second time they requested that the airplane be made available for their return to Colombia. They also had consulted with President Santos. He agreed with their position. That the FARC delegates quickly accepted the second government proposal clearly shows their relatively weak position in the bargaining.

This was the second case when the guarantor countries played an essential role in preventing the negotiations from ending. The government made another proposal that was similar to the first one. The FARC delegates quickly accepted it.[92]

The 2013 negotiations ended on December 20, with chief negotiator Humberto de la Calle optimistically stating, "We close a year of intense and productive work at the table of talks in Havana. We would have liked better results, but we are moving forward. . . . Never before have we advanced so far in terms of agreements with the FARC as on this occasion."[93] Negotiations were scheduled to resume on January 13.

Yet the new year did not begin in a promising way. Presidential elections were approaching, and since one of the major candidates was against the peace process, opposition to the negotiations gained more importance throughout the first half of 2014. Members of Congress and civilians in political parties increasingly disapproved. There was actual and potential opposition from the armed forces. This situation probably led to faster negotiations.

President Santos again bargained by warning the FARC that, if it took certain actions, he would end the talks. Even he seemed pessimistic when he pointed out that the FARC members were not angels and added, "What worries me? Well, that they will commit an act of irrationality that makes it impossible to continue, an attack on an important figure, something that will really blow up the process into a thousand pieces."[94] As mentioned in chapter 1, an attack on Senator Jorge Gechem Turbay was the immediate incident that led to the end of the Pastrana negotiations with the FARC. However, President Santos did not give a definition of an "important figure," and there was no FARC attempt against one who apparently was important.

Despite all of this, by mid-February the negotiators in Havana announced that they had a first draft on illegal drugs. Difficulties reemerged later in the month, first when FARC negotiators strayed from the agenda in their public announcements and later when the guerrilla group changed its negotiating team, adding Fabián Rodríguez. He came from the Bloque Sur, the second-most powerful FARC bloc and the one from the coca-producing areas of the Amazon rainforest. Rodríguez's presence caused a problem when General Jorge Enrique Mora Rangel was upset and declared, "I'm not going to sit down with a narco at the table. I announce my withdrawal from the delegation."[95] However, the general did remain.

At the end of March, once again departing from the agreed-upon agenda, FARC leaders called for a truth commission. Government negotiator de la Calle rejected their demand, saying that a truth commission should be created only after the signing of the final agreement, and that there all the parties must provide "all the truths."[96]

The political debate during the 2014 presidential election continued to be important. Negotiator de la Calle insisted that opponents were using false information in the campaign to frighten voters, "to create a negative climate around these conversations, to frighten Colombians about the progress of these dialogues and their consequences for the future of the country." The opposition to the agreement also used this tactic later during the plebiscite debate, as shown in chapter 6. At the same time, after rumors began that the role of the military was being negotiated, retired general Jorge Enrique Mora Rangel, a member of the government's negotiating team, called for support from the military. Mora assured them that "at no point has the theme of the armed forces been discussed at the table," and that, under instruction from President Santos, "the armed forces are not on the agenda."[97]

Several stumbling blocks arose as April neared its end. The FARC protested that it was not a drug-trafficking group, questioning a recent report of the US Department of State that offered rewards of US$5 million for its leaders, including Iván Márquez and Pablo Catatumbo, two of the group's negotiators. The guerrilla group pointed out, "Both the president of the republic and his plenipotentiaries at the table have affirmed that the FARC guerrilla group is not a drug-trafficking organization, and that is why they are in dialogue with it."[98] The FARC again threatened to stop the peace process if the creation of a truth commission were not approved. Finally, as the presidential election intensified, there was electronic hacking of the peace negotiations apparently to help the campaign of Centro Democrático candidate Óscar Iván Zuluaga.[99]

Despite all these difficulties, in mid-May 2014 the two sides agreed on a solution to the drug trade. The newspaper *El Tiempo* called it a "historical step," adding that "for the first time in nearly thirty years of the attempts of the Colombian state and the FARC to make peace, the guerrilla group promised 'to end whatever association that, as a part of the rebellion, there might have been with drug trafficking.'"[100] The outline of the agreement on illicit drugs was as follows:[101]

The government will establish a National Comprehensive Program for the Substitution of Illicit Crops.

The substitution of crops will be done with the agreement of communities and with manual eradication to generate employment.

In the exceptional case that a community does not collaborate in the substitution of illicit crops or carry out the agreements, other forms of eradication can be used, including the spraying of glyphosate.

The government will create a National Program of Comprehensive Intervention against the Consumption of Illicit Drugs. This program will have a focus on human rights and public health.

The government will fight against organized crime and its networks. To that end it will launch a strategy of criminal policy and a new strategy against the assets involved in drug trafficking and laundering of assets in all sectors of the economy.

The government will revise and establish strict controls over the production, import, and marketing of inputs and precursor chemicals.

The agreement also included the provisions that the government would stop its fumigation program and would stress voluntary manual eradication; the FARC would take part in the removal of antipersonnel mines; and the government agreed that solutions were needed for the estimated sixty thousand families who made their living through the cultivation of illicit drugs.[102]

CONCLUSION

The Completion of the Negotiation of Three Agenda Topics

After the talks in Colombia, Venezuela, and Havana that preceded the negotiations and the approval of three items of the agenda, it was clear that Juan Manuel Santos faced fewer difficulties in his negotiations with the FARC than his predecessors had and that the Santos negotiations went further than those of any of his predecessors. That leads to the question of why.

While it is appropriate to leave some conclusions to the final chapters, the following are some of the opinions that were expressed after the negotiation of the first three topics on the agenda. María Isabel Rueda, a lawyer, professional journalist, and former member of Congress who has been active since the 1980s, wondered if the hour for peace had finally arrived. In comparing the Santos initiative with those of other presidents, she concluded that there was a remote possibility of success because of a change of scenario in which the military forces had begun to strengthen under the presidency of Andrés Pastrana and to win the war during the presidency of Álvaro Uribe. Nevertheless, she suggested that there would be difficulties because of a negative national attitude and the Uribe opposition to the peace talks.[103]

Foundation head León Valencia, former member of the guerrilla group the National Liberation Army (Ejército de Liberación Nacional, ELN) and critic of the Uribe administration, when comparing the Santos peace process with that of Andrés Pastrana, said something very similar in these words: "This peace negotiation with the guerrillas has profound differences from the one carried out in Caguán and also with the one conducted in Ralito with the paramilitaries. This time the state has the initiative and a big advantage over the irregular forces; in contrast, at the end of the century, the guerrillas were on the offensive and had achieved great military victories in the south and in the east of the country."[104]

A third analyst, Rafael Nieto Loaiza, while not challenging the assessments of the other two that the Colombian military was stronger, was dubious that the negotiations would be successful for two reasons. One was because of the ability of the FARC leaders and troops to retreat to Venezuela. The second was because of the income that the guerrilla group still received from the drug trade. For those reasons, Nieto argued, "In those circumstances, I doubt that the FARC will do anything other than take advantage of the benefits that the dialogue produces for them. On the one hand, of legitimacy. When a government negotiates with insurgents, it validates them."[105]

Another critic was Óscar Iván Zuluaga, ally of former president Uribe and the 2014 presidential candidate of the Centro Democrático party. Zuluaga, like the former president, argued that the government was still negotiating from a position of weakness. As he explained it, "The mistake of the president is not his wanting to negotiate peace, but the obsession to negotiate it prematurely and at the expense of the security policy." There was no doubt, he continued, that peace was a noble goal and was the desire of Colombians. However, it was a desire that the FARC had turned into one more of its tactical control tools. For that reason, Zuluaga concluded, being against negotiations was not being an enemy of peace.[106]

Clearly, the government and FARC had made a good start, but difficulties remained. At the beginning of the negotiations, a comprehensive analysis by Gustavo Palomares, president of the Instituto de Altos Estudios Europeos and director of the program Gestores de Paz en Colombia, used the term "hurting stalemate." As mentioned in the introduction to this book, it is defined by I. William Zartman as "where each side is willing to change policies only if it believes that it cannot achieve its desired ends by violence at a tolerable cost and that its relative position will decline in the future. The hypothesis would be that a stable agreement is possible only if both sides believe this at the same time."[107]

Viewing the Colombian case and considering both the positive and negative factors, Palomares stated that this question of a hurting stalemate is not easy to answer, and even more so if we consider that this conflict has been, and continues to be to a lesser extent, a very profitable way of life, especially as the "revolutionary" military objectives gave way to other, much more profitable, "transactions," where kidnapping, extortion, and especially drug trafficking became the priority objectives of that particular way of understanding. Palomares then pointed out the reasons that the FARC might not be ready to negotiate seriously, including the money it was making from the drug trade, estimated to be between US$1 million and US$1.5 million a year, and the land it had seized from the victims during the conflict, perhaps as much as 1,995,682 acres (807,624 hectares). He concluded, "However, doubt—if not pessimism—persists with respect to the fact that in this process there will probably not be a solution agreed upon to definitively overcome the war in Colombia, as long as in such agreements territorial control is not well assured, and there is a continuation of the business of the production and distribution of drugs. Unfortunately, drug trafficking will be that actor formally absent from the table but, nevertheless, the actor always present and decisive in this negotiation."[108]

The Opposition

The opposition to any peace process appeared in Colombia even before President Santos formally announced that negotiations were taking place. In a country in which leaks of secret information are common, rumors began that the government was talking with FARC leaders. On August 19, 2012, former president Uribe reported that the government was negotiating with the FARC in Cuba and warned that the FARC was deceptive. *Semana* magazine reported that Uribe was setting up a group in opposition to Santos. The fundamental reason for creating this group was because of Santos's criticism of Uribe's security policy and what Uribe considered the worsening of the conflict with the FARC in the two years Santos had been president.[109] The Uribe opposition to the negotiations increased as time went on. The former president thought that a military victory by government forces was possible.

After President Santos announced in October 2012 that a peace process had begun, Óscar Iván Zuluaga, who would later criticize the results of the negotiation of the first three agenda items, immediately said that there were many reasons to be pessimistic, "probably the most obvious of which is the improbability that the FARC will abandon the extravagant earnings from the narcotics trade." To that concern Zuluaga added the FARC control of illegal mining, the vast amounts of land it had seized, its lack of the will to make peace, and its continuing terrorist activities such as kidnapping. He concluded, "A legitimate, democratic state like ours cannot negotiate with terrorists in these conditions. The model of development cannot be put on the table, which is exactly what the government did when it permitted the agrarian theme to be the first of the negotiation agenda."[110]

Using the terrorist label put Zuluaga alongside his mentor Uribe, who during most of his presidency refused to accept that there was an internal conflict in his country. Instead, from his perspective, the FARC and the ELN were terrorists. The terrorist label fit well with the war against terrorism waged by the US government under President George W. Bush and was one of the reasons for Plan Colombia. Zuluaga was mistaken in the claim that the model of development was on the table, because this matter was explicitly omitted from the earliest conversations.

There was also resistance from the military. Some of the commanders doubted that Timochenko had issued the FARC communiqué expressing a willingness to consider talks. They pointed out that the military had just initiated a new offensive against the guerrilla group, that a bilateral cease-fire that the FARC had proposed would help the guerrillas while harming the military, and that the FARC was still carrying out hostile activities.

In February 2014 the newsmagazine *Semana* reported that an elite army cyber unit had spied on the digital communications of the government team. The possibility of opposition from the military complicated the negotiations.[111] Interior Minister Aurelio Iragorri said that the Santos administration had not authorized this espionage.[112] In addition, Army Commander General Juan Pablo Rodríguez advised the country that a cease-fire was not appropriate at that time because a military offensive was the only way to contain the terrorism of the FARC. He continued, "The FARC is a terrorist organization that commits crimes throughout the national territory. For example, the famous truce they mentioned was in reality a time in which they built up logistics and intelligence, and after that truce they carried out terrorist acts at the national level and generated a sense of insecurity in the country. Thanks to the efforts of our soldiers, it has been possible to control."[113]

Political opposition to the peace process heated up in January 2014 when unnamed individuals began calling the process a "revolution by contract," saying, "In Havana they are giving the country away." Government negotiator Humberto de la Calle called these "myths." Demonstrating the importance that he gave to the opposition, de la Calle replied at length. To those who were saying that the government would give the FARC the essential institutions of the state and throw away Colombian democracy, he asserted, "Nothing could be farther from reality."[114]

De la Calle assured the public that one should not confuse the habitual FARC speeches with what takes place in the negotiations. While the agreements to this point had been about the first two items of the agenda, and there were transcendental agreements that implied constitutional reforms, nothing in them meant a change from the essence of democracy. The argument that there would be a reduction in the armed forces and in its status was false since the agenda of the conversations explicitly omitted the status of the armed forces. As for the accusation that the rural reform affected private property, everything in the reform respected private property: "Those who had property legally had nothing to fear."[115]

To the criticism that the conversations were secretive, de la Calle noted that experience showed that such conversations needed some confidentiality to be successful: "Negotiating by microphone is the best way to have frustration." And, as negotiated by the two sides, the final agreement would be submitted to a referendum of the people: "Nothing will be done behind the country's back."[116]

To the suggestion that there would be impunity for those responsible for crimes against humanity, de la Calle pointed out that the judicial framework for peace already approved by Congress contemplated a strategy of transitional justice that would be within the international obligations of the Colombian state. Therefore, the legal treatment of those who might have participated in serious violations of human rights would depend on their having recognized their responsibility and having participated in stating the truth and making reparations.[117] Although the juridical framework had not been considered by the delegates of the two sides at this point, a subcommission had begun work on the topic. The agreement reached is analyzed in chapter 4. Subsequent chapters show that it became one of the most controversial parts of the agreement.

New potential opposition to the peace process appeared in March 2014 when Rafael Mejía, president of the Agricultural Association of Colombia (Sociedad de Agricultores de Colombia, SAC), one of the most powerful interest groups in the country, said that members were concerned about the lack of clarity and the lack of leadership in the government.[118] At about the same time, Centro Democrático leaders complained that no one was educating the public about the agreements, something that would be important when the referendum on the agreements took place.[119] In addition, former president Andrés Pastrana stated that the peace process was "a pot that is beginning to smell bad." He insisted that the peace process was a "blank check" for the FARC with the date erased, and he perceived the current balance of the negotiations to be "languid": "Two suspicious 'partial agreements,' cooked up behind the backs of the Colombians, of which not even the one who has to succeed Juan Manuel Santos in the presidency knows anything."[120] Pastrana would later enter a coalition with his former adversary Uribe in opposition to the final agreement.

This opposition was not so intense as it was to be in later stages. One reason was the lack of information about what had been agreed to in Havana. As knowledge increased, and as the date for a plebiscite got nearer, the opposition increased. As shown in chapter 6, the availability of additional information did not prevent the opponents from using half truths and lies.

There is no indication that the Santos administration attempted at this point to talk with the opposition centered around former president Uribe. One person whom I interviewed argued that this was a major problem, that Santos should have met with Uribe and worked together on the negotiations with the FARC.[121] This political scientist believed that there were some points on which Santos and Uribe could have agreed. Events of later years indicated that was not the case.

CHAPTER FOUR

Victims and Justice

June 2014 to September 2015

AFTER THE SIGNING OF TENTATIVE agreements about rural reform, political participation, and illicit drugs, the negotiations with the FARC had already shown more favorable results than any other earlier negotiation. To an extent, every success in reaching an agreement made the following negotiations more promising. However, there still were doubts about the successful completion of a final agreement. Despite the apparent momentum, each item considered seemed to be more difficult than the previous ones. At the same time, the opposition to the Santos-FARC negotiations was increasing. As a result, it took over a year to reach an agreement in Havana about the next item on the agenda, victims and justice. That agreement led to intensified objections from Álvaro Uribe and other opponents, an opposition that continued during the debate before the plebiscite and afterwards.

NEGOTIATIONS WITH THE FARC

At the time of the signing of the agreement on illicit drugs, the FARC suggested that there was much left to do. After acknowledging that the drug negotiations had been difficult, the FARC added, "On this subject—as with the issues related to land and political participation, too—there remained pending issues or details, which must be addressed and resolved, either before signing an eventual final agreement or letting the sovereign settle the disagreements, within the framework of a National Constituent Assembly." The FARC listed four items in its statement, the third of which was clearly beyond the agenda:[1]

1. A new penal code that would focus on the prosecution and imprisonment of the main beneficiaries of the illicit drug market, as well as on the dismantling of transnational trafficking and money laundering networks.

2. Immediate suspension of aerial spraying with glyphosate . . . and full compensation for its victims.

3. Structural transformation of the public health system.

4. The need to hold a national conference on a policy to combat drugs . . . with a focus on human rights in the production, consumption, and marketing of illicit drugs.

When the negotiations resumed in June 2014, the representatives of the two sides faced another complicated subject. As university professor Medófilo Medina wrote in an op-ed article in *El Tiempo*, "The matter of victims surpasses in complexity the points previously agreed upon. It relates to serious issues concerning the violation of International Humanitarian Law; it touches the sphere of the jurisdiction of the International Criminal Court; it is a definitive part of the model of transitional justice that is being designed."[2]

Chief negotiator Humberto de la Calle stressed that this was an essential part of the negotiations. He stated, "As we have said in the past, the victims are at the center of the process," and added, "We have not come to negotiate their rights, but to agree on how the government and the FARC may respond to them in the best way. How do we satisfy their rights to truth, justice and reparation and ensure that the pain and tragedy that they experienced are not repeated? They are of the highest interest to the government in this chapter of these dialogues."[3] High Commissioner for Peace Sergio Jaramillo also considered the victims an integral part of the end of the conflict. He believed that ending the violence required a "logic of recognizing and reassuring victims, that would guarantee their rights, placate the resentment eating away at people and fueling hatred in society, and promote conditions of coexistence and reconciliation."[4]

In early June 2014, the FARC attempted to broaden the scope of the discussion when, in a news conference, its leaders stated, "The victims are not only those of the armed confrontation and the mistakes of war; economic and social policies are the worst perpetrators, because they have caused the majority of deaths in Colombia by denying fundamental human rights such as the right to a decent life, to food, to employment, to education, to housing, to health, to land, to political participation and to good living when enough natural resources are available to solve our social problems."[5] Although, as shown below, the two sides did make the definition of victims broader, it did not become that inclusive. If the two sides had defined victims in that way, they would have added to the agreed-upon agenda.

The two sides agreed that the following ten principles would frame the discussion:

1. Acknowledgement of all victims of the conflict.

2. Acknowledgment of responsibility.

3. Satisfaction of victims' rights.

4. Participation of victims.

5. Clarification of the truth.

6. Reparation for victims.

7. Guarantees for protection and security.

8. Guarantee of non-repetition.

9. Principle of reconciliation.

10. Perspective of human rights.[6]

To tackle all the questions about victims and the transitional justice system, the two sides agreed to establish three commissions to speed up the process of reaching the justice agreement. The first commission would deal with victims of the conflict, the second with the history of the conflict, and the third with the judicial process for those who had violated international humanitarian law and committed crimes against humanity. It was of note that, at least tacitly, the government recognized that it too was the cause of victims. Iván Márquez, number two in the FARC hierarchy and lead negotiator in Havana, said that those responsible for the victims of the conflict went all the way to the presidency and other "powerful leaders" such as in the political parties, the media, the Roman Catholic Church, and the government of the United States.[7] Government negotiating team member retired general Jorge Enrique Mora Rangel defended the role of the state in the conflict: "FARC leaders have been speaking for several days about Colombia's military forces: on the doctrine, on the budget, on the reduction of forces. And I just want to tell you that Colombia's military forces are the legitimate forces of the state. They are the ones that have a more than 70 percent approval rating from Colombians, and the FARC has been the organization that has declared war on the Colombian state, on Colombian society. They are the ones that have brought despair to the Colombian countryside."[8]

The second commission was to study the history of the conflict. It consisted of twelve academics, as well as two rapporteurs. It began discussions and agreed in August to discuss the origins and causes of the armed conflict, a concession to the FARC, which had called for such a study for some time.[9] The FARC peace delegation published a communiqué in which the members welcomed the commission, stating that they had insisted on the importance of its immediate creation because they were aware that it could provide a better understanding of the complexity of the conflict and also open the ways to reconciliation. In addition, this "new intellectual and academic construction of the history of the conflict should provide new interpretations, in many fields which, until today have been insufficiently (or not) treated or analyzed in a biased way."[10]

Defending the guerrilla conflict, the FARC communiqué continued, "To consider that the FARC has invented a war against society, that we are a victimizing machinery and an organization of perpetrators, isn't a demonstration of common sense and a proper analysis of history." The FARC thought that there was enough evidence from documents, testimonies, and historical sources that showed the structural causes of the armed uprising against the state and the dominant classes. Finally, the FARC expressed its commitment to the clarification of the facts that marked the development of the confrontation, and that is why it also proposed the creation of a truth commission in addition to the historical commission.[11]

In January 2015 the government delegation proposed a transitional justice court but made no progress on it for six months. FARC delegate Iván Márquez asked instead for a general amnesty for his organization, reminding the government negotiators that an amnesty had been given to the M-19 guerrillas in the 1990s. Sergio Jaramillo replied that the Rome Statute of the International Criminal Court did not allow such amnesty. A transitional agreement was necessary. FARC leader Timochenko then suggested a commission of judicial experts, an idea that, according to him, had come from Álvaro Leyva. Timochenko added that the FARC would like Leyva to be on the commission.[12] The negotiators established this third commission to work on the judicial process component of the fifth item of the agenda. It functioned in addition to the other two commissions, which were set up to deal with the victims and the history of the conflict.

When President Santos and Álvaro Leyva met on July 29, 2015, Santos said, "I know that Dr. Leyva has played a very important role, and I thank him for all the efforts. For this reason, I would like him to be in the final part of this process officially." Leyva replied, "If you agree, I promise to complete the legal agreement in Havana in a month."[13] The FARC named Leyva as one of its three members on the commission along with Diego Martínez, a leftist lawyer from the Universidad Libre, and Enrique Santiago, a Spanish jurist. The arrival of Leyva was the only reason that the FARC agreed to return to the discussion of the transitional justice system, a fact that Sergio Jaramillo and de la Calle accepted, albeit with a certain discomfort.[14] Three advisors made up the government delegation to the third commission. They were Manuel José

Cepeda, former president of the Constitutional Court and legal advisor to the government in the writing of the 1991 constitution; Juan Carlos Henao, rector of the Universidad Externado de Colombia and former president of the Constitutional Court; and Doug Cassel, professor from Notre Dame University and an expert on human rights.[15]

This deconstruction of the topic of victims into three specific groups, working separately but in the end taking their conclusions to the negotiation table, was theoretically a rational way to deal with a complex topic. In the end, it was also advantageous in practice.

Events in Colombia during 2014 negatively affected progress in the bargaining in Havana. In the congressional elections, Álvaro Uribe's Centro Democrático party increased its representation to 20 of the 102 senators and 19 of the 166 members of the lower house of Congress, weakening the power of the Unidad Nacional coalition of President Santos. The presidential election affected the peace process with competition between Santos and Centro Democrático candidate Óscar Iván Zuluaga. Support for the peace process was the principal plank of the Santos campaign. As lawyer, professional journalist, and former member of Congress María Isabel Rueda wrote, "In today's elections . . . the FARC will be decisive. If the winner is Juan Manuel Santos, it will show that most Colombians want to continue exploring the path of the negotiated solution. . . . If Óscar Iván Zuluaga wins, it will also be thanks to the FARC. Because most Colombians will have decided to reject a negotiation that, for them, includes the cost of widespread impunity, which they are not willing to pay."[16]

In the first round, Santos received 25.6 percent of the vote while Zuluaga had 29.2 percent. Santos won the second round with 50.95 percent. The closeness of that vote was like that of the plebiscite of October 2016, discussed in chapter 6.

Armed conflict in Colombia also complicated the negotiations. In July, twenty months into the peace negotiations, FARC members planted bombs that destroyed infrastructure and killed campesinos. The four hundred thousand inhabitants of Buenaventura, the leading port for foreign commerce, were left without electricity, while citizens of the eastern plains and the Amazon region had seen so much violence that Putumayo governor Jimmy Díaz said, "In this region we are living in one of the most difficult times of our history."[17] As is always the case, it is not clear whether these activities on the Pacific coast (Buenaventura) and the Amazon rainforest (Putumayo) were at the direction of the central leadership of the FARC or were actions that guerrilla fronts took at their own initiative. Plan Colombia had made communications from the central leadership to the fronts more difficult and dangerous.

President Santos had said that he hoped that the negotiations would not take place through public declarations of the leaders of both sides. However, in one of his strongest statements to this point in the negotiations, he said on July 29, "They themselves [the FARC] are digging their own political graves, because that is exactly what makes people increasingly reject them. And that is what we are telling them: you continue with that, you are playing with fire and this process can end, because we cannot continue indefinitely in this situation, because the Colombian people get confused and do not understand."[18] *El Tiempo* columnist Jorge Restrepo asked how much more the Colombian people would take and said that "the obvious question then is whether the guerrilla leaders in Havana control their bases, or whether the inertia of war will repeat with them what happened with the paramilitaries and their continuation in criminal gangs."[19] However, it should be remembered that the FARC had proposed a bilateral cease-fire and the government had rejected it.

On August 7, 2014, in the inaugural speech for his second term, Juan Manuel Santos celebrated: "We signed the General Agreement for the Termination of the Conflict, which established the structure and agenda of the process, and we have not deviated even a single minute from that roadmap. We also reached agreements on three of the five substantive points." He added, "More than celebrating our successes, I remind you that we are already entering the final phase of the talks. And this, as every ending, will be the most difficult and most demanding stage. It will require sacrifices of all of us and, above all, it will require decisions."[20]

On August 16, the first of four groups of fifteen victims testified in Havana. Of the almost forty-eight million citizens of Colombia, the estimated number of victims was six million. The United Nations Development Programme (PNUD) and the National University's Center for Reflection and Monitoring of the Peace Dialogues, with advice from the Roman Catholic Church, chose those sixty persons to travel to Havana to testify. The government and FARC negotiators had been specific that the people should have suffered directly from the conflict. In addition, they "should reflect the universe of violations of human rights and infractions of International Humanitarian Law that have occurred throughout the internal conflict, keeping in mind the different social sectors and populations and the regional focus."[21]

The following month, the FARC in a communiqué responded with ten minimum proposals for the rights of victims:

1. Clarification of the historical truth of the conflict and its impact on the population.

2. Recognition of the victims of the conflict.

3. Special recognition of collective victims; political and social organi-

zations, trade unions and peasant and afro-descendant communities, and indigenous peoples.

4. Systemic responsibility, primary responsibility of the state and multiple responsibilities, including responsibilities of the guerrilla, towards the victims of the conflict.

5. Full recognition and real and effective materialization of the rights of the victims of the conflict, with special attention to women's rights.

6. Full compensation for the victims of conflict and creation of the Special Fund for Comprehensive Compensation.

7. Direct participation of the victims of the conflict and their organizations in the definition of policies for the effective protection of their rights.

8. Agreed definition of legal mechanisms and tools to ensure the rights of the victims of the conflict.

9. Provision of real and material guarantees of non-repetition.

10. Political and social pardon as a foundation for a national reconciliation process.[22]

As part of point 1, the FARC had demanded the creation of a truth commission, of independent nature, with full autonomy in the exercise of its work. It would "contribute to revealing the truth about the process of victimization and the serious violations of human rights and international humanitarian law"; "provide victims with an explanation of the factors, circumstances and people responsible for the acts of victimization"; "help realize the right of the victims of the conflict to truth, justice, reparation and guarantees of non-repetition"; "recommend and promote structural and institutional reforms, needed to prevent future repetition of human rights violations and violations of international humanitarian law"; and "contribute to the necessary process of national reconciliation, derived from the final agreement."[23]

The discussion of reparation to the victims began on August 12. In one of the most complex and sensitive items in the negotiation to this point, the different sides accused each other of being responsible for the victims. The position of the FARC negotiators, as mentioned above, was full compensation and the creation of a special compensation fund. The FARC made the reparations issue more complicated when it asked that imprisoned FARC members be included as victims because "they have been and continue to be victims of serious violations of human rights."[24] Not to be left behind, the government stated that, as a result of its participation in the armed conflict, members of the armed forces had been victims of serious violations of their human rights and infractions of international humanitarian law. As a result, they should be included because of their status as public servants.[25]

As the discussion continued, individuals or groups suggested that victims of spousal abuse, sexual violation, and violence against gays and homosexuals be added to the victims who could testify in Havana. FARC delegates went along with this broader definition of victims when it proposed a fund for the complete reparation of victims, including women and diverse LGBTI groups "who have been victims of regulations, violence, and exclusion throughout the conflict."[26]

The government might have been surprised, but activities by the women's and LGBTI groups led to this change. As one leader of a women's group said to me, "When the photos came out from the meeting in Oslo, all the people were men. That's when women's groups began putting pressure on the government to include women. Sergio Jaramillo had some very capable women in the office of the High Commissioner for Peace, and they helped get the message to him. Later, when the first drafts of the first three agreements were released, it was obvious that women had not been included as much as they should have been. Pressure was put on in the rewrites of them. The establishment of the gender commission was very important. Women became involved for the first time."[27] A sociologist, referring to the final agreement, said, "You should remember that this was the first peace agreement in the world that had the themes of women and of gender crosscutting all the issues agreed upon."[28] As shown in chapter 6, this consideration of women and the LGBTI community gave a minefield of issues for the opponents of the agreement to use.

Representatives of two LGBTI advocacy groups, Colombia Diversa and Caribe Afirmativo, participated in the peace talks. Mauricio Albarracín, a lawyer and LGBTI rights advocate, said that it was the first time that a peace deal had specifically included LGBTI people. "It is very important for the agreement to include the rights of the LGBTI community," he said.[29]

Although the period of bargaining was supposed to be about justice and victims, from time to time the negotiators brought up matters that more properly were part of the final points of the agenda or had already been tentatively decided. The latter could be justified because of the "nothing is decided until everything is decided" clause in the agenda. In some cases, one side or the other made statements on issues such as the extradition of FARC leaders wanted by the United States for their activities in the drug trade, the nature of the Colombian armed forces after the peace treaty, the FARC political movement, a rural police force, and political reform. Both sides made proposals about the way that the Colombian people would approve the peace treaty.

One statement that did not address the agenda item under consideration came in February 2015 when the FARC said that it would create a political movement once the peace process was completed. This seemed redundant since it had agreed to that in the agreement on political participation in November 2013. Nevertheless, the guerrilla group said again that "the FARC will agree in that which corresponds to its contribution to no repetition with the end of the armed conflict and its decision to change itself into a political movement that stimulates structural transformations."[30]

In December 2014 the FARC proposed political and judicial reforms in Colombia. These were to be "profound," but the proposal had no detail. Clearly this was not on the agenda the two sides had agreed to. At the same time, the FARC repeated its earlier comment that no members would spend time in jail.[31]

In the same month, two of the FARC negotiators insisted that after the conflict ended the Colombian armed forces should have a change in mission and a reduction in numbers. They said, "Without conflict it is normal to think of the reduction of the size of the armed forces and the change of its doctrine so that it is dedicated to the defense of sovereignty and natural resources."[32] This statement applied to the armed forces and the national police. However, as noted, the government had already specified that it would not negotiate the status of the military. While not replying explicitly to this suggestion, President Santos suggested in January 2015 that, after the peace agreement, Colombia should establish a rural police force similar to the French gendarmerie. To bring security to the countryside, the objective of the rural police would be to consolidate the development of regions most affected by the violence.[33]

Although the talks at that time formally concerned the fifth agenda item, victims and transitional justice, the two sides made important progress in February 2015 when they set up a technical subcommission for the third agenda item, the end of conflict. As discussed in chapter 5, the subcommission, composed of ten members of each delegation, had the task of considering the issues of the bilateral cease-fire and surrender of weapons. The activity of the subcommission was to focus on the review and analysis of models and the best national and international experiences related to the topic of surrender of weapons. Again, the establishment of a smaller group with a specific focus proved to be a successful tactic in the negotiations.

Since the agenda item specified that this was a comprehensive and simultaneous process, in addition to the cease-fire and the surrender of weapons, the subcommission would consider additional matters:

1. Guarantees for the economic, social, and political reincorporation of the FARC into civilian life.

2. Review of the situation of prisoners for belonging to or collaborating with the FARC.

3. The intensification of the fight to end criminal organizations and their supporting networks, including the fight against corruption and impunity.

4. The review, reform, and institutional adjustments needed to cope with the challenges of peace building.

5. Security guarantees.

6. The clarification of the phenomenon of paramilitary groups.[34]

In March 2015 the positive direction of the peace process continued when President Santos announced the possibility that members of the FARC would not be extradited to the United States, even for drug trafficking. Several of the FARC negotiators in Havana were on the list of those wanted. The president pledged to have conversations with President Barack Obama about this matter. As he stated in an interview with a Spanish newspaper, "No one is going to turn in their arms to you to go to a North American prison. That is totally unrealistic. My responsibility, in my relations with the United States, is to find another solution."[35]

At times during 2015 progress seemed very slow. One sociologist, who said he had been optimistic throughout the negotiations, reported, "The only time I thought the process might fail was in 2015 when things were taking so long."[36] The governments of Cuba and Norway, guarantor countries in the peace talks, aided in the positive direction of the process, when on May 27 they communicated "their profound concern at the current escalation of the armed conflict in Colombia." In addition to regretting the loss of lives this had caused, "The achievements made at the talks, with important agreements on three agenda items, need to be preserved. Never before has Colombia been closer to finding a peaceful solution to the armed conflict."[37]

The issue of how the Colombian people would approve the agreements came up again. The two sides had different positions, the government being in favor of a referendum and the FARC preferring a constituent assembly. While this was supposed to be the final matter negotiated, during this period President Santos made his position clear, saying in December 2014 in a radio interview, that if the peace agreement were concluded, the Colombian people would get to vote on it.[38] He said nothing about how many of the people would need to vote on the agreement, which would prove to be a complicated matter.

Former president Álvaro Uribe, who at times had agreed with the FARC about the constituent assembly, presented yet another view at this time when he suggested the creation of a temporary legislative body, or "little congress." It would evaluate and authorize the agreements made by the FARC and the government in Havana.[39] As I show in chapter 6, the government and the FARC would later decide on the plebiscite. After the Colombian people voted against the agreement, a revised agreement would be approved by Congress.

The Justice Agreement: Beginning Steps

Even before the negotiations began on a post-demobilization justice system, FARC leader Iván Sánchez made the position of the guerrillas clear when he said, "For the guerrillas, no prison. No peace process in the world has ended with the leaders of the insurgence behind bars." Sánchez also said that the FARC members would not turn in their weapons but would simply stop using them.[40] Leaders of the FARC repeated the same "immovable position" the next month, giving as a reason their having exercised the right to rebellion. They claimed armed resistance was not a crime but instead "highly valued by humanity, in order to put an end to the injustices that our people have suffered."[41]

The government seemed to be making a concession to the FARC when in late March chief negotiator Humberto de la Calle announced that there was a high-level commission that was designing a way for transitional justice to be applied to members of the armed forces and the police for crimes they had committed during the war. However, he added, "Of course one cannot apply the same framework as for the members of the FARC, since the security forces are state-run and constitutionally formed."[42]

By May the negotiators on the justice agreement were engaged in a serious struggle over key issues, including the sentences that FARC leaders would have to serve. While the FARC position was clear, so was that of President Santos. He said in a newspaper interview, "A process with complete impunity is impossible." The interviewer explained, "He said it because the FARC still do not accept the Legal Framework for Peace, approved in 2012 by Congress and whose basis is transitional justice, which allows, in exchange for truth, justice and reparation, giving alternative penalties to those responsible for serious crimes. This type of justice is applied precisely to make possible the transition from critical states of violence to peace."[43]

Discussions continued in Havana, with the FARC reporting on May 5 that talks on the revision of sentences for rebellion needed to be unblocked.[44] Negotiations slowed again later in May when the FARC ended its unilateral cease-fire after a governmental attack on one of its bases in the Cauca department. Nevertheless, in the following month the two sides agreed on the establishment of a truth commission. The joint communiqué specified clearly what its functions and objectives would be. As stated in *Semana*, it was a first step, but it lacked answers to the questions of who, where, and when. However, "with the creation of the truth commission, both parties will embark on the painful task of recognizing their substantial responsibility in the war, something that is indispensable for the negotiations to win the support of Colombians."[45]

Although the Santos administration appeared to be accepting a FARC demand with the agreement to set up a truth commission if a peace deal was reached, the government team also thought it was a good idea. According to the joint communiqué, the commission would be independent and impartial and would make sure to hear from all sides of the conflict, particularly victims. The commission would not have the authority to impose sentences, nor could it give information to judicial authorities. Rather, it would try to achieve a broad understanding of the complexity of the conflict, recognize its victims, and guarantee Colombians they would never again have to go through a conflict like the FARC insurgency. The commission would share with the public all information obtained; the government would be responsible for ensuring that the commission had access to public media to allow this. The government would also handle securing the safety of the commission members and those who testified before it. The truth commission would consist of eleven members who would be elected in a process that would "ensure legitimacy, impartiality and independence" to all of Colombian society, especially the victims. A nine-member representative group would elect the eleven members of the commission. The government and the FARC would each elect three of the representatives while the remaining three would be delegates from independent organizations. After the signing of a peace deal, there would be six months to elect the commission members, after which the entity would hold hearings for three years and present a final report.[46]

President Santos expressed his thoughts about the truth commission on Twitter: "We celebrate the agreement in Havana of a truth commission. An important step. We need to keep advancing on other points."[47] María Victoria Llorente, director of the Bogotá policy group Ideas para la Paz, said that FARC had long supported the formation of a truth commission because "the FARC is saying: 'We are not the only ones responsible for the Colombian conflict.'"[48]

By July the position of the FARC negotiators on the matter of transitional justice became clearer when their advisor, Spanish jurist Enrique Santiago, said, "If this peace process is considered the stage for judging one of the parties, of course they will reject it. That is not an alternative because this is not a defeat or a surrender. The FARC will not accept that they alone be judged."

Later in the same interview he added, "From the legal point of view, those most responsible for the crimes committed during the conflict are not only those who have taken up arms. It is clear who are the most responsible ones of the insurgency. But who are the most responsible ones of the state? For international justice, no political office has immunity."[49]

The Justice Agreement: From Announcement to Completion

On September 23, 2015, the government and FARC negotiating teams issued a joint communiqué (Memorandum 60), which, in addition to reaffirming their commitment to the first three agreements, announced the creation of the Special Jurisdiction for Peace. In the end, however, the agreement was not complete until December of that year.

At the time of the September announcement, President Juan Manuel Santos proclaimed, "Today is a crucial and very positive day in the progress of our country toward peace and toward the end of the armed conflict that has bled us for more than half a century." He added that on the afternoon of that day he had met with FARC commander Timochenko and that they had agreed on a deadline of March 23, 2016, to sign the final agreement that would end the war: "At the latest, that day—in exactly six months—will be a definite good-bye to the last and longest war in Colombia, and not only in Colombia but in all of America."[50] The FARC commander said, "The current peace process is the only one in the world that has agreed on a comprehensive system that gathers and relates all the elements described by international law as 'inalienable rights of victims': truth, justice, reparation and non-repetition." He also underlined the need for a special day of contrition, a proposal made by the peace delegation some months previously, and the need for all participants in the conflict to assume their responsibility and offer truth to the Colombian people.[51]

There was a last-minute problem. President Santos later said that Timochenko tried to back out of a crucial part of the newly negotiated framework, seeming to reject an agreement, negotiated just the night before, to set a six-month deadline for the signing of the final accord to end the war. Recalling the problem in an interview in New York the next week, Santos said, "'What is this? Did you not inform this guy about the deadline?' And he said, 'Yes, we did.'" Santos said the rebel leader worried that the government would use the deadline to force the guerrillas to make concessions at the last minute, but he assured Timochenko that he wanted only to speed up the end of the talks. That ended the impasse.[52]

Memorandum 60 gave the impression to some that the government and FARC had reached a deal, mentioning agreements on a comprehensive system of truth, justice, reparation, and non-repetition and on the creation of a commission for the clarification of truth, coexistence, and no repetition. Chief negotiator Humberto de la Calle seemed to mean the same when he said, "The ten points announced constitute a firm agreement. There is no doubt in this. I repeat, this is a firm agreement, there is no doubt about this matter."[53] While it is not clear whether the government was being disingenuous or simply sloppy, if one looked carefully at the sentence construction in the second major point, it was "we are constructing," present progressive instead of past perfect tense (we have constructed) or past tense (we constructed).[54] It would take until December 15 to finish that agreement.

Before an examination of the agreement in its final form, two other matters need analysis. The first is the agreement as it existed in September. The second considers the issues that came up during the next three months.

The Agreements Accepted through Joint Communiqué 60

After reiterating the first three agreements already reached in the negotiations as its first point, Memorandum 60 included nine additional points conveying important information about the justice accord reached up until then:[55]

2. A commission for the clarification of truth, coexistence, and non-repetition would be created, and important agreements about reparations for victims had been achieved.

3. A Special Jurisdiction for Peace (Jurisdicción Especial para la Paz, JEP) with Justice Chambers and a Tribunal for Peace would be created. The membership of the two would be primarily Colombian, although foreigners could compose a minority.

4. In accordance with international humanitarian law, the state would give the broadest possible amnesty for political crimes and those crimes connected to them. In no case would there be amnesty for crimes against humanity, genocide, or serious war crimes such as hostage taking, torture, forced displacement, disappearances, extrajudicial executions, or sexual violence.

5. The JEP would have competence in the cases of all who had taken part in the conflict, directly or indirectly, including the FARC and state agents.

6. The JEP would have two kinds of procedures: one for those who acknowledge the truth and their responsibility and another for those who do not or who do so belatedly. In the first case, they would receive sentences based on precedents determined after comparing in-

vestigations by the Office of the Prosecutor General, penalties imposed by other organs of the state, and existing court rulings, as well as information provided by victims and human rights organizations. In the second case, they would face an adversarial trial before the Tribunal. For all who recognize their responsibilities, the penalty would have a restriction of liberty and rights that guarantees compliance with reparation by the carrying out of work and activities to satisfy the victims.

7. The sentences for those who confess serious crimes would be a minimum of five years and a maximum of eight in special conditions. Those who belatedly confess crimes would be sentenced to five to eight years of prison. To have a right to the alternative punishment, the beneficiary would have to agree to resocialization through work, training, or study. The people who refuse to confess their crimes and are found guilty would be sentenced to prison for up to twenty years.

8. To receive any special treatment through the JEP it would be necessary to confess completely, give reparation to victims, and guarantee non-repetition.

9. In the case of the FARC, participation in the system would be subject to the surrender of weapons that should begin no later than sixty days after signing the final agreement.

10. The transformation of the FARC into a legal political movement was a shared goal that would have help from the government.

Points 2–10 were to be the subject of intense debate during the following months, and several of the statements are of special note here. As point 5 shows, government agencies (primarily meaning the armed forces and the police) would also be subject to the judicial process. This clearly was something that the FARC negotiators wanted. Some later criticized this provision as it punished some agents of the state, putative holders of the monopoly of force. Second, points 6–8 did not indicate exactly what the punishments were going to be, something discussed at length in the months between September and December. Point 9 did not say specifically what "surrender of weapons" would mean, and, finally, there was no mention of where the FARC troops would demobilize. Both of these last two issues were important in the following months.

It soon became apparent that significant issues divided the government and the FARC. The first was what they had agreed to on September 23 in

Memorandum 60. Others issues still open to negotiation included the cease-fire, the location of former FARC troops, and the method for the Colombian people to approve the agreement.

The first disagreement had to do with determining exactly what the two sides had agreed to in the justice part of the agenda. The euphoria of September 23 became a kind of skepticism in only a week. President Santos, chief negotiator Humberto de la Calle, and High Commissioner for Peace Sergio Jaramillo spent seven days explaining the agreement. This, however, produced FARC statements expressing bewilderment at the "unilateral interpretations" of the government, which, in the FARC's opinion, were different from the agreement.[56]

Those statements led to feelings that the FARC guerrillas might go back on what they had agreed to, although both Iván Márquez and the group's Spanish jurist, Enrique Santiago, rejected that contention. Both insisted that they had closed, edited, and signed the agreement on the justice theme. De la Calle was to say several days later in a radio interview that the signed document was the spirit of the agreement, and they still needed to agree to details. "The agreement is being constructed," he explained. The FARC, on the other hand warned or threatened that the agreement could not be modified, arguing that the justices chosen through the agreement would have the function of interpreting it, and if any doubt was cast on the agreement as a whole or any of its points, "that will put in doubt the date agreed upon for the end of the conflict."[57]

De la Calle added, "In response to the recent statements of the FARC delegation, allow me, as chief of the negotiating team of the government of Colombia, to make the following clarifications." He then listed four points: First, that the document released on September 23 gave the "fundamental elements" that are a fixed agreement. Those points included the creation of a special judiciary for the investigation, judgment, and sanction of the most important crimes. It would cover FARC members, state agents, and third parties. Second, it promised the greatest amnesty possible for political crimes with the understanding that amnesty would not apply in the case of international or serious crimes. Third, the rights of victims would be guaranteed through justice, truth, and non-repetition. Finally, a system of differentiated sanctions would be created, depending on those who recognized truth and responsibility and who contributed to reparations and the guarantee of non-repetition.[58]

The chief governmental negotiator reiterated that it was a solid agreement about which there was no doubt, but also it was a summary of a longer text of seventy-five points, drafted by a group of legal experts. Finally, the chief negotiator said that, because of recent public statements by lawyers and members of the FARC delegation, the government thought that there were other cases of clauses that might be ambiguous. Those needed to be written in a more precise way.[59] This was an attempt to avoid "the devil is in the details" problem, common in the unsuccessful Andrés Pastrana negotiations.

On October 6, in a "report from Havana" the FARC peace delegation, headed by FARC negotiator Victoria Sandino Palmera, agreed that the justice agreement needed more specificity and then made ten minimum proposals. The first was "legal formalization of institutional adjustments and reforms needed to address the challenges of peace building." This point was divided into five subpoints that included reforms and institutional adjustments designed to achieve peace as well as new rules and regulations for the legal system. In turn, public policy should reflect the entire process. For this purpose, the FARC proposed the creation of a commission for policy development, to be composed of six experts appointed by the table. Finally, the peace delegation proposed the definition of a mechanism to deal expeditiously with the pending issues of the partial agreements and the peace talks in general.[60]

In the interim between the announcement of the justice agreement and its finalization, three other issues came up at the bargaining table. They were the location of former FARC troops, the end of the conflict, and the paramilitary groups.

On October 28, Humberto de la Calle reported that a subcommission was making progress on the issue of where to locate demobilized FARC troops. He said that it would be "one of the largest operations of verification and monitoring in the world, therefore it is a topic that we are making progress on and for which we have inputs." He concluded that he had encouraged the government's delegates to speed things up and hoped that FARC leader Timochenko would do the same.[61]

This matter was still controversial in early December when the FARC delegation said, "Some see us concentrated in a kind of confinement. . . . That idea is far from what should happen since we are searching for a peace between equals and not a surrender." In this "necessary clarification," the FARC delegation then quoted from the agenda point concerning the end of the conflict: "Reincorporation of the FARC to civil life in its economic, social, and political aspects, in agreement with its interests." FARC members could do that by living with their families and not in pens: "In none of our proposals have we talked about 'demilitarized zones.' Our interest is to live in community and with the communities."[62]

The FARC proposed that peace territories be set up. Negotiator Carlos Antonio Lozada said that these would not be demilitarized areas but rather that these were meant to become real laboratories of reconciliation, of reunification, not only of the two parties but also of the two Colombias, divided and separated by inequality and social and economic imbalance. When asked about the functions of the military in these zones, he said that local security was more a police issue, not a task of the military forces: "The role of the police can be carried out in multiple ways, while the army must fulfill others, for example, defend the sovereignty, recover the identity of our sovereign and independent nation."[63]

The question of the end of the conflict came up again in late November when the FARC, through a communiqué read by Commandant Ricardo Téllez, presented its eighth proposal on the question. Regarding the "comprehensive security guarantees for the population in general and for the future FARC political movement," the FARC proposal included eight initiatives, among other safety guarantees for mobilization and social protest, including the dismantling of the infamous riot police, according to the spokesman.[64]

Likewise, the guerrillas talked about security guarantees for political and social organizations on the left, victims, and human rights defenders. These guarantees should also apply to the recently proposed "special territories for peace building" and to the political movement the FARC would form. To this end, a "special and permanent security commission" should be created, in charge of designing a security plan for the post-agreement phase. This special plan would require exceptional regulations and a new institutional framework for its implementation. All the initiatives would be in order to provide guarantees not only for the future FARC's legal political movement, but also for all existing political and social movements and others that might arise, with the participation of people and their communities as well as the participation of other countries and organizations like the Union of South American Nations, the Community of Latin American and Caribbean States, and the United Nations.[65]

Another disagreement between the two sides during this September–December period had to do with paramilitary groups. The position of the government was that paramilitary groups had ended with demobilizations during the Uribe administration and that the organizations that existed were "emergent or criminal bands."[66] FARC negotiators, however, made a proposal that suggested that they did not acknowledge a difference between paramilitary groups and the criminal bands. They wanted an "action plan to dismantle paramilitary structures." A document read by FARC spokesman Pablo Catatumbo called for the creation of a "specialized unit of investigation and analysis for the dismantling of paramilitarism," created by the government and the FARC. A specific task of this unit would be to draft within four months a report on the current location of criminal counterinsurgency structures, especially of a paramilitary nature. Based on the report, an "action plan for the dismantling of paramilitarism" should be in operation before the signing of a final agreement.[67]

The FARC also proposed emergency legislation for the dismantling of paramilitarism; to do so, Catatumbo first asked for the elimination of any legal or administrative provision that allowed the creation of counterinsurgency structures. Also, there would be sanctions for those proven to have links to those structures, and penalties for those who created, financed, promoted, or concealed them. The expropriated goods or sources of financing from those structures would go to comprehensive victims' reparation.[68]

The Final Agreement on Victims

On December 15, 2015, the government and FARC negotiators released the "Full Agreement on Victims."[69] Humberto de la Calle emphatically stated, "Today from Havana, we Colombians have very good news for the world. It is not rhetorical, IT IS NOT RHETORICAL, to say that the announcement of the agreement on the recognition of the rights of the victims predicts the possible end of the conflict and the advent of a firm peace. Not any peace. We want a lasting peace, which can only be achieved by placing the victims at the center, as we have done."[70] The full agreement was much more specific than the communiqué of September 23 had been, and it was to become a major source of controversy, especially the part having to do with the adjudication of the FARC leaders. This controversy was notable during the debate before the plebiscite and even afterward.

The agreement called for a transitional justice system, called the Special Jurisdiction for Peace, that would apply to all those who had directly or indirectly participated in the armed conflict, even if they were not members of the armed rebel organizations. The justice agreement would cover only combatants in organizations that had reached a final agreement with the government. Using a different set of rules, it would also have authority over government agents who had committed crimes in the armed conflict. Presidents would not come under its jurisdiction. They would still be judged by the Chamber of Representatives, which would act according to its powers as granted by the constitution.

The imposition of any punishment would not prevent political participation, nor would it limit the exercise of any right of political participation. Persons who were part of rebel groups that signed the peace agreement would receive amnesty or pardon for political and related offenses committed as part of rebellion. The membership of a rebel group would be determined by a list handed over by the group. Included among political and related crimes were rebellion, sedition, and military uprising, as well as illegal possession of weapons and killing in combat as defined by international humanitarian law.

Some political crimes would qualify for pardon and amnesty. Those included were offenses related specifically to the development of the rebellion, committed within the context of the armed conflict. Those excluded were crimes as established by international law, according to the Rome Statute. Not eligible for pardon or amnesty were crimes against humanity, genocide, serious war crimes, hostage taking or other severe deprivation of physical liberty, torture, extrajudicial execution, forced disappearance, violent sexual intercourse and other kinds of sexual violence, child abduction, forced displacement, and the recruitment of minors.

Administering justice for crimes excluded from amnesty had two procedures: one in the case of the acknowledgment of truth and responsibility and another in the case of the absence of it. A very important stipulation stated that under no circumstance would imprisonment be a punishment for crimes that had been acknowledged. The sanctions for very serious offenses would require some alternative to imprisonment: a deprivation of liberty from five to eight years. Yet this provision lacked specificity, and the nature of punishment became one of the major issues in the debate about the agreement before the October 2016 plebiscite.

The sanctions imposed for individuals who did not acknowledge truth and responsibility would comply with existing penal law and could include imprisonment. However, those individuals could receive a reduced sentence if they participated in social rehabilitation through work, training programs, or study. In the case of state agents, sanctions with a special prison jurisdiction would be applied. Once again, the agreement lacked specificity concerning key aspects of this procedure, including the places for and monitoring of the sanctions.

Extradition would not be allowed. The guarantee of non-extradition included all FARC members and persons accused of belonging to the group, for any conduct carried out before the signing of the final agreement, and for those persons who submitted themselves to the comprehensive system of truth, justice, reparation, and non-repetition. The date of the signing of the agreement became important later.

There was a list of sanctions that the Peace Tribunal might impose, which could be added to later. The list considered the extent of truth disclosed by the person, the gravity of the sanctioned conduct, the person's degree of participation and responsibility, and the commitments the person made in terms of reparations of victims and guarantees of non-repetition. Activities accomplished personally and directly by any individual under the Special Jurisdiction for Peace would be considered, provided that they led to victim reparation or had a restorative impact.

There were two kinds of sanctions. First, for persons who acknowledged truth and responsibility, the sanctions were of a restorative nature, to guarantee non-repetition. They promoted such things as comprehensive rural reform, political participation, and the solution of the problem of illicit drugs. Other sanctions related to the damage inflicted on minors, women, and other affected subjects, and addressed the need for reparation and restoration of victims of the armed conflict, to the largest extent possible.

Second, there were sanctions applicable to persons who did not acknowledge truth and responsibility in the process and who were found guilty by the tribunal. Sanctions would correspond to the criminal code. The effective deprivation of liberty would not be less than fifteen years or more than twenty years in cases of serious breaches or violations. Substitute penalties might be applied, provided that the beneficiary committed to resocialization through work, training, or education during the time spent deprived of liberty, and engaged in activities aimed at non-repetition following release. Once the sanction had been complied with, if a reduction in sentence had been received because of a commitment to engage in such activities, the convicted person would be released on probation. The probation period would expire upon completion of the activity, and in any case, would expire when the sentence imposed by the Peace Tribunal had been served.

Despite all the specificity shown in the preceding paragraphs, the agreement on the judicial process still had vague points. There was no specific decision about the method to elect the judges of the special court. Nor was the method for making reparations clear. That was irrelevant according to FARC negotiator Iván Márquez because the FARC had no money.[71]

INCREASING CRITICISMS FROM THE PEACE PROCESS OPPONENTS

Criticisms of the peace process, especially from former president Álvaro Uribe and members of his Centro Democrático party, increased throughout this phase of negotiations. In May 2014, CD member Carlos Holmes Trujillo maintained that his party favored peace, but it should be arrived at with justice. He also asserted that the CD was against political participation of any former FARC member who had committed war crimes or crimes against humanity.[72] At about the same time, CD member Rafael Nieto Loaiza criticized President Santos and the media for calling anyone who disagreed with how the negotiations were proceeding "enemies of the peace, extreme right, neo-Nazis, fascists, Black Hand, and countless epithets and disqualifications of similar caliber." Nieto continued that those accusations were dangerous as well as false.[73]

Along the same lines, the next month Óscar Iván Zuluaga, the CD presidential candidate, called the FARC the "principal aggressors in Colombia," adding, "President Santos did not demand the surrender of weapons, nor does he demand that they hand over all the money, the fortune they have accumulated with drug trafficking and kidnapping, to be able to compensate the victims. The victims need reparation, truth, and justice, and the big aggressors are the FARC."[74] Zuluaga was wrong about the surrender of weapons. Right after his reelection, Santos replied that he was bored with the Uribe accusations and said in a radio interview, "I want to leave behind that chapter of false testimony, of false accusations; the country is bored by that."[75] As shown in chapter 6, the false testimony and accusations were far from over.

In early July think tank leader and former ELN member León Valencia took Uribe to task in an op-ed column in *Semana* magazine. Valencia pointed out that the former president had sent letters to former chief executives of Brazil, Chile, the United States, Spain, and Great Britain in which he had said, "During the negotiations between the government under President Juan Manuel Santos and the FARC, the criminal actions of this terrorist group have increased against Colombians and the future of new generations, as shown by the statistics on murders, kidnappings, and attacks on the country's infrastructure." Valencia said that the statement just was not true and that data collected by his think tank showed that.[76]

In August, Uribe and his movement rejected the presence of military officers in active service in the Havana negotiations. Óscar Iván Zuluaga said that made the legitimate forces of the state equal to terrorist actors. Senator Alfredo Rangel added that the CD considered it illegal to have active military officers in Havana, that it humiliated and demoralized the armed forces, and that it might gravely affect national security.[77]

In October an article appeared in *Semana* recounting Uribe's attempts to connect with the FARC during his own presidency. President Santos asked Uribe to stop "sabotaging" the peace process. The president accused Uribe of having a double standard since Uribe himself had made many attempts to negotiate with the FARC.[78]

One of most intense debates between the government and the Centro Democrático party to that point came in October 2014 when the CD listed fifty-two objections to the agreements that the government and the FARC had made up to that point. Presenting those points, the CD called the agreements a "capitulation to terrorism," and asserted that the agreement about agrarian reform had expropriation in it and threatened seriously the rule of law in the countryside. Senator Alfredo Rangel added that the reforms would take more than ten years and that the FARC would give up its arms only when the agrarian program had been completed.[79] This was not the case in the final agreement.

Humberto de la Calle replied that suggestions were welcome, but these criticisms were based on incorrect information. He said that the Centro Democrático members' points were subjective, their own opinions, and wrong: "I categorically state that what has been said about expropriation and forfeiture is not true." He added that the agreement about agrarian development "does not change a comma of the legislation in force" and that "expropriation for reasons of social interest and public utility in the matter of land issues has been a legal concept for more than twenty years." On this topic, de la Calle concluded, "The Centro Democrático may be against current law. But that does not allow it to attribute to the agreements something that they do not say nor to use their dissatisfaction with rules in force since the last century to provoke alarm among legitimate owners and businessmen."[80]

As for the suggestion that the FARC would be armed while taking part in politics, Humberto de la Calle and Sergio Jaramillo were emphatic. They said, "There will be no armed peace." The implementation of the agreements "requires the full and simultaneous fulfillment of all the obligations contracted, including the laying down of arms."[81]

President Santos also replied to the CD criticism of the peace process, saying that some persons "for political reasons prefer for the country to continue at war because they know how to manipulate fear very well or because they believe that continued violence does not give space to some leftist groups that have suffered politically due to the existence of the conflict." Referring to the fifty-two "capitulations" to the FARC that the CD had alleged, the president was categorical: "What an irrational position, so lacking in support, simply by criticizing or opposing a process that the Colombian people want. Well no, we will not allow them to oppose that peace. The Colombian people will continue to back a process that will change one future for a much better future."[82] As shown in chapter 6, the president was wrong in his evaluation of what a majority of the Colombian people wanted.

CONCLUSION

The decision to create a transitional justice system proved difficult at the bargaining table and was to be one of the most controversial parts of the final agreement. The FARC delegates could not accept prison terms, and President Santos recognized that such punishments were not possible. Nor was complete amnesty a possibility. Even if the government had been willing to go along with that FARC position, the Rome Statute made amnesty impossible in certain cases.

The question was whether the compromise would be acceptable. While it might have been a reasonable compromise for the government and the FARC, former president Uribe and his followers would not approve it, especially with the ambiguities in the final agreement.

An important change in the negotiation pattern between the government and the FARC became evident during the consideration of the transitional justice system. In the Pastrana negotiations there had been a negative tit for tat, with each side replying negatively to the negative statements of the other, leading to a failure in the peace process.[83] No longer did one side "freeze" the negotiations as had happened then. Instead, now both the government and the FARC demonstrated that they wanted the negotiations to succeed. Both sides feared failure. Each side took actions, issued positive statements, and made goodwill gestures. Each party participated—individually, together, or with the help of governments and international organizations outside of Colombia. The pattern changed from the vicious cycle of the Pastrana negotiations to a beneficial cycle. No longer were there sequences of reciprocal causes and effects in which two or more elements intensified and aggravated each other, leading inexorably to a worsening of the situation. Instead, in the new tit for tat, a positive dynamic prevailed in which causes and effects led to a better situation.

This change in dynamics had been seen previously in the Santos negotiations, both in the preliminary talks in which the government and the FARC made agreements about the place for the negotiations and the accompanying countries and in the preliminary talks in Havana that resulted in an agenda.

The beneficial cycle continued in one of the most difficult incidents during the negotiations. On November 15, 2014, President Santos suspended the peace dialogues with the FARC after FARC troops in the Chocó department kidnapped General Rubén Darío Alzate Mora, commander of the Fuerza de Tarea Conjunta Titán. Addressing the Colombian people, the president announced that "the important thing is that the FARC, we already know, were responsible for this kidnapping. A totally unacceptable kidnapping. We already have information that makes us certain that it was the FARC. And that is why we hold the FARC responsible for the life and security of these three people: the general, the corporal and the lady. And we demand that they release these three people as soon as possible."[84]

As a result, the president ordered the negotiating team not to return to Havana for the next round of talks, an action that came close to the freezing that occurred in previous negotiations. The FARC leaders first replied that they did not know if their troops in that remote area had the general or not, and leader "Pastor Alape" called the government action "impulsive" and said that the peace process should not be put at risk in that way.[85] The FARC peace delegation in Havana responded, "The peace process, whose results have renewed the hope for reconciliation, cannot be put at risk with impulsive decisions. To the astonishment of the world, this decision is made by a government that has stubbornly refused the opportunity for the peace process to be carried out amid a truce or armistice, which could help to de-escalate the conflict. The position to be at peace talks while under fire seems more senseless every day."[86] At nearly the same time, the FARC representatives announced

Table 4.1. From a vicious cycle to a beneficial cycle

	FARC	Government	Together
2014			
November 18	Puts bilateral cease-fire on the table.		
December 17	Announces unilateral truce.		
December 27	Declares willingness to withdraw children under 15 years old.		
2015			
January 17	Asks to start discussion of a cease-fire soon.		
March 7			Reach demining agreement.
March 11		Military operations decline.	
April 9		Another month passes without bombing the FARC.	
April 16	Timochenko talks about peace dialogues.		
April 19		Despite an attack in Cauca, the peace talks do not stop.	
April 24	Says peace process must be carried out.		
July 8	Announces unilateral cease-fire as of July 20.		
July 22	Promises to stay at the table until they reach peace.		
July 25		Santos suspends bombing of camps.	
August 30	Says the process moves in the direction of a final agreement.		
December 7	Acknowledges guilt to the victims of the massacre of Bojayá.		

Continued on the next page

Table 4.1. *Continued*

	FARC	Government	Together
December 15			Agree on transitional justice.
December 30	Secretariat says that agreement will be reached in 2016		
December 31		Santos says that in 2016 the country will see the signing of peace.	
2016			
January 28		Santos wants to remove the FARC from the terrorist list.	

that the general and the four other captives would be released.[87] The general was released on November 30.

In an op-ed column in *El Tiempo*, Marisol Gómez Giraldo correctly argued that this was a "signal of peace without precedent." It was such, she argued, because if this had led to the end of the negotiations, the FARC would have gone down in history as being responsible for ending the peace process: "It is clear that they never have been predisposed to assume the political cost of the failure of the negotiation."[88] While that was the case in 2014, it was far from it during the Barco, Gaviria, and Pastrana negotiations. During those dialogues, the guerrilla group was ready to end negotiations on many occasions, always blaming the government for the rupture of the talks. Either the government or the FARC froze negotiations when incidents like the Alzate kidnapping happened.

A lead editorial in *El Tiempo* concluded that 2014 had been the year in Colombian history with the greatest success in peace negotiations: "What happened in Havana is, without doubt, the big event of the year that ends today. The reason is, as has been said, that never before had there been such progress in a matter, although sometimes not seeming to be statistically significant to the extent that fewer and fewer Colombians are affected by the conflict or die because of it, to which it is clear are tied a handful of unresolved issues, which are nothing less than the impediment to the country fully developing its immense potential."[89]

Yet while the negotiations were headed in a positive direction, two sets of uncertainties remained. The first was whether either side would attempt to complicate the bargaining. For example, as late as January 20, 2016, the FARC presented a new proposal—to create a national commission to rid the country of paramilitarism. The fight against the paramilitary groups, the proposal argued, should be a state policy, as well as of different parts of society. To do that, the FARC proposed the creation of a national commission to combat paramilitary groups and impunity. That commission would be an independent organ made up of state entities, civil organizations, and FARC members "moving to a political movement without weapons."[90]

The second set of reservations, also at the Havana bargaining table, was whether the two sides would reach agreements on the end of the conflict and on the method for ratification of the agreements. The government and the FARC had very different ideas on the ratification method. Little had been made public about disagreements about the end of the conflict, but they were likely to exist since they included disarming the guerrillas, placing them in certain zones of the country, and providing for their adjustment to civilian life.

At the same time, opposition to the peace plan intensified. While criticisms of the possible agreement had already risen, the increase would be much greater later. Francisco Barbosa anticipated this when he wrote in a November 2014 op-ed piece in *El Tiempo*, "One of the important debates about the current peace process is related to the possibility that the members of the FARC may be condemned to prison terms for the commission of atrocious crimes. This aspect cannot be resolved with agreement between the parties, nor with endorsement by the people, due to international restrictions established for the state by the inter-American system of human rights and the International Criminal Court."[91]

The same month columnist Álvaro Sierra Restrepo wrote in *El Tiempo*,

To the FARC are attributed more than 20,000 kidnappings; at least 3,000 child recruitments; most of the 4,200 civilian victims of antipersonnel mines (1,100 are children); thousands of homicides, such as those of the two indigenous guards of Toribío; and major responsibility for forced displacement. Not to mention incidents like the massacre of 11 deputies of Valle in 2007 or that of 34 workers who harvested coca leaves in La Gabarra in 2004.

With such a burden of "mistakes" and "imponderables," sooner or later they will have to make the decision. It happened to the government. For years it denied that there were victims and even that there was armed conflict. With the Law for Victims and acts such as forgiveness for the massacre of El Salado, it finally began to accept that it is a victimizer. It still has a way to go. But the FARC lack that essential step.[92]

CHAPTER FIVE

The Final Negotiations

March to August 2016

DURING 2016 FOUR IMPORTANT THINGS happened in Colombia: the Colombian government, under Juan Manuel Santos, and the FARC reached a final agreement; in a plebiscite in October the Colombian people rejected that agreement; the government and the guerrilla group negotiated a second final agreement; and Congress approved that agreement. The process through which the two sides reached the first final agreement is the subject of this chapter.

While negotiations in 2016 officially focused on the issues of the cease-fire, demobilization, and surrender of weapons, the two sides had begun the process of bargaining about those issues through subcommissions during the previous year. In March 2015 President Santos announced that five generals and an admiral would go to Havana to negotiate a bilateral cease-fire and the surrender of arms as part of a subcommission on the topic. The officers were Álvaro Pico Malaver, Carlos Alfonso Rojas, Martín Fernando Nieto, Orlando Romero Reyes, and Oswaldo Rivera Márquez. General Jorge Enrique Mora Rangel, a member of the governmental negotiation team, also participated. The members from the FARC leadership were Carlos Antonio Lozada and Joaquín Gómez.[1]

The decentralization of the negotiations to meetings between military experts from the parties proved to be among the most important procedural decisions. To reach an agreement on the difficult issues of a cease-fire and the laying down of weapons, the bilateral cease-fire subcommission consulted experts and practitioners to draw on lessons learned from other peace processes. They also invested considerable time in agreeing to a common methodology before drafting a text. The direct participation of the Colombian security forces in the talks was an innovative feature of this process compared to other attempts to negotiate peace with nonstate armed groups. Their participation was controversial among many members of the armed forces, and those who participated were subjected to considerable criticism in Colombia.

The parties agreed to invite the United Nations to assist the subcommission at a time when it became essential to receive input from the body that had agreed to monitor and verify the laying down of weapons and the cease-fire. The UN secretary-general appointed an experienced UN envoy as the secretary's delegate to the subcommission on August 13, 2015. The UN Security Council passed a resolution in January 2016 establishing a political mission in Colombia with the task of monitoring and verifying the laying down of weapons. The three parties designed a mechanism comprising the UN, the Colombian armed forces, and the FARC to monitor and verify the definitive bilateral cease-fire and cessation of hostilities. The Community of Latin American and Caribbean States committed to providing the staff needed for the special mission, demonstrating the support of regional organizations for the peace process.

The reintegration of former combatants probably received too little attention during the talks. Reintegration has normally been the least successful dimension in Colombian peace processes and has resulted in fresh cycles of violence. The issue was not sufficiently defined in the peace agreement, partly because of time constraints, and partly because of very different perspectives on how it should be resolved.[2] Problems with it characterized the post-agreement phase, discussed in chapter 7.

REACHING THE FINAL AGREEMENT WITH THE FARC

On September 23, 2015, President Santos and FARC leader Timochenko had named March 23, 2016, as the deadline to sign the final agreement that would end the war. While the deadline might have been reason for 2015 to end and 2016 to begin with optimism, the negotiations were not always productive. In December 2015 the FARC delegates once again attempted to stray from the agreed-upon agenda. They proposed changing the security policy of the government by reducing the size of the army and the police and, most importantly, by demilitarizing the peace territories. Retired General Jorge Enrique Mora Rangel, former commander of the armed forces and one of the government negotiators, made it clear that this was not something to be negotiated: "The FARC must be absolutely clear that the process we are carrying out does not include counterclaims, or redefinitions of the mission and budgets, the size of the forces, or of their organization. As a team, we are not going to do it, and the instructions that we have received from the president of the republic have been clear and precise. Therefore, the extensive and daily communications of recent days laden with issues, proposals, and messages related to Colombian military forces and the national police, simply reflect aspirations of the FARC that have no future."[3]

Nor did the negotiations progress rapidly during the first weeks of the new year. Marco León Calarcá, a member of the FARC peace delegation, placed the blame on the government, saying that the FARC had given a fundamental contribution to the climate of peace. He "recognized as positive the government's decision to suspend bombings. However, it cannot be said the same of the measures taken against the interests of the majority, like the miserable minimum wage increase and the road towards tax reform." Living conditions were deteriorating and that should not be allowed in the name of peace.[4]

On February 18, 2016, FARC leaders Iván Márquez and Joaquín Gómez, as well as some twenty other armed guerrilla members, paid a "pedagogical visit" to the settlement at El Conejo in the municipality of Fonseca in the Caribbean coastal department of La Guajira, causing a major incident. While FARC delegates did have the right to visit Colombia to explain the peace process to members of the guerrilla group, that did not include armed contact with civilians as took place in this case. The encounter caused a general uneasiness in the Colombian government. High Commissioner for Peace Sergio Jaramillo cautioned that this incident was not a "small impasse" and that it put the peace dialogue in crisis.[5] FARC leaders claimed, "These protocols do not stipulate that you cannot talk to the people. Educating for peace is not equal to armed proselytism. That is the agreement. There is no such violation of the protocol by the FARC."[6] The government suspended the pedagogic visits of the guerrillas and ordered the guerrilla leaders to go back to Cuba. However, this incident, just as the one with General Alzate described in chapter 4, did not lead to a "freezing" of the process and had no lasting effect on the peace process. The El Conejo episode showed once again that the negotiation dynamics had changed from those of previous administrations.

The negotiators did not meet the March 23 deadline that Santos and Timochenko had set for the final agreement. After a long day of conversations in Havana on that date, Humberto de la Calle explained why the two sides had not kept the promise made six months before. He said, without being specific, "We must inform the public that at this time there are major differences with the FARC on fundamental issues." An *El Tiempo* article speculated that the real reason had to do with armed campaigning, such as had happened in El Conejo. De la Calle's statement substantiated this. He stressed that the agreement about the surrender of arms would affect political participation and that disarming would be necessary to apply the transitional justice system and to reincorporate the guerrillas into civilian life.[7]

In his official declaration, however, de la Calle became more specific, making three demands. First, the FARC would have to disarm before taking part in political activities. Second, the government demanded a "clear, precise and fixed date for the end of the disarmament." Third, the government would not allow any citizen to be unprotected in the zones where the disarmament was taking place. This, the government's chief negotiator said, was to avoid what had happened in El Caguán during the Pastrana negotiations.[8] In that case, the absence of the military and national police resulted in the complete authority of the FARC. Some of the policies of the guerrilla group led to discrimination against LGBTI individuals, divorced people, and others who disagreed with the puritanical policies of the guerrilla group.[9]

Referring to the failure to finish by the March 23 deadline, FARC leader Iván Márquez was vague when he stated, "It could not be accomplished because of the obvious demands of a prolonged war that has brought us to engage seriously in the roadmap that we hope will be agreed upon during the next negotiating cycle." However, he implied what the difficulties might have been when he added, "We are outlining the most propitious way to move forward in the specification of crucial issues such as amnesty, the bilateral cease-fire and the end to hostilities, the process of surrendering arms, and the undertaking of measures that will guarantee [. . .] the legal protection and the effective implementation of all commitments."[10] It is important that, unlike in previous negotiations, Márquez did not blame the government and claim that the FARC was not the problem.

El Tiempo analyst Marisol Gómez Giraldo argued that the major reason for missing the deadline was the FARC negotiators who resisted setting a date for the total surrender of their arms. She believed that although the guerrilla group's proposal had not specified a concrete date, the FARC had counted on the government accepting it anyway due to time constraints. In addition, she suggested that the FARC wanted the arrest warrants for its members lifted in the entire country while the government only wanted them lifted in the transitional zones. Also, she said, the FARC wanted its political campaigning to begin before disarmament, and it wanted mobility for its members throughout the nation.[11]

A similar analysis in *Semana* contended that while it was true that the two sides disagreed on the number of transitional zones, the major problem was the government proposal about the rules within the zones.[12] For the government, the zones were where the FARC members would be identified, receive their citizenship cards, and join a state reincorporation project. For the FARC, on the other hand, the transitional zones would be the beginning of its political work. The disagreement brought up a sensitive matter—that the demobilized guerrillas would interact with civilians and with institutions.

In addition, the government's position was that the zones would be in distant, rural areas, preferably without civilians and schools, to avoid violations of international humanitarian law. This idea of living in an isolated area made the FARC delegates unhappy because they thought that their transition to politics would mean intense contact with the civilian population. The government wanted to avoid the possibility that the civilian population would claim to be at the mercy of the FARC since the group would not yet have definitively surrendered its arms.

Importantly, each side also had fears. The guerrillas worried most about the time of surrendering arms. *Are they going to kill us? Are they going to put us in jail? Are they going to betray us?* The members of the government also had fears and mistrust. *Are they going to keep their word? Will they really turn in all their weapons? Will they begin their political activities before they turn in all their weapons?*

According to the *Semana* analysis, the matter of justice and the surrendering of arms were the two issues that touched the FARC the most and were also the thorniest in the face of public opinion. The legitimacy of the peace process, and therefore its eventual approval, depended to a considerable extent on people understanding that there would be no impunity and believing that the FARC would lay down its weapons and not use them in politics. The analyst concluded, "That's the difficulty. And although their positions are still very distant, what is clear to both sides is that the agreement will be signed this year. In fact, the surrendering of weapons must also be done before the end of 2016. But, now, no one risks setting a date."[13]

In an interview in *Semana*, Carlos Antonio Lozada, a member of the FARC secretariat, explained the insurgent group's position on the concentration in placement zones, the cease-fire, the relinquishment of arms, and the transition to politics:

Semana.com: What does that proposal consist of?

Lozada: It is that at the time we reach agreement, it is not known if, at one time or in stages, all the weapons will be placed in the hands of a third party, be it a group of countries or an international organization. All verified by the international component of the tripartite monitoring mechanism that was already agreed on.

Semana.com: What are these pending issues?

Lozada: There are pending issues in all the agreements, such as the election of the judges of the special peace tribunal and the terms of the amnesty law and the date when it would take effect. It is necessary to synchronize the timing of this, and there is a very clear proposal on the table.[14]

Regardless of which side might have had greater responsibility for the slow progress, several matters remained to be negotiated. The two pending items of the agenda were the end of the conflict, that is, the cease-fire and demobilization, and how the Colombian people would ratify the agreement. In addition, minor points from previous items needed to be made more specific, including the establishment of the land fund. There were questions about the amount of land that would be in the agrarian reform, from both unclaimed lands and lands confiscated through asset forfeiture, and about a special system for food security.[15] In the political participation agreement, the two sides had agreed that there would be special transitional electoral districts for those territories that had been especially damaged by the conflict, but the two sides had not defined those territories nor determined the number of seats for them in the lower house of Congress. In addition, both sides had agreed that there would be a commission to recommend changes in the electoral system, but there was no agreement on how they would set up that commission. On the matter of illicit drugs, how the FARC would contribute to the effort against the trade still was not clear. As expert Juan Carlos Garzón put it, "It needs to be specified how they are going to contribute to crop substitution and the disarticulation of drug trafficking criminal groups."[16]

The FARC had another major concern: how the agreement would be protected after its signing. The guerrilla group still did not trust the government or the political establishment. The FARC's fear was that if it did not have sufficient guarantees, the government would rescind the agreement once the FARC had disarmed. The statements being made by Álvaro Uribe and the silence of other political leaders strengthened those fears.[17]

In June the FARC made a major concession, agreeing that Congress would protect the agreement. More specifically, the legislative body would give juridical stability to the agreement through two constitutional reforms and a law. This was a dramatic change after years of saying that Congress was illegitimate and rejecting its laws.[18] President Santos celebrated this decision, saying that for the first time the FARC recognized the governmental institutions of the nation, and the FARC recognition practically guaranteed that the Colombian people would have the final accord through a plebiscite.[19]

Nevertheless, decisions remained to be made in the justice agreement. No specific method to choose the judges of the special court had been determined. Nor was the process for making reparations clear. FARC negotiator Iván Márquez had said that the FARC had no money.

The cease-fire and disarming of the FARC were complicated, as was the way to verify those actions and the zones that the former guerrillas would occupy. President Santos had said there would be between seven and ten areas while FARC spokespersons talked of a higher number. In addition, this point included the conditions under which the guerrillas would transition into civilian life.

From the beginning of the negotiations, the two sides had disagreed on the way that the Colombian people would approve the eventual agreement. FARC delegates argued for a constituent assembly. The government representatives wanted a referendum. As President Santos said in December 2014, "I am sure that when we say to the Colombian people—if we reach these accords—vote for peace, . . . the Colombian people, I know it, are going to vote for that peace . . . because that peace is not going to be a peace at any cost. That peace is going to be a sensible peace."[20] The president's assessment proved to be wrong. A majority of the Colombian people did not vote for peace as called for in the agreement. Before this came to pass, during the negotiations two questions remained about the process for approval by referendum: first, would this be a vote on each one of the agreements or a yes-or-no vote on the entire package? And, second, what percentage of the Colombian people would need to vote?

The first progress of the year had come on January 19, 2016, when the two sides communicated through a joint memorandum that they had decided to create a tripartite mechanism of monitoring and verification of the agreement, as mentioned above. The next issue they resolved was the way that the Colombian people would approve the agreement. While in early May the two sides had remained firm in their preferences, the FARC then changed its stance and agreed to a plebiscite. From the beginning, the FARC had sought a constituent assembly, but it would have been a rubber stamp one, not one that could change the constitution in any way.[21] It is not clear why the FARC changed its position. One possibility is that, fearing that the process of a constituent assembly would be slow, the guerrilla group was concerned that its demobilized members could be threatened in the meantime. Therefore, it had proposed a two-step process with the assembly approving the constitutional changes sometime after the two sides had approved the agreement. Another possibility, as explained by an interviewee, was that the governmental negotiating team convinced the FARC team that the Uribe forces would win the election for a constituent assembly and make changes that the guerrilla group did not want.[22] A third possibility is that this concession was a trade-off that the FARC delegates made to achieve what they wanted in another of the pending issues.

In early May, the government began its planning for the ratification of the agreement by the Colombian people. Senator Roy Barreras, one of the government's negotiators and president of the Partido de la U, asked the National Electoral Council for a date for an open vote by the people on the agreement.

His proposal was very similar to that suggested by FARC negotiator Iván Márquez the previous week. The law stated that one-half of the national electoral list, or almost seventeen million voters, would have to take part. This, the government negotiators thought, would make a "No" vote more likely. They also feared that the treaty would not be ratified because of abstention. If the necessary number of people did not vote, the agreement would not be accepted, even if the majority of the people voting approved it. The government and its allies in Congress made the decision that 13 percent of the eligible voters would have to participate, an arbitrary number the reason for which is uncertain. As explained by a sociologist, "The constitution leaves to Congress the regulation of referendums and plebiscites. A statutory law had previously set the threshold for plebiscites at 50 percent of the electoral roll. For the vote on the peace agreement, Congress approved a law to lower it to 13 percent. . . . Many people perceived it as a trick by Santos."[23]

One of those people was Senator Carlos Fernando Galán, a member of the Cambio Radical party. He protested, "In the text of the provisional article that has been put forward, we do not see where it has been stated explicitly that the procedure to protect the agreements is contingent on popular endorsement. In my opinion there is a gap. It is not clear; and it should be clear, that it is essential . . . that this article be subject to popular endorsement." Senator Claudia López was more explicit, saying, "They are pulling a fast one with the plebiscite, the popular mandate that we Colombians have to give on peace agreements."[24]

Despite these objections, the Constitutional Court approved the new law in July. Only 13 percent of the eligible voters would have to participate in the plebiscite. The Santos administration had permission to make it easier to get the approval of the agreement by the Colombian people.

Also in May the two sides decided on additional details of the agreement. One was the exact meaning of a surrender of arms. There were three sub-issues in this matter. First was when the turning over would start. Would it be when the FARC troops arrived at the transitional zones, as the government wanted, or at an official time after that, as the FARC wanted? Second was how the laying down of arms would take place. Would it be 30 percent when the FARC troops arrived at the zones, as the government wanted, or would it be in a progressive way, as the FARC wanted? Third had to do with the arms, destroying them, as the government wanted, or having extradited leader Simón Trinidad coordinate the process, as the FARC wanted. In the end, as shown below, the FARC position prevailed in the first two points and that of the government in the third.

On May 12 the two sides issued a joint communiqué in which they reported that they had agreed that "once Congress has approved the Final Agreement signed as a Special Agreement under common article 3 of the Geneva Conventions, the National Government, by means of the special legislative procedure for peace, will immediately promote a Legislative Act whereby the Final Agreement shall be entirely incorporated into the Political Constitution in a transitory article, in which the Agreement on the Special Jurisdiction for Peace dated December 15, 2015 must be expressly stated. Said transitory article will enter into force once the Final Agreement comes into force."[25] This addition was important because it made it more difficult for later governments to make changes, something that seemed possible given earlier Uribe opposition to the negotiations. In addition, the situation at the end of the guerrilla insurgency in Guatemala was something that the FARC wanted to avoid. In the Central American country, the guerrilla groups had demobilized after negotiations; however, some parts of the agreements later were not passed as constitutional amendments.[26] Putting the agreement into the constitution would be one of the objections to it in the debate before the plebiscite.

While progress was taking place, the two sides still disagreed about the number of areas in which the FARC troops were to demobilize. FARC negotiators insisted on more than sixty while the government proposed fourteen. On May 25 in Joint Communiqué 72, the two sides assured that matters were going very well in the solution of their differences about the end of the conflict and that they would be in a "permanent session" to arrive at agreements as soon as possible.[27]

When negotiations began again on June 20 in Havana, President Santos was optimistic that a successful end was near. The negotiators had made progress on the final two issues—the end of the conflict and the implementation of the agreement. They were getting closer to an agreement on the number of zones in which the FARC would demobilize, the government having increased its proposal from eight to fourteen. Sources indicated that, once the number was decided, the two sides would determine what to do with the weapons that would be turned in.

One of the greatest fears for the FARC in the reincorporation of its members into civilian life was that the persecution suffered by the Unión Patriótica would be repeated. The FARC and the Colombian Communist Party founded that party in 1985, as part of the peace negotiations that the guerrillas held with the Conservative Belisario Betancur administration. As a result, the FARC wanted a guarantee of personal security for its members when they demobilized.[28] A member of the government's negotiation team said that the presence of military officers on the joint subcommission took care of this concern. Those officers guaranteed that former FARC members would be able to move throughout the country without fear.[29]

The two sides resolved the issues of the number of zones and the surrender of arms, and on June 22 they announced that they had reached agreement on the third topic of the agenda, the end of the conflict. Their joint communiqué stated, "The delegations of the National Government and the FARC-EP hereby inform the public opinion that we have successfully reached the Agreement for the Bilateral and Final Ceasefire and the End of the Hostilities; the Laying down of arms; the security guarantees and the fight against the criminal organizations responsible for homicides and massacres or those that target Human Rights' advocates, social movements or political movements, including the criminal organizations labeled as successors of paramilitarism and their support networks, and the prosecution of criminal conducts that threaten the implementation of the agreements and the construction of peace."[30]

An emotional President Santos assured the Colombian people that the agreement meant the end of the FARC as an illegal armed group, and complimented the guerrilla group when he said, "I specifically want to show appreciation for the step the FARC is taking today in agreeing that the struggle for its convictions will no longer be armed, but, as it should be, political, with ideas and arguments. The truth is that we became accustomed to the horror of war. It became part of everyday life. Today, fortunately, with what has just been signed, we turn this tragic and long page of our history." Timochenko proclaimed that, with the agreement, "neither the FARC nor the state are defeated forces," and that it should not be interpreted as "the imposition of one party or the other." He added that in the past the armed forces and the FARC had been adversaries but now, for the good of Colombia, they had become allies.[31]

The agreement about the bilateral cease-fire and the turning in of arms announced in Joint Communiqué 76 was as follows.[32] The two sides reached a compromise, approving twenty-three zones where the agreement would be implemented without any limitation on the normal life of the surrounding civilian communities. Beginning on an agreed-upon day (D+1), the armed forces and police would facilitate the movement of the FARC troops to the zones to carry out the cease-fire and turning in of arms. Beginning on D+5, FARC troops would begin moving towards the zones, following routes previously established through an agreement between the government and the FARC. In each zone, the FARC would designate a group of ten of its members who could move around the municipality and department to carry out activities related to the peace agreement. For these movements, the government would guarantee the safety of FARC members. No civilians would be in the zones and none could enter. In addition, the government and the FARC would jointly agree on security protocols to minimize the threats to people who were taking part in the cease-fire and who were turning in their weapons. The United Nations would receive all the arms which would be used in the construction of three monuments agreed to by the government and the FARC. The collection of arms would take place in three stages: 30 percent by D+90, another 30 percent by D+120, and the final 40 percent by D+150. The guerrilla group would also contribute, in part by giving information, to the cleaning and decontamination of territories affected by antipersonnel mines, explosive artifacts, unexploded munitions, or any other explosive remnants of war. Finally, on D+180 the zones and cease-fire would end.

In the days that followed, government officials issued optimistic statements. Minister of Defense Luis Carlos Villegas was confident that the government would have complete authority in the zones and that the military supported the agreement completely since the negotiations were successful because of "the triumph of our armed forces."[33] Chief negotiator Humberto de la Calle said that the zones would not be like the demilitarized zones of the Andrés Pastrana negotiations, in which all military and police left the area, because "the state will have presence," perhaps even more than in other areas of the countryside. Even the comments of FARC leader Timochenko made it sound like the insurgent group desired peace. He said, "We hope to reach an agreement soon on endorsement that will allow the widest popular participation in the determination of the fate of the country, just as we want to be able to bring about agreements that are precise and guarantee implementation and reintegration."[34]

The international cooperation also contributed to the late June optimism. The first UN observers arrived in Colombia. As a leader of a women's group said in an interview, "The international component was very important, not only the United Nations but also the government of Norway."[35] In addition, in 2014 President Obama had named former US undersecretary of state Bernard Aronson to be an envoy to the process. Aronson, who had helped negotiate the end of the civil war in El Salvador in 1992, made twenty-five visits to the Havana negotiations. The guerrilla commanders soon warmed to Aronson's quiet pragmatism and willingness to listen. He helped troubleshoot the accord. Sergio Jaramillo said, "He did a brilliant job in helping us get the FARC to understand the constraints of the real world and to agree to things that no guerrilla force has ever agreed to before in a negotiation: to be accountable before a tribunal for their war crimes, to repair their victims and to get out of the drug trade."[36] Aronson stated, "I am convinced that the war has ended and that the agreement cannot be reversed," and added that the important thing at that point would be the support of the accord by the Colombian people to guarantee its legitimacy.[37]

On July 4 the FARC publicly renounced extortion and the recruitment of new troops. Timochenko disclosed, "I have just given the order to all FARC structures to suspend all taxes there are in the regions on all legal economic activity, taxes that we have on ranchers, on the various sources of funding, on big business."[38]

On July 7 Congress passed Legislative Act No. 1, which created a fast-track approval procedure for the implementation of the agreement. For six months, the number of committee meetings was reduced, and bills and legislative acts could only be amended if they conformed to the content of the final agreement and had the prior endorsement of the government.[39]

While the peace process showed so many positive aspects, it soon became obvious that not all of the FARC fronts would follow the central leadership of the group. In the same month, the Armando Ríos front said that it would not turn in its arms and would not abide by any of the agreement. While not the largest of the FARC fronts, this group dedicated itself more than most other fronts to the drug trade. The front stated that its members did not feel defeated, and as a result, "We have decided not to demobilize; we will continue the struggle for the takeover of power by the people and for the people, regardless of the decision made by the rest of the members of the guerrilla organization. We respect the decision of those who withdraw from the armed struggle, lay down their arms and return to civilian life; we do not consider them our enemies."[40]

Within days it was clear that at least one other FARC front would not adhere to the agreement. FARC leaders replied immediately. They said that free expression of ideas and concerns was a right of all FARC guerrilla combatants, provided through statutory mechanisms, but after the majority made decisions, they were binding for all: "Those who distance themselves from the leadership's guidelines separate themselves from the FARC and thus must not use its name, weapons, or goods for any purpose."[41] President Santos was equally categorical: "Let me take this opportunity [. . .] to give a message to those people from the First Front who have doubts: do not hesitate, avail yourself of this process because it will be your last chance."[42]

At the end of July, the FARC and the Colombian government announced something in their peace agreement that had no precedent in others: the victims agreement included a gender perspective that was, "fundamentally, to create conditions for women and persons with diverse sexual identity to have equal access to the benefits of living in a country without armed conflict."[43] The provisions of this gender perspective were controversial during the plebiscite debate.

Yet details remained to be worked out. In early August, there was a chicken-and-egg argument about when amnesty for the former guerrillas would happen. The greatest concern of the FARC was that its troops would demobilize before the government complied with its promise of amnesty. Chief FARC negotiator Carlos Antonio Lozada asked that amnesty be before the final agreement and therefore before the guerrilla troops demobilized. He cautioned, "Without legal and political security, there would be no final accord and no march to the transitional zones."[44]

In Joint Communiqué 83 on August 5, the two sides clearly established the planning and execution phases, defined the operation of the twenty-three Transitional Local Normalization Zones (Zonas Veredales Transitorias de Normalización, ZVTN) and the eight Transitional Normalization Spots (Puntos Transitorios de Normalización, PTN), and itemized the specific procedures and the timeline to be developed during the cease-fire and the laying down of arms. At this point the weekly magazine *Semana* reported, "Everything is ready for the end of the war," quickly adding, "Only lacking is that the people approve it and that it come into force." The article pointed out that the chief of the UN delegation, Jean Arnault, had said that there were eighty international observers already in Colombia and that the number could reach five hundred. Using hyperbole, the article concluded that "all appears ready for the guns to be silenced forever in Colombia."[45] Government chief negotiator de la Calle was positive, stating that "the progress of the process to date is really substantial. The announcement we make today is a sign that we have reached agreements on issues of great importance, such as the abandonment of arms and the transition to civilian life of the members of the FARC-EP." He added, "The steps we have defined in recent weeks ensure that the process will be done transparently, safely, and with a robust monitoring and verification system."[46]

However, FARC leader Iván Márquez made it clear that the plebiscite needed to approve the agreement. Márquez said that the movement of FARC troops would be suspended until rules were approved that guaranteed their legal, social, and political security.

Progress continued August 12 when the two sides, in a joint communiqué, announced that they had agreed on a mechanism for the selection of the judges of the Special Jurisdiction for Peace. A committee would be set up with one member named by each of the following: Pope Francis, the secretary-general of the United Nations, the Penal Section of the Colombian Supreme Court, the Colombian delegation to the International Center for Transitional Justice, and the Permanent Commission of the State University System. They were charged with selection of members who were people "with high ethical qualities and a recognized professional background."[47]

On August 17 the government's representatives went back to Cuba with the intention of ending the negotiations by the end of the month. The government added as reinforcements Juan Fernando Cristo, minister of the interior; Rafael Pardo, councilor for the post-conflict; and María Ángela Holguín, foreign minister. The two sides worked constantly on the question of amnesty and the FARC presence in Congress as the two key issues to resolve. FARC spokesperson Marco Calarcá warned, "There will be no final agreement until the amnesty law is in place. Nobody ends their armed political struggle to be in jail."[48] Some thought that this statement was an isolated one, but Carlos Antonio Lozada, head of the technical subcommission of the FARC and member of its national secretariat, expressed the same sentiment and said that the FARC could not move until it had legal security.

The negotiators also addressed the issue of the FARC's representation in Congress. While they had tentatively decided this during the political rights debate earlier in the negotiations, there was that statement in the agenda that "nothing is decided until everything is decided." At this point, the FARC wanted the legislative body to seat its representatives as soon as the guerrilla group completed the disarmament, and it would choose the representatives. The government wanted the terms to begin in 2018 after the FARC's political movement had offered candidates.[49]

Chief government negotiator Humberto de la Calle also stressed that FARC participation in politics was important. He advised, "We Colombians must face that debate. I have said that it is not just a topic for the table. We believe that the central purpose of a peace process is to cast aside weapons and open the political space, obviously, with no combination of forms of struggle. I think we should be generous in that, which is an essential effort, for the achievement of the ultimate goal of the conflict."[50]

The negotiators completed their deliberations by August 24, having resolved issues concerning the political rights to be granted to the FARC, the economic reincorporation of the FARC members, and the implementation of the agreement. The political rights document first stated that the FARC political party would have ten seats, five in each house of Congress beginning in 2018. They would be chosen through elections, but the party would not have to receive the plurality of votes: the state would guarantee the seats, and the candidates of the FARC party with the most votes would be elected. The FARC would immediately have three members in the Senate and three in the Chamber, with voice but without vote. The party established by the FARC would have legal identity right away and would receive 10 percent of the state fund for political parties, or about COL$7 billion. Until 2026 the party would not have to have the minimum number of members nor the minimum number of votes required for other parties to maintain legal identity. The party would have guarantees including use of public media and security. In addition, beginning in 2018 and for two electoral periods, the party would have five seats in the Senate and five in the Chamber. FARC party candidates would receive the same financial support as candidates of other parties. However, those FARC members who had been found guilty of atrocious crimes could not be candidates. Finally, if the Colombian people approved the agreement through the plebiscite, Congress could approve elements of it by fast track.[51] All parts of the political rights agreement were favorable to the FARC.

The agreement on economic reincorporation of former FARC members was also favorable to the guerrilla group. The process would be centered on a private institution called Cooperative Solidarity Economies (Economías del Común, Ecomún), to which former guerrilla members could voluntarily affiliate. Each former member would receive COL$8 million (about US$2,600) to invest in an individual or collective project. If it were collective, the government would send the funds to Ecomún after the project had been approved. Each demobilized FARC member would receive a basic monthly stipend of 90 percent of the minimum salary for two years (about COL$620,000 or US$207). In addition, people who followed the reintegration programs would receive other incentives, especially if they were students. Finally, everyone would become affiliated with the social security system.[52]

The third set of agreements on August 24 concerned implementation. The two sides established a commission for that purpose, as well as for follow-up and verification of the final peace agreement and dispute settlement. Each side would name three members of the commission, which would exist for ten years. By the end of August, the United Nations had agreed to monitor the cease-fire and turning in of weapons. The processes would be joint ones with monitoring by the UN, the Colombian government, and the FARC. Three-party groups would visit the twenty-three zones during the 180 days of the cease-fire.[53]

CONCLUSION

The Colombian people then were to vote on a complex agreement, the PDF version of which was nearly three hundred pages long. There is no evidence of what percentage of the Colombian people read the entire agreement, or even the executive summary of it condensed to six points in the four pages of the introduction, as posted online by the government.[54]

Point 1 was the comprehensive rural reform that would contribute to the structural transformation of the countryside, closing the gaps between the countryside and the cities and creating conditions of well-being and a good life for the rural population. It aimed to bring regional integration, contribute to the eradication of poverty, promote equality, and assure the full enjoyment of the rights of the citizens.

Point 2 was the agreement about political participation. It called for an amplification of democracy that allowed for the emergence of new political groups so as to enrich the debate and deliberation about the major national problems. In that way it would fortify pluralism and therefore different visions and interests of society, with suitable guarantees for political participation.

Point 3 included the agreement about the bilateral and definitive cease-fire and surrender of arms with the goal of the definitive end of military actions between the armed forces and the FARC. It included the reincorporation of the FARC into civilian life in its economic, social, and political aspects. There was an agreement about the guarantees of security and the fight against the criminal organizations that were responsible for homicides and massacres and that threatened human rights groups, social movements, or political movements. It included the criminal organizations that had been labeled as the successors to paramilitarism.

Point 4 was the agreement about the solution of the problem of illicit drugs. It stated that, to construct a peaceful country, it was necessary to find a definitive solution to the problem of illicit drugs, including the cultivation, production, and marketing of them. For those reasons, Colombia needed a new vision of the problem, while assuring a general focus on human rights, public health, and gender.

Point 5 was the agreement about victims, which the two sides agreed should be the central point of any agreement. The agreement created the Comprehensive System of Truth, Justice, Reparation, and Non-repetition that would contribute to the struggle against impunity with legal mechanisms that would allow the investigation of and punishment for grave violations of human rights and the serious infractions of international humanitarian law. The system would consist of the Commission for the Clarification of Truth, Coexistence, and Non-repetition and the Special Unit for the Search for the Missing.

Point 6 had the agreement for mechanisms of implementation and verification in which the Commission for Implementation, Monitoring, and Verification of the Final Peace Agreement and for Dispute Resolution would be created, made up of representatives of the government and the FARC with the purpose of, among others, evaluating the following of the agreements and verifying compliance, serving in the resolution of differences, and encouraging and following the legislative implementation.

PART THREE

The Plebiscite and the New Final Agreement

IN THIS PART OF THE book, I turn in chapter 6 to the debate about the final agreement between the Santos administration and the FARC and to the unexpected defeat of the plebiscite. One of the tactics of the president and other officials was to say that the final agreement could not be renegotiated, yet in chapter 7 I analyze how it indeed was renegotiated. At no point did the three sides—the Santos administration, the FARC, and the opposition to the agreement—all meet to reach an agreement. However, as described in chapter 7, the Santos administration first talked with the opposition and then to the FARC. The part ends with an analysis of the second final agreement. It concludes that no one of the three sides was completely satisfied with the final compromise.

CHAPTER SIX

The Debate about the Peace Agreement and the Plebiscite

THROUGHOUT 2016, AS MORE WAS known about the Santos-FARC agreement, the intensity of the opposition to it became greater. In many ways it became a personal conflict between Juan Manuel Santos and Álvaro Uribe. As pointed out in chapter 3, the fundamental reasons for the disagreement were Santos's admission that there was an internal conflict in the country, his criticism of Uribe's security policy, and Uribe's claim that the war with the FARC had worsened in the two years Santos had been president. This personal animosity between former president Uribe and then president Santos lasted beyond the October 2016 plebiscite.

While conflicts between presidents and their predecessors were not new in Colombia, and for that matter are common in many countries, the one between Santos and Uribe was particularly intense. Alejandro Reyes, a longtime student of the Colombian case, believed that the basic reason for their dispute was that Santos, unlike Uribe, thought that there was an internal conflict. Uribe argued that the negotiations were giving up the country to what he called "Castro-Chavismo." He believed the country's agenda was being negotiated with a terrorist group, which would guarantee impunity for atrocious crimes and the political eligibility of those who had destroyed Colombia with their terrorist struggle.[1]

In addition, the agreement included many points that individuals or groups might oppose. Were the possible punishments for FARC members strong enough? After over fifty years of conflict, thousands of Colombians had been negatively affected, either through the death of or injury to family members or through having been forced to leave their homes. Should the national military be subjected to a judicial process similar to the one devised for the former FARC members? In a very conservative country, was it proper to consider women and LGBTI individuals as victims of the FARC conflict? Why were demobilized FARC members receiving economic benefits that were greater than what millions of poor Colombians had?

As I show in this chapter, these questions and the Uribe-Santos personal dispute led to the victory of the "No" forces in the plebiscite. In chapter 9, I analyze how the conflict made the implementation difficult when Congress considered the revised treaty. One political scientist even went as far as to say that "the peace agreement was not a success. The biggest mistake in the negotiation was that it was not based on a national consensus, as previous ones had been, like the National Front and the M-19 demobilization. There was no consensus this time because of the conflict between Santos and Uribe."[2] This chapter shows how difficult a possible agreement between the two would have been.

The debate intensified as the negotiations neared their end in 2016. Many analysts expressed their views in the media, especially about the Special Jurisdiction for Peace (Jurisdicción Especial para la Paz, JEP). The 2012 Legislative Act No. 1, passed on June 14, 2012, before the negotiations began, had established the method of transitional justice. Much of it was later incorporated into the agreement. Most importantly, crimes against humanity could not lead to either pardon or amnesty. Other crimes might be tried in a special court if the perpetrators disarmed, confessed, and made reparations.[3]

One of the early analysts who made an argument against the JEP was journalist, lawyer, and former member of Congress María Isabel Rueda. She wrote in *El Tiempo* that, after years of slow progress, now in Havana "they have resolved to incapacitate it [the Colombian justice system] and take from it the responsibility for one of the most important trials in the history of Colombia, to end a war of fifty years. We will invest millions of pesos in a special jurisdiction, within the framework of an alternative justice copied from models from failed countries worldwide. They will create a super justice on top of the Colombian justice system."[4] Rueda's argument was just the beginning of the criticisms of the Transitional Justice Agreement.

THE PASTRANA-CEPEDA DEBATE ON THE TRANSITIONAL JUSTICE AGREEMENT

One clear case of the debate about the Special Jurisdiction for Peace took place in an exchange of opposing views that appeared in the newspaper *El Tiempo* in February 2016. First, former president Andrés Pastrana published an op-ed article entitled "They Gave the Country Away in 24 Hours." The following day, Manuel José Cepeda, former member of the Constitutional Court and one of the three authors of the JEP, responded in "Advisor Replies to Criticism of the Transitional Justice Agreement."[5]

Shown in the Pastrana-Cepeda exchange, and in much of the debate about the peace agreement between the Colombian government and the FARC, is the kind of argument that can be considered "proof texting." As defined in the case of theological debate, "proof texting uses certain short passages, many times only a single verse, pulled from the Bible in support of a particular belief or doctrine. The problem with this method is that the person who is proof texting usually gives their selected verses a meaning that may be entirely different from what the writer intended."[6] Much of the Colombian debate was similar in that an agreement of some three hundred pages is subject to proof texting just as the Bible is. The practice was also clearly shown in the Pastrana-Cepeda exchange. The major points of the Pastrana-Cepeda debate appear in table 6.1.

Former President Andrés Pastrana ended his op-ed article with a strong statement, leaving little doubt about his opinions and suggesting the position he was to take in the plebiscite debate and afterward: "With this court, President Juan Manuel Santos is carrying out a coup d'état by destroying the institutional structure from its foundations. This antidemocratic monster that—without exaggerating—exposes us to a totalitarian future is what the president hopes for his compatriots to endorse. The 72-hour agreement, as clearly shown here, destroys the separation of powers which is the essence of liberty in a democracy. We friends of peace and democracy should say to these totalitarian pretensions, 'For this absurdity, don't count on us.'"

At the end of the interview with Manuel José Cepeda, the reporter asked if he thought that former president Pastrana was reading the agreement incorrectly or had bad legal advisors, or that Pastrana was correct that a monster had been created in Havana. Cepeda replied, "The political readings of the agreement, which are respectable in a democracy, are one thing and another is what the text of the agreement really says."

This was a debate between two lawyers, one a former president and the other a former member of the Constitutional Court. The two had conflicting values, Pastrana as a representative of the previous governmental system and Cepeda as one of the authors of a dramatic change. The two presumably had read the entire 297-page document and had the training to understand it. As shown below, the general debate about the agreement was not similar to the Pastrana-Cepeda one. Individuals, without the training and most often without the time to read the entire agreement, stressed only those parts of the agreement that they thought were good or bad. The debate many times was over political issues and not what the agreement said.

URIBE'S OPPOSITION TO THE AGREEMENT

Just as Álvaro Uribe had been the chief critic of the Santos-FARC negotiations since rumors first appeared that they had started, he was the chief opponent to

Table 6.1. The Pastrana-Cepeda debate about the Special Jurisdiction for Peace (Jurisdicción Especial para la Paz, JEP)

Pastrana statement	Cepeda response
JEP was created in only 72 hours.	The three-person commission worked at least 250 hours over five months.
JEP creates an all-powerful tribunal with extraconstitutional powers, without time limits, and with the power to examine decisions made in the past and in the future, in matters legislative as well as judicial and disciplinary.	Instead of destroying Colombian institutions, the agreement does the exact opposite by applying the constitution and the laws.
JEP is above the agreements that the country had made in matters of human rights, international humanitarian law, and international penal law.	The norms are in accordance with the Statute of Rome, international human rights law, and international humanitarian law.
Point 15 gives the JEP court the right to exercise a dominant authority in the case of future laws passed by Congress.	The powers of Congress and the executive are respected.
Point 33 implies the repeal of the power given by the constitution to the inspector general.	No reply.
Point 49 takes away the constitutional powers of Congress and the president to grant amnesties and pardons.	The power of Congress and the executive are respected.
Point 51 creates an investigative and accusatory unit that takes the place of the Prosecutor General's Office.	On the contrary, the agreement gives full credit to the investigations carried out by the Prosecutor General's Office.
The new tribunal will have power greater than the Supreme Court, the Constitutional Court, the Council of State, the Superior Council of the Judiciary, and supervisory bodies of the inspector general and the comptroller.	It is certain that the Peace Tribunal has final authority but only for the Special Jurisdiction for Peace. The JEP is a new jurisdiction but with competence restricted to the crimes related to the armed conflict.
The agreement creates impunity. It does not fit with the minimum penalties and justice of the Rome Statute.	There will be no impunity. The serious crimes will be punished by the court.
Drug traffickers fall under the authority of the JEP.	By no means. Drug trafficking is a common crime.

Sources: Information from Andrés Pastrana, "'Se entregó el país en 72 horas': Andrés Pastrana," *El Tiempo*, February 28, 2016, https://m.eltiempo.com; "Refutan críticas de Andrés Pastrana a acuerdo con las Farc," *El Tiempo*, February 28, 2016, https://m.eltiempo.com.

the agreement in the debate before the plebiscite. In addition to his rhetoric, in early May 2016 he began collecting signatures against the agreement. Calling the movement "civil resistance," the former president himself took part in the first day of signature collection. He stated, "If you ask Colombians if they want peace, everyone says 'yes,' but if you ask citizens if they accept that in the Havana agreement the ones responsible for kidnapping children, for raping girls, for the drug trade will not go to jail and will be elected? Many of us have to say that we want peace, but we do not accept impunity because it causes more violence."[7] Impunity was to be Uribe's principle theme from then on. President Santos accused his predecessor of having offered even more to the FARC during his presidency, and claimed, "We have all the letters, all the evidence that what we are doing is exactly what President Uribe wanted to do. He even went further. He made offers that we have not made."[8]

In July President Santos, in an attempt to have more unity within the civilian political establishment, wrote a letter to Uribe using conciliatory language. He let him know that "from his heart" he was pleased with the results that the two had enjoyed while carrying out the policy of democratic security when he was Uribe's secretary of defense. Because of the current division over the peace process, the president called for a collective effort to make it stronger. He said, "I am ready, together with the government's negotiating team, to meet with you to listen to your concerns and to open a constructive dialogue."[9] There is no evidence that this meeting took place. Indeed, as one political scientist told me, "They did not talk, they did not even have a cup of coffee together."[10]

After President Santos had sent the letter to Álvaro Uribe, the former president tweeted his thirteen objections to the agreement:

For FARC leaders responsible for massacres, car bombs, there is no prison, not even repentance. Is this not impunity?

For FARC leaders responsible for the kidnapping of thousands of Colombians, there is no prison, but eligibility to run for office. Is this not impunity?

For FARC leaders responsible for the recruitment of children and the rape of girls, there is no prison, but eligibility to run for office. Is this not impunity?

For FARC leaders responsible for attacks on ambulances, there is no prison, but eligibility to run for office. Is this not impunity?

For FARC leaders responsible for attacks on commercial airlines, there is no prison, but eligibility to run for office. Is this not impunity?

For FARC leaders responsible for the taking of and destruction of many towns, there is no prison, but eligibility to run for office. Is this not impunity?

Six years ago, the FARC got no attention in the media; today it gets it all. Is this not permissiveness?

Six years ago, the FARC were weak, today powerful. What is the responsible authority?

The government does not require the FARC, millionaire terrorists, to give money to the victims. Is that a peace agreement or surrender?

The government agrees to take our military to FARC court. Is that fair to the armed forces of our democracy?

Military and civilians in many cases will have to admit to crimes not committed to avoid going to jail. Is this justice?

The government negotiates with FARC terrorists the rights of the political opposition. Is terrorism an opposition party?

The government negotiates the national agenda with FARC terrorists. Is Castro-Chavismo coming here?[11]

In these objections, Uribe stressed the impunity that FARC leaders would receive, the lack of justice, and the weakness of the government. Bringing up the image of the disliked, leftist leader of Venezuela, his last tweet asked, "Is Castro-Chavismo coming here?" This was the first of many opposition statements that attempted to raise emotions to defeat the agreement, rather than to educate people about the details of it.

Uribe also opposed the procedure for approving the agreement. Concerning the method, the weekly magazine *Semana* asked, "When did the rules of the game get twisted up so that the agreement could go forward?" The complex reply was that the Constitutional Court and Congress had accepted everything that the president requested. At first Santos wanted a referendum at the same time as the local elections. Later he changed that to a plebiscite, lowering the necessary level of participation among eligible voters from 50 percent to 25 percent and eventually to 13 percent.[12]

President Santos had called for this plebiscite from early on in the conversations. However, the constitution did not require that the peace accord be approved in that way. In my interviews, the reactions of analysts to that choice were consistently negative. A historian concluded, "The plebiscite was unnecessary and a bad idea."[13] A sociologist was blunt when he said, "The idea of the plebiscite was the most important error that Santos made. He was certain that the majority of the country would back the agreement."[14] A political scientist saw the plebiscite as a way for President Santos to look better than Álvaro Uribe.[15]

High Commissioner for Peace Sergio Jaramillo, however, defended the idea of the plebiscite in the following way: "Many people asked us, not without reason: why submit a peace agreement to a plebiscite? There was an inherent tension between ending a war, which clearly does not require a vote, and other parts of the agreement, such as comprehensive rural reform, which we believe needed democratic legitimation. We also had the problem of distance and the necessarily closed nature of the negotiation, which separated the process from the Colombian people, despite the extraordinary efforts of Humberto de la Calle to transmit to Colombia what was being done in Havana, and the peace pedagogy efforts in the territories of the members of the Office of the High Commissioner for Peace."[16]

After the Constitutional Court approved the plebiscite, including the 13 percent threshold in mid-July, Álvaro Uribe said categorically that the plebiscite was illegitimate. At this point the Centro Democrático had not decided whether to encourage its followers to abstain or to vote "No." One of its members, Senator Iván Duque, considered this process to be a series of tricks and added that, after lowering the percentage of voters, the Senate did not approve public funding for either the "Sí" or the "No" campaigns.[17]

Former president Andrés Pastrana went even farther, calling the plebiscite a coup d'état and encouraging people to vote "No." He took a position in opposition to the leadership of his Conservative Party, saying that it was blackmail for President Santos to call the plebiscite a choice between peace and war. He argued that the FARC had already said that it would not return to war, win or lose at the polls. The guerrillas had left open the door to the possibility of adjusting the agreements in the eventuality of a victory of the "No" vote.[18]

TAKING POSITIONS FOR AND AGAINST THE AGREEMENT

Other political parties also continued considering their positions as July ended, with many having difficulty deciding whether to support "Sí," "No," or abstention. The members of two parties of the Santos coalition, the Partido de la U and the Liberals, favored the agreement as did the opposition Polo Democrático and Alianza Verde parties. The Conservative Party was divided, and two of its leaders, David Barguil and Marta Lucía Ramírez, debated the issue on Twitter. It seemed that the party would support the agreement, but the decision was a difficult one.

The debate in August and September took place in two distinct ways. The first was about what the agreement contained, most often using the proof-texting technique. The second had more to do with arousing the emotions of the Colombian people, often using up-to-date, twenty-first-century tactics and social media.

In August former President César Gaviria insisted that whoever supported the "No" vote did not necessarily want armed conflict. He also made it clear that the arguments of the "Sí" sector, the one calling for an affirmative vote in the plebiscite, were easy to support because peace would not bring impunity. He said, "We are obliged to formulate the answers in a different way. I recognize that the one who intends to vote for the 'No' is not someone who wants war, it is difficult to imagine that, but the consequence of rejecting the agreements is going to be war, even if one does not want it. It is not automatic, but war is the consequence of winning the 'No' vote. . . . They also talk about a possible renegotiation, but it cannot be done."[19] This last argument was incorrect, as would be seen later in the year.

Also in August, former president Álvaro Uribe's Centro Democrático party strengthened its criticism of the peace agreement when Senator Paloma Valencia made it clear that she did not consider the proposed sentences in the JEP to be enough: "They will spend zero days in prison, they will be awarded with political representation."[20]

As the October plebiscite approached, the campaigns for and against the agreement continued to be led by former presidents—César Gaviria for "Sí" and Álvaro Uribe for "No." Uribe proclaimed, "We undertake the campaign for the 'No' in the plebiscite because with impunity, hatred does not die but more violence is born; because they deny victims the right not to repeat the tragedy; because the FARC with their crimes rewarded, justified, and without atonement, prevent many Colombians from feeling the spiritual relief of forgiveness." In his long speech, the former president continued, "It is a courageous reaction of those without options that we must vote 'No' to the illegitimate plebiscite. Illegitimate because it just presents a question and lowers the threshold from 50 percent to 13 percent, with the excuse that it will be one time only and with the precedent that later they will do something similar for the ELN, the criminal gangs or any other dictatorial contrivance." The former president addressed other themes, including gender policy and reparations. As to the latter, Uribe contended, "To vote 'Yes' for the illegitimate plebiscite is to accept that the FARC, the third richest terrorist group in the world, will not contribute a single cent to compensate victims, will go into politics with a wealth of illegal money, and will buy arms to substitute for surrendered ones."[21] Clearly, the agreement did call for the FARC to compensate victims; however, the former president was skeptical that the guerrilla group would comply with that requirement.

Uribe added to his earlier tweets that, if voters accepted the agreement, it would mean higher taxes for Colombians. Then he raised the fear that "in this trip we will have to cure ourselves of the habit of sleeping in order not to have the plague of 56 years of Castroism or 14 of Chavismo."[22] Raising the fear of Colombia becoming like the Cuba of Fidel Castro or the Venezuela of Hugo Chávez continued to be one of the themes of the "No" campaign, using emotion as a tool.

Carlos Holmes Trujillo, who had been the Centro Democrático candidate for vice president in 2014, brought up another "No" theme when he replied on behalf of his party to a statement by César Gaviria. Holmes said that the International Criminal Court might intervene if the treaty were not changed "because the government-FARC accord was an agreement of disguised impunity." He added that the triumph of the "No" vote would not be for the continuation of the war but for the renegotiation of the agreement. Chief Negotiator Humberto de La Calle replied that thinking that the treaty could be renegotiated was a "tremendous error." "To resist taking the step is to condemn the country to a period of uncertainty. Putting an end to the conflict is a certainty," he said.[23] De la Calle was incorrect about renegotiation, just as Gaviria was, as stated above.

Although it appeared that Álvaro Uribe was the natural leader of the "No" campaign, the former president decided instead not to take an active role in the campaign throughout the country. In his place, the Centro Democrático named Juan Carlos Vélez Uribe to be the operations manager. Like the ex-president from Antioquia, Vélez was a lawyer and a former senator. His tasks were to include communications, publicity, legal matters, and finances.

THE SEPTEMBER DEBATES ON THE AGREEMENT

By the end of August, the procedure for the plebiscite was known. The question was formulated, and after the president announced it, the interested parties would have thirty days to make their appeals. The National Electoral Council announced rules for that period. An unlimited number of advocacy committees could promote one of the two sides. They needed to register with the commission by September 15. Limits were set on how much money the committees could spend, how much money they could receive in donations, how many billboards they could post, and how many radio and television spots they could broadcast. Public employees could participate, either on the "Sí" or "No" side. Public opinion polls could take place until September 27 but not afterward.

In an analysis in late September, *Semana* concluded that there were five salient issues in the debate about the agreement:

1. The ones most responsible for atrocious crimes would not go to jail;

2. FARC leaders could participate in politics and be elected by popular vote;

3. The drug trade would be considered a crime connected to the rebellion;

4. The FARC could hide its fortunes and not make reparations; and

5. The justice system would be replaced with one separate from the constitutional one to satisfy the FARC.[24]

Of these five points, there were two in which there was much misinformation and three in which the critics had some sound arguments. The three with good arguments had to do with economic reparation, the justice system, and the political eligibility of those found guilty of atrocious crimes.

Importantly, as intense debate between the two sides took place, a political scientist pointed out, it was the "No" forces who set the agenda, making the debate not about the majority of the content of the agreement but about impunity, gender, and the threat of Colombia becoming like Cuba or Venezuela.[25] In his analysis, sociologist Eduardo Pizarro wrote, "Nobody had a clear awareness of the degree of national polarization that the country was experiencing, nor of the level of public opposition there was to the FARC and the agreements signed." The opposition used "a systematic campaign of lies and the generation of fear; a long agreement that is difficult to read and assimilate."[26]

Family members often took different positions in the debate. Some people hated the FARC because of its violent activities during more than half a century. Others thought that those who were against making peace with the FARC had selfish reasons. The Colombian tradition that "the family that votes together stays together" was replaced with disagreements within the family, loud arguments, and insults. One was a "fascist" or a "Castro-Chavista." A period of polarization prevailed in the country, unmatched since the end of the partisan violence in the 1960s. As expressed in the weekly magazine *Semana*, "A peace agreement involves a change of scenery, with new actors, with unknown scenarios, and from there arise emotions of a wide variety. And this applies as much to a citizen who overnight will encounter guerrillas on TV, in a park, or in a restaurant, as it does to a member of the FARC, who from one moment to another lays down arms to enter a completely unknown life. That produces fear, because of uncertainty, but also confidence, to the extent that perceived risks are being overcome."[27]

Following the customary Colombian policy of "the enemy of my enemy is my friend," Álvaro Uribe and Andrés Pastrana agreed to work together in the "No" campaign. Even though Uribe had criticized the Pastrana peace process in his 2002 presidential campaign, as he put it in 2016, "Anyone who is in favor of the 'No' will be my ally."[28] In his debate with Manuel José Cepeda, Pastrana showed his reasons for opposing the agreement. For others, it was difficult to decide which side to take. After an intense deliberation, the Conservative Party chose to support the "Sí" side.

The previously mentioned criticisms of the agreement were far from the only ones. The arguments of the "No" forces included the following:

The Special Jurisdiction for Peace did not conform to international humanitarian law, which the FARC had violated.

There was no guarantee that the FARC would totally disarm.

Adding the agreement to the constitution would weaken it by making changes more difficult.

The agreement would cause a disequilibrium of the political parties by giving the FARC party immediate seats in Congress and communication abilities that other parties did not have.

The government could renegotiate the accord.

The "Sí" leaders made contrary arguments:

The agreement would be good for the economy, with the government estimating that GDP growth would double to 6 percent a year.

Countries of the world and multinational organizations supported the agreement, including the European Union, the Vatican, the United States, the International Monetary Fund, the World Bank, and the Organization of American States.

There would be no immunity for the guerrilla group. To receive the alternative punishment, the members of the FARC would have to collaborate with the justice system and promise reparation to the victims. In the cases of crimes committed post-agreement, the normal sentences of more than twenty years would apply.

No part of the agreement implied that the government would stop fulfilling its obligation to combat crime. The government would seize any illicit goods of the guerrilla group that it did not turn in.

The FARC would help in the manual eradication of illicit crops. If that were not possible, the government reserved the right to use aerial fumigation.

The sum of money that the FARC members would receive upon demobilization was equivalent to that given by the Uribe administration to paramilitary troops who demobilized.

The government assured that it negotiated the best agreement possible after four years of arduous negotiations.

The gender perspective complied with UN resolutions.

The clear regulation was that in a maximum of 180 days all of the weapons of the guerrillas would be destroyed. The FARC troops would locate in specific zones, under supervision.

The FARC delegates had arrived in Havana expecting amnesty and complete pardon. However, the Rome Statute of the International Criminal Court requires countries not to give amnesty and pardon to crimes against humanity, war crimes, and atrocious offenses. As a result, the FARC had to accept the transitional justice system and its punishments as stated in the agreement. Therefore, there was no impunity according to the definitions of the International Criminal Court. However, the "No" proponents argued that the FARC leaders were responsible for the most serious crimes, should spend time in jail, and should not be able to participate in politics.

However, the FARC would not be held accountable for its drug crimes. According to the agreement, they were to be considered part of the rebellion and would not be punished. The argument for this stipulation was that the guerrilla troops were not drug dealers but insurgents who took part in the drug trade to finance their ideological struggle to overthrow the political regime. If this proviso had not been in the agreement, all the FARC negotiators in Havana and the guerrilla secretariat would have had to be tried as drug dealers.[29]

AROUSING EMOTIONS AND USING TWENTY-FIRST-CENTURY POLITICAL TACTICS

Many of the declarations of spokespersons on the two sides were honest, stressing the parts of the agreement that they thought were good or bad. However, there were others who used lies and distortions.

One very important example concerns what the agreement said or did not say about the rights of the LGBTI community. Those rights had been issues in Colombia previously. The Constitutional Court had made several controversial decisions about same-sex marriage and the right of same-sex couples to adopt children. In 2015 the court ruled on the rights of LGBTI students, and not long before the plebiscite, it ruled twice that transgender students in two different schools must be allowed to wear clothing appropriate to the sex with which they identified.

As a result of the Constitutional Court decisions mentioned above, Education Minister Gina Parody issued a decree that required all public and private schools to revise their student manuals to protect students from discrimination over their sexual orientation or gender identity. Parody's plan for revising the student handbooks included a pamphlet she designed in conjunction with the United Nations Population Fund to instruct schools on how to encourage students to respect and value transgenderism and homosexuality.[30] Parody is lesbian and had acknowledged publicly her relationship with Minister of Commerce, Industry, and Tourism Cecilia Álvarez-Correa. Thousands marched in protests held throughout Colombia to object to Parody's initiative to implement homosexual and transsexual gender ideology programs in Colombian schools.

In the debate about this issue, some in the "No" group emphasized the gender perspective, arguing that although the agreement never used that expression, it was encrypted in it. On July 14, 2016, the government and the FARC had agreed that men, women, homosexuals, heterosexuals, and people of diverse identity should benefit equally from the agreement. Religious groups, saying that they were defending the rights of traditional families, argued that this agreement camouflaged the "ideology of gender," an expression that included the theory that sexual identity and gender roles were not a social construction but a biological condition.

A number of individuals and groups made this argument. Ángela Hernández, a member of the departmental legislature of Santander and a member of the Partido de la U, stated, "It is not right that they mix a matter as important as the termination of the conflict with gender ideology. Under these conditions, and even wanting peace for my country, I feel morally held back from voting for the 'Sí.'"[31]

A similar statement was made by Ilva Myriam Hoyos Castañeda, deputy prosecutor for the rights of children, who, after an analysis of the joint communiqués, the statements of the negotiators, and the official documents from the Havana negotiations concluded, "Gender ideology may be encrypted in the final agreement; it is not easily noticed, but it can be uncovered." According to her, in the 297 pages of the final agreement the word "gender" was used 144 times, which "seems to demonstrate that this is an approach that cuts across the entire final agreement." Hoyos also said that, in her judgment, the expression of gender perspective in the peace agreement had two goals: on the one hand, to claim the rights of women, and on the other, to promote "the recognition of the LGBTI population as a maker and a beneficiary of public policies." According to her, the latter will involve changing "institutions as essential to society as marriage, family, adoption, marital status." Hoyos concluded her analysis asking why there was no reference to God in the agreement. In addition, she said that there was no reference to the freedom of religion: "Can stable and lasting peace be made without taking Colombian believers into account?"[32] The document written by Hoyos was reproduced in the social networks of churches and foundations that defended the traditional or nuclear family. They argued that the gender ideology was the backbone of the agreement and invited their cohorts to vote "No" for that reason.

The gender perspective became one of the most important issues in the plebiscite debate. Evangelical Protestant churches played a significant part in it. The Evangelical Council of Colombia, which was established in 1950, maintained a neutral position, with its president, Édgar Castaño Díaz, making it clear that the organization would not support either the "Sí" or the "No" vote. Castaño advised, "Peace is essential in the Christian church and this causes us to differentiate between peace and the referendum on the Havana agreement. We invite people to keep this difference in mind and to vote according to the how the Holy Spirit inspires them for the best decision for the good of our nation."[33]

However, other evangelical leaders were definitely for the "No" vote. Pastor Miguel Arrázola, of Iglesia Ríos de Vida of Cartagena, called on the members of his church to vote "No" on the agreement and called President Santos the "antichrist." Another influential voice was Eduardo Cañas, of Iglesia Manantial, one of the largest evangelical churches in Bogotá, who told his followers that "the future of Colombia cannot remain in the hands of Satan." A similar position was that of Iglesia Familiar Internacional, whose leader Marco Fidel Ramírez, also a Bogotá city council member, counseled, "Vote 'No' in the plebiscite. The 'Yes' vote tramples biblical principles and attacks the family."[34]

The idea that the ideology of gender was camouflaged in the agreement was of great importance. My reading of the agreement several times leads me to the same conclusion as two university professors whom I interviewed. A sociologist said, "It was a lie, the idea that there was a bias in favor of homosexual groups in the original agreement."[35] A political scientist who has studied in the United States was blunter when he said, "Raising the gender issue was pure bull shit."[36] That notwithstanding, this issue was crucial in what turned out to be a very close vote. One feminist leader said that she had heard that a million and a half of the "No" votes came from the evangelical groups because of this allegation.[37]

The gender perspective issue shows that Colombia is still in many ways a very conservative country. One political scientist reported that when his students, in rural areas near Bogotá, asked people why they were voting "No," they sometimes replied it was because of what the agreement gave to the "queers."[38] A sociologist said that she had heard anti-gay sentiments during the plebiscite debate even in Bogotá.[39]

Two interviewees suggested there was resistance to the "politically correct" language of the agreement. A historian observed, "While there was no hidden gender ideology in the agreement—that just was not true—the attempt to be 'politically correct' hurt."[40] Another historian correctly said that there were many reasons that people voted "No" in the plebiscite and added, "One was that the agreement was 'politically correct,' including expressions like 'guerrilleros y guerrilleras.'"[41] *Guerrilleros* in Spanish has traditionally referred both to a group of all men or to a group of people of any mixture of genders.

Campaigners also used current methods of projecting negative statements and visions. Playing on the doubt and resentment of many Colombians, billboards appeared in various places with the face of FARC leader Timochenko, warning about the possibility that he might become president. While the government and other "Sí" supporters used figures, statistics, and economic projections, the "No" forces focused on issues that caused a negative emotional reaction. Juan Carlos Garzón, a researcher at the Ideas para la Paz foundation said, "The opposition used that argument regarding gay marriage, abortion, and religion to attract and rally against the peace accords. It was an effective strategy to drive the most conservative voters against the peace agreement."[42]

Juan Carlos Vélez Uribe, the leader of the "No" campaign, to the dismay of former president Uribe, later revealed the strategy of his forces. Vélez disclosed that the campaign early on discovered the power of social networks: "On a visit to Apartadó, Antioquia, a town councilor gave me an image of Santos and Timochenko with a message about how they would give money to the guerrillas even if the country were in economic trouble. I posted it on Facebook and last Saturday I had 130,000 shares with a reach of six million people." Vélez also said that the campaign soon decided to concentrate its message on indignation instead of analyzing the negative parts of the agreement. According to Vélez, the messaging was selective: "On radio stations for middle- and high-income levels we relied on impunity, political eligibility, and tax reform, while on radio stations for the lower classes we focused on subsidies. As for each regional group, we used their respective accents. On the coast, we individualized the message that we were going to become Venezuela."[43] Leaders of the Centro Democrático did not receive the Vélez interview well, especially Álvaro Uribe. The former president tweeted, "Compañeros who are not careful with their communications do harm."[44]

Because of the polls that showed that "Sí" was going to win easily, because of the lack of coordination within the executive branch of government, or because the government thought that people wanted peace so much that they would accept the agreement, the campaign in favor of the agreement lacked the intensity of the "No" campaign. President Santos did warn that if the plebiscite failed, the war would continue, and that it might affect urban people more than ever: "We have ample information that the FARC are prepared to return to war and urban warfare, which is more devastating than rural war."[45] Santos also cautioned, "People have tried to say that if the plebiscite is rejected, we will be able to negotiate a better agreement. No, make no mistake. If the plebiscite is not approved, we return to war. As simple as that."[46] As shown later, the president was incorrect, either intentionally or inadvertently. The Colombian people would not approve the agreement in the plebiscite and it was renegotiated.

Throughout September, public opinion polls concluded that the "Sí" vote would prevail, and although the "Sí" percentage was going down, the last polls suggested that the plebiscite would pass. In the nationwide sample of 1,524 voters conducted September 21–25, the results predicted that 66 percent would vote "Sí" and 34 percent would vote "No." Several days before the plebiscite, the opinion firm Datexco, in a study sponsored by *El Tiempo*, predicted that 55 percent would vote "Sí" while only 36.6 percent planned to vote "No." Cifras y Conceptos, another public opinion firm, predicted a similar margin with 54 percent voting "Sí," while the Ipsos-Napoleón Franco firm predicted a 66 percent "Sí" result.[47]

In the final days before the plebiscite, both sides argued for the vote they wanted. Former president Uribe issued a list of ten reasons to vote "No," adding repression of the "No" forces to his previous list of tweets. Chief negotiator Humberto de la Calle argued that a victory by the "No" forces would be a disaster for the country.[48] President Santos called for the people to vote for the agreement, saying that it was a historic opportunity. He reasoned that he preferred to see the FARC members in the national congress rather than to see them recruiting children and committing atrocities. He also pointed out that there had been no deaths since they had proclaimed the bilateral cease-fire. On another occasion in September, the president added that "a peace, although it might be imperfect, is much better than a perfect war."[49] He assured that there would be no new taxes since all the revenue needed for the stipulations of the agreement had already been secured. Responding to the question of impunity, the president promised that there would be punishment and noted that in previous peace processes there had been blanket amnesties.

María Jimena Duzán reported that a week before the plebiscite she heard the president say, "We're going to win it. Not by much but we will win, there is no doubt." Juan Manuel Santos thought that seeing the guerrilleros dressed in civilian clothes, without weapons, was a sign. How was it possible that the plebiscite would not pass when people saw this?[50]

CONCLUSION

On October 2, the Colombian voters rejected the peace agreement with 50.23 percent (6,424,385 votes) against the agreement and 49.76 percent (6,363,989 votes) in favor of it. Only 37.4 percent of the eligible voters cast ballots. In

Bogotá, on the Atlantic and Pacific coasts, and in three departments of the Amazon voters supported "Sí." In the interior of the country, with one exception, the "No" vote prevailed. Boyacá was the only department in the interior part of the country that voted "Sí," but just barely, 50.08 to 49.91 percent. On the day of the plebiscite, Hurricane Matthew hit the Caribbean coast of the country, the weather perhaps keeping voters from going to the polls in a part of the country in which people favored the agreement. In the Atlántico department, where Santos had received over one million votes in the presidential election, only 24 percent of the eligible voters participated.[51]

People saw diverse reasons for this unexpected result. University professor Francisco Barbosa pointed out that some Colombians reacted negatively when guerrilla groups were shown on television approving the agreement, as was their right to do.[52] Some Colombians were even more disturbed to hear FARC leader "Romaña" declare, "In the FARC, we are determined not to serve a single day in jail, not only ourselves but also the rest of the people who were in the context of the war and who were fighting."[53]

When I asked for opinions about why the plebiscite failed, a leader of a victims' group stressed that the Santos administration did not have an effective campaign selling the agreement to the Colombian people.[54] A sociologist and a historian each emphasized that the Roman Catholic Church, a long-time supporter of peace initiatives, did not take a strong position, instead encouraging believers to make up their own minds.[55] Another sociologist pointed out that there were many factors in the "No" victory, "including the hurricane on the Atlantic coast, the gender issue, and the use of emotion instead of the stipulations of the agreement. The most important, in my opinion, was the Christian opposition, especially from the leader in Cartagena who came out publicly for a 'No' vote. Although the traditional family is a minority in Colombia, the Christian opposition used the fear of the disappearance of it and the negative effects that would have on Colombian life. The Roman Catholic church joined the evangelicals in this."[56]

One clear statement was that the plebiscite failed because it took place. After pointing out that in previous peace agreements plebiscites did not occur, in an op-ed piece in *El Tiempo*, Vladimir Flórez remarked, "I do not know where the president got such an idea; but I am inclined to think that he believed that he lived in a normal country, in which people would opt for peace with their eyes closed. In his naiveté, he must also have believed that he could finally defeat his former boss and mentor, Senator Uribe, killing two birds with one stone."[57]

Another likely reason why voters failed to approve the agreement in the plebiscite was because Álvaro Uribe Vélez opposed the accord. When he left the presidency in 2010, more than 70 percent of Colombians gave Uribe a positive approval rating. Many remembered the state of the country when he became president in 2002 and gave him credit for the favorable changes.

Perhaps every plebiscite on multiple issues suffers from the problem that a political scientist pointed out in this case: "The plebiscite was a mistake because in an agreement of three hundred pages different groups were able to see something they did not like. So, while most of the agreement was acceptable, that one thing would cause them to vote 'No.' And other groups could see other things."[58] I agree with that opinion.

CHAPTER SEVEN

The Renegotiations and the Second Final Agreement

AFTER THE VICTORY OF THE "No" forces on October 2, 2016, Colombians had five key questions about what would happen next. The first three dealt with the immediate response of the actors while the last two had to do with the renegotiation and approval of the accords:

Could the agreement be renegotiated?

Would the FARC be willing to make changes?

How would Santos deal with the leaders of the "No" vote?

What changes would be made to the agreement in the renegotiation?

How would the second final agreement be approved?

THE IMMEDIATE RESPONSES OF THE ACTORS

A certain amount of confusion reigned in Colombia after the unexpected victory of the "No" forces in the plebiscite. Before the vote, the government had stated that the "final" agreement could not be renegotiated. However, afterward there were questions. Could it be renegotiated? Would the FARC be willing to renegotiate? Which of the "No" groups would the president consult? If renegotiations were possible, what role would the "No" forces play in them?

Could the Agreement Be Renegotiated?

As pointed out in chapter 6, during the debate preceding the plebiscite, both chief government negotiator Humberto de la Calle and President Santos had said that it was an error to think that they could renegotiate the agreement if the "No" forces won the vote. However, when the results came in on the evening of October 2, President Santos and some of his allies immediately began talking about a new political pact to save the peace process. Either the two leaders realized that they had been incorrect in their earlier statements, they had been less than honest with the Colombian people before the plebiscite, or they had changed their minds.

When he found out the results of the plebiscite, Santos first met with his family and with chief negotiator Humberto de la Calle. He then met with his ministers and the president of Congress, Mauricio Lizano. Later that evening, Santos said, "Tomorrow (Monday), I will convene all the political players—and especially those that supported the 'No'—to listen to them, to open spaces for dialogue, and to determine the way forward."[1] The president said that it was clear that that dialogue would have to include the forces led by former president Uribe. Santos had suffered a double defeat: the plebiscite had not only been a way to achieve peace but also "for the less altruistic purpose of defeating Álvaro Uribe."[2]

Within two hours after the results were known, the FARC officials in Havana said that they would continue their search for peace. Showing that the negative vote in the referendum had not led to changes in their attitudes, the leaders clearly wanted to find a solution after the "No" victory, even at one point suggesting that the result of the plebiscite should simply be ignored. Leader Timochenko said that the agreement remained in force and that "the plebiscite has no legal effect, only a political one." Other FARC leaders made similar arguments.[3]

This is another clear indication of the relative weak position of the guerrilla group in the Santos negotiations. In the Pastrana and other previous negotiations, the FARC had been ready to return to conflict if there were problems while negotiating. In this case, the FARC did not have that desire, even after the vote of the Colombian people against the agreement. By October 2016, the FARC troops had already left their safe places and had begun to move to the zones where they would be demobilized. Some feared that because the "No" position had prevailed, they would be an easy target for the armed forces.

Meanwhile, members of the Centro Democrático and others celebrated the "No" victory through social media and the traditional means of communication. José Félix Lafaurie, president of the Colombian Federation of Ranchers (FEDEGAN), commented that the vote showed that a silent majority did not want the agreement. Centro Democrático senator María Fernanda Cabal said, "Human dignity is not negotiated; it was clear that principles are not negotiated. They have to think about the whole country; a peace without justice is not peace." Francisco Santos, the president's cousin, vice president during the Uribe presidency, and former mayoral candidate in Bogotá, declared that the "No" victory was a "message of greatness and dignity." However, he added, "We will work with the government to renew this agreement," so that "this peace will succeed, so that it will have justice, reparation, reconciliation and forgiveness, a peace where we all fit and not where only half of the Colombian people are included."[4]

At the same time, in Antioquia former president Uribe was meeting with the three potential presidential candidates of the Centro Democrático: Carlos Holmes Trujillo, Iván Duque, and Óscar Iván Zuluaga. The purpose of their meeting was to come up with their requests for changes in the agreement, therefore demonstrating a more moderate attitude than during the debate before the plebiscite. That the Centro Democrático would support a change in the agreement became apparent when, at about nine on the evening of the plebiscite, Uribe said, "We want to contribute to a great national pact." On television Uribe appeared conciliatory and calm. He did not call members of the FARC "narcoterrorists" as he had during the debate before the plebiscite. This time he said, "Gentlemen of the FARC: It will contribute much to the unity of Colombians if you, protected, allow the enjoyment of the tranquility." He did, however, call for changes "so that the agreement would not substitute for the constitution, abolish institutions, reward crime, or jeopardize the state." Addressing himself to the president and Congress, Uribe called for a judicial solution that did not include impunity.[5] His message was in keeping with his statements during the debate before the plebiscite. During that time, he had said, "If the 'No' wins, we ask that the table not be broken, that the dialogue not be broken, that the dialogue be reoriented."[6]

Although at the end of October 2, it was not clear what the post-plebiscite process would be or whether the president and Uribe would meet, it was apparent that the peace process was not completely dead. The idea of continuing was soon endorsed by the presidents of the Conservative Party, the Partido de la U, and the Liberal Party. Liberal leader Horacio Serpa stated, "President Santos has the support of the Liberal Party because he took a chance on peace, and we support that path on which we have always been. Our duty now is to be with him."[7]

Would the FARC Be Willing to Make Changes?

The immediate response of FARC leader Timochenko was that "the FARC maintains their will for peace." The organization regretted the rejection of the peace agreement but ratified its willingness to disarm after fifty-two years of conflict. The FARC "lamented that hatred and resentment had influenced the opinion of the Colombian population."[8]

The question of whether the FARC would be willing to renegotiate was resolved very quickly. On October 3, chief government negotiator Humberto de la Calle and Sergio Jaramillo met with FARC leaders in Havana.[9] On October 6, the government and FARC delegations met a second time along with the guarantor countries and the head of the United Nations special mission.

The following day, the two sides issued a joint decree in which they said that it was appropriate for them to listen to the proposals for changes from the "No" groups to find adjustments that the government and the FARC would discuss. The two sides pledged to continue the bilateral cease-fire and asked the secretary-general of the United Nations, through the Security Council, to authorize the mission to monitor and verify the agreement, as previously decided. Finally, the memorandum stated, "We will continue to make progress in the implementation of confidence-building measures of a humanitarian nature, such as the search for missing persons, the pilot plans for humanitarian demining, the voluntary substitution of crops for illicit use, commitments relating to the departure of minors from the camps, and to the situation of persons deprived of their liberty."[10]

How Would Santos Deal with the "No" Leaders?

The next step that the Santos administration took was to consult with the leaders of the "No" groups. On October 5, President Santos met with Álvaro Uribe—the first time the two had met since Santos became president. He also had meetings with other "No" leaders from the Centro Democrático including former procurator Alejandro Ordóñez, Marta Lucía Ramírez, and Óscar Iván Zuluaga, as well as others. Given the importance of the evangelical Christian vote, the president contacted pastors of those groups and met with fourteen of their representatives in the presidential palace. In all, as reported by the Office of the High Commissioner for Peace, the following individuals and organizations also met with government representatives: Andrés Pastrana, Ilva Myriam Hoyos, Pedro Medellín, Augusto Ibáñez, Diana Sofía Giraldo, Rafael Guarín, the Association of Retired Officers of the Military Forces, the Colombian Federation of FARC Victims, the World Revival Center, the Christian Covenant for Peace, the Colombian Evangelical Council, Centro Democrático, and Ricardo Arias of the Significant Group Free Citizens.[11]

Of all the groups that made up the "No" coalition, without doubt the Centro Democrático and its leader, Álvaro Uribe Vélez, were the most important. The day after the plebiscite, Uribe made three proposals that, from his perspective, would make a continuation of the peace process possible. First, the former president proposed amnesty for FARC foot soldiers who had not committed atrocious crimes, somewhat surprising because it was already in the agreement. During his presidency, Uribe had sought amnesty for former foot soldiers of the paramilitary groups. Uribe's second proposal was for effective protection for members of the FARC who immediately stopped their violent activities, including extortion and the drug trade. The third was for relief of members of the armed forces who faced judgment for their actions during the armed conflict. He said, "I would ask that the same dialogue committee study the possibility that Congress consider judicial relief, without impunity, for the members of the armed forces."[12]

Doubts still existed about the possibility of finding common ground on which to renegotiate the agreement. How could an agreement of almost three hundred pages change if ex-president Uribe and his followers completely opposed some of the major points of the pact? To some, it seemed that the Centro Democrático and others of the "No" forces had the upper hand after the vote. Although Uribe repeated his willingness to take part in a dialogue, he asked, "Is there a willingness in the government and in the president (Juan Manuel Santos) to listen? Is there a willingness to listen in order to introduce changes to the agreement?"[13] So, the first task that the government had was to negotiate with the "No" forces.

Five issues were most important for Uribe and his followers:[14]

1. Political participation: For Uribe, the agreement opened up the possibility of political participation for the terrorists, without excluding those responsible for atrocities.

2. The armed forces: For Uribe, it was not acceptable to include the armed forces and civil society in the same justice system as the terrorists. The former president said, "The armed forces, guardians of the nation who are not terrorists, need a dignified treatment separate from the criminals."

3. The drug trade: Uribe thought it was not acceptable to consider the drug trade as a crime connected to rebellion. His thesis was that "drug trafficking, as financial backing of terrorism, has not been a political offense; on the contrary, it has been a continuing atrocity, never pardonable."

4. The terminology referring to the abandonment or surrender of arms: One of the most common terms in the agreement was "abandonment" of arms. Uribe preferred "surrender" of arms because "abandonment" might mean that the terrorist groups would keep the arms and use them later.

5. Justice without impunity: It was unacceptable to Uribe that the government had agreed that criminals responsible for atrocious crimes would not go to jail if they confessed their responsibility for them. He believed that transitional justice was too lenient because it called for restorative actions like social work and the effective restriction of liberty, but never used the word "jail." In other words, Uribe wanted the FARC leaders to be in prison uniforms behind bars, but

the foot soldiers who had not committed atrocious crimes could receive amnesty.

Without doubt this last point was one of the most difficult ones. While it was implausible that the FARC would sign a peace agreement in which some of its members would end up in jail, the Uribe movement had already proposed an intermediary solution: restriction of liberty not by imprisonment in an ordinary jail but by confinement in specific areas.

At the same time, FARC leaders were skeptical that anything good would result if Uribe had too much influence in changing the agreement. As the Santos-Uribe meeting drew nearer, FARC leaders began expressing their concerns and expectations through a number of tweets. Timochenko repeated his desire for peace, but, after President Santos stated that the government would honor the cease-fire only until the end of October, he and other FARC leaders, including Pastor Alape, Iván Márquez, and Carlos Lozada, voiced their doubts. They recommended that FARC troops move to secure positions "in order to avoid provocations so that the FARC would not break the cease-fire."[15]

By the end of the first week after the plebiscite, there were complications, and the ability of the government to compromise with the "No" leaders was looking unlikely. A brief meeting that the president had with former president Andrés Pastrana made some people less uncertain after Pastrana, admitting that 98 percent of the Colombian people wanted peace, agreed to lessen his criticism of the government.

The Santos-Uribe meeting lasted more than four hours, ending with the agreement that the two leaders would exchange their viewpoints. To that end, the two agreed to meet again the following week. The government clearly had decided to listen to suggestions from the "No" groups. It had also decided to take the suggestions to Havana to discuss with the FARC. This latter decision meant that the "No" groups would not participate directly in the Havana renegotiations.

However, not all conditions were favorable for a renegotiation. In the Santos-Uribe meeting, the former president wanted to reopen the debate about whether there was "internal conflict" or "terrorism" in Colombia. This Uribe position, coming six years after Santos had first signaled a change in policy in his inaugural speech, showed the importance that the former gave to the terminology. Likewise, despite its conciliatory language, the FARC did not seem ready to change some of the key points in the first final agreement. According to a sociologist who is a long-term student of peace processes in Colombia, in the Havana negotiations the government negotiators had attempted to have the agreement require punishment in jail and limited political participation but had been unsuccessful.[16]

The thesis of an article in *Semana* magazine on October 8, 2016, was that President Santos was negotiating simultaneously with the FARC and Uribe and, as a result, "maneuvering space for President Santos, even with the Nobel Peace Prize, is very small. He is sandwiched between an emboldened opposition that has a convincing argument—the popular mandate of 6.6 million people—and a guerrilla group that also has its own: an agreement signed with the government before the international community, placed as well in the hands of the United Nations and the Swiss Federal Council. The distance between the positions of Uribismo and the FARC do not give reason for much optimism."[17] This statement underlines the argument of this book: that Santos negotiated simultaneously with the FARC and with Uribe from the very beginning of the meetings of government and FARC representatives. The difference was that while before the three-part negotiation might have been implicit, at this point it had become very explicit.

In addition, Álvaro Uribe was no longer the only powerful actor against the first final agreement. One of the priorities of President Santos was to call the evangelical Christian leaders, inviting them to meet with him. They were the other major group in the "No" coalition, second only to the Uribe-led one. For that reason, the day after his meeting with Uribe, Santos met with fourteen evangelical representatives. Immediately after the "No" victory, the evangelical leaders had said that they wanted to assist in making changes, especially to preserve the "concept of family." While Colombia has long been considered to be one of the most Roman Catholic countries in the world, according to the Colombian Evangelical Council, there were some ten million evangelical Christians in the country in 266 churches, seminaries, and businesses. There were 145 evangelical radio stations and dozens of television programs as well as an international cable channel that broadcast twenty-four hours a day, every day of the year. The question of gender was the major problem that evangelical groups had with the first final agreement.[18]

RENEGOTIATION AND APPROVAL

After these meetings, the government compiled a document based on the 410 proposals for changes and 700 pages of commentaries it had received.[19] From that collection, the government constructed a matrix of sixty changes proposed by the "No" groups to take to Havana to negotiate with the FARC.[20] President Santos told the negotiators to come to a solution as soon as possible. The renegotiations lasted for nearly two months, and, as María Jimena Duzán recounted, "It was an agonizing fifty days in which the smallest mistake could have caused a catastrophe." Duzán pointed out that, even though it was unknown to the Colombian people, during that time nearly seven thousand FARC combatants were moving towards their demobilization zones.[21]

The cease-fire continued, however, and nothing happened during this "final march," as the FARC called it.

The proposals that High Commissioner for Peace Sergio Jaramillo took to Havana were in two groups. In the first were changes that would not affect the central goal of the peace process—to end the conflict between the two sides that shared responsibility for the violence. The second group of proposals, on the contrary, was based on the idea that there was no armed conflict and that the agreement should be to disarm and punish the FARC. According to the "No" leaders who wanted this result, the guerrillas were the only ones responsible for the serious crimes.

The least problematical parts of the change proposals were misunderstandings, ambiguities, and matters that negotiators had left to define later. One example of this was that "No" leaders thought the accord should explicitly express the right to private property. The first final agreement did not do that even though its intention was to strengthen private property. Another similar case was that of the family. After the government explained to the church groups and other conservative sectors that "gender ideology" and sexual liberty were in fact not in the first final agreement, those groups made specific suggestions. One was that the agreement should stress the importance of the traditional or nuclear family. Secondly, based on the number of their ministers who had been assassinated, evangelical churches wanted the agreement to include them as victims.

In addition, the "No" groups had proposed changes in the transitional justice agreement, insisting that there be no Special Jurisdiction for Peace (Jurisdicción Especial para la Paz, JEP) and that the traditional justice system play a part. The changes in the transitional justice system that the government was prepared to make did not satisfy the "No" groups. However, the exclusion of foreign judges and the extension of the time period of the JEP seemed likely to pacify them.

Many of the proposals of the "No" leaders were contradictory to the central backbone of the peace process, including the political opening for the former guerrillas. The "No" leaders considered this a step towards Castro-Chavismo. For that reason, they proposed that the accord limit the possibilities of the new FARC-created political party. In the same manner, the "No" groups wanted to limit the amnesty law so that it would not include extortion or illegal mining.

There were four key points on which the "No" and FARC leaders were unlikely to find compromises. First, for punishment the "No" side wanted a real "privation of liberty" instead of an "effective restriction of liberty." The FARC definitely would not accept prison sentences. The original agreement put the punishments in the hands of the judges, which was not specific enough for the "No" leaders.

A second obstacle, perhaps the most difficult of all, was political eligibility. "No" leaders wanted a stipulation that the FARC chiefs that the court found guilty of serious crimes would not have the right to be political candidates, even after they had finished their sentences. This was an impossible stipulation for the FARC.

The third complicated matter concerned the assets of the FARC and effective reparation for the victims. The first final agreement was general. The "No" forces wanted more specificity, with the FARC supplying a complete list of its goods and an explicit promise to make reparations.

Another contentious point in the agreement was that it would become part of the constitution. That condition was unacceptable to the "No" leaders. The FARC wanted a legal guarantee for the agreement. However, the "No" leaders thought that some parts should not be irreversible. Making the agreement part of the constitution would mean that only votes from both houses of Congress in two consecutive sessions could change it.[22]

The question was whether the FARC delegation would accept any of the proposed changes; many thought that it would be difficult for the FARC to agree to most of them. Some changes would be unacceptable to the guerrilla group while others would be objectionable to the political establishment. The government representatives realized that it was going to be challenging to come to an agreement that would please both the FARC and the "No" leaders.

After the meeting of the FARC and government delegates, negotiators for the guerrilla group accepted fifty-eight of the proposed changes, "many more than we would have ever imagined," according to Sergio Jaramillo. This is a clear indication that the FARC leaders knew that even a modified agreement was better than none. However, there were limits for the FARC. As Jaramillo reported, "The two points that it was not possible to modify—closing the door to the political participation of the FARC and making the conditions of imprisonment more severe—are the two things that made this or any peace negotiation impossible. No guerrilla signs an agreement not to participate in politics."[23]

Lead negotiator Humberto de la Calle reported that the government made various proposals for compromises on FARC political participation. One was that instead of immediate representation in Congress, the FARC themselves would state that they had made the decision not to participate during the first congressional session. Another government proposal was that the FARC could choose as its representatives people who were close to them in ideas but who had no judicial processes against them. The FARC delegates rejected those government proposals.[24]

What happened next was close to the magical realism of Colombian Nobel laureate Gabriel García Márquez. While taking a walk to calm down, de la

Calle coincidentally heard a telephone conversation between FARC delegate Iván Márquez and leader Timochenko. Márquez expressed his feeling that it was time to alert the guerrilla troops that the process had ended. De la Calle called President Santos, who happened to be in Rionegro, Antioquia, talking with former president Álvaro Uribe. Uribe wanted the negotiators in Havana to return to Colombia for additional negotiations with him. De la Calle told Santos that he thought that time was of the essence and the agreement would fail if there were a delay.[25] The government agreed to immediate FARC representation in Congress.

This was another occasion when the peace process could have failed. If de la Calle had not overheard the Márquez-Timochenko conversation, he might have agreed with the Uribe request that the government delegation return for more negotiations with him. The FARC leader in that case might have instructed the organization's troops to stop their march toward the demobilization areas and to return to their safe places. Then the war would have started again.

On November 14, 2016, the representatives of the Colombian government and those of the FARC approved a new agreement of 310 pages.[26] The Office of the High Commissioner of Peace also published another document called "The Final Agreement for the Termination of the Conflict and the Construction of a Stable and Lasting Peace," showing all the deletions and additions. An analysis published in *Semana* identified ten as being the most important.[27]

First, the new peace agreement did not become part of the constitution. The "No" forces had insisted on that. Instead the new agreement specified that its contents, which corresponded "to norms of international humanitarian law or fundamental rights defined in the political constitution and those related to the previous, will be obligatory parameters of interpretation and a guide for implementation and validity of the rules and the laws for the carrying out of and development of the Final Agreement." Also, the new accord established the obligation of all public authorities to comply in good faith with its provisions.

Second, the Supreme Court could consider appeals of decisions of the Special Jurisdiction for Peace. The "No" forces wanted "to clarify that any review of judgments by the JEP is not done in detriment to the court official who issued the judgment." The change made was that "the Supreme Court of Justice shall be competent to review the judgments that have been made."

Third, the characteristics and mechanisms of effective restriction of liberty were spelled out more precisely. The "No" forces wanted "to specify the scope of effective restriction of freedom, the criteria that should guide judges to impose these sanctions, and the system for supervision and control." The changes were that the judges would set specific areas for complying with sanctions, with a maximum size equivalent to that of the transitional zones;

set schedules for the fulfilment of restorative penalties; determine the place of residence for a person complying with a sanction; and designate the body that would verify compliance and the regularity with which it should submit reports.

Fourth, some drug trafficking crimes would come under the Colombian penal code and could not be pardoned as part of the guerrilla conflict. The "No" leaders wanted to make amnesty for drug trafficking conditional upon the delivery of relevant information for the fight against it. The new agreement specified that crimes that were categorized as those committed only to finance the rebellion would not include any that resulted in personal enrichment or that could be considered crimes against humanity, a serious war crime, or genocide.

Fifth, foreign judges would not be part of the Special Jurisdiction for Peace, going along with the position of the "No" forces. The change was to specify that the Peace Tribunal would be composed of Colombian magistrates in sections of five members.

Sixth, the political party set up by the FARC could not offer candidates for the sixteen transitional seats. These seats would be given to communities and victims affected by the conflict. However, the final language went further: "The parties that have representation in Congress or with legal status, including the political party or movement that arises from the transition of the FARC-EP to legal political activity, will not be able to register candidates for these constituencies."

Also eliminated was the provision that the FARC party would receive 10 percent of state funds for parties, leaving it at an equal level with the other parties. The "No" position had been that the resources granted to the FARC party should be additional, without affecting the common fund of the other parties, should be in accordance with the rules that applied to the others, and should be the only resources that the FARC party would receive. The new agreement stated that the FARC party or political movement would receive annually, between the date of registration and July 19, 2026, a sum equivalent to the average received by political parties or movements with legal status for their functioning in the elections prior to the signing of the agreement.

Seventh, freedom of religion would be respected and gender focus was defined as "the recognition of equal rights of men and women and of the special circumstances of each." The "No" forces had asked that the agreement reiterate respect for the constitutional right to religious freedom and of worship.

Eighth, during the cease-fire process the FARC would present an inventory of its goods and assets to be used for the reparation of victims. The "No" groups had asked for two things: the agreement should specify the terms for the FARC's contribution to the reparation of its victims, and the FARC must report the list of assets it had for that reparation. The new agreement stated that while the FARC members were in the transitional zones handing over weapons, their authorized representatives would agree with representatives of the government on procedures to inventory all types of goods and assets and to report on them. The FARC should proceed to the material reparation of the victims, observing the criteria established by the authority of the Constitutional Court regarding war resources.

Ninth, the Special Jurisdiction for Peace could judge third parties if they requested that they be judged. It would be competent to review behavior of noncombatant third parties who by funding or collaboration had participated actively or decisively with the actors of the conflict in the most serious crimes. The "No" forces had said that the competence of the JEP should be clarified in relation to members of the FARC, individuals, and state agents. The change was that the new agreement specified that it would also define the legal status of those third parties who voluntarily submitted themselves to the jurisdiction within three years of its start-up and who had processes or convictions for offenses that were the responsibility of the JEP. The important change was that third parties would be judged if they requested it.

Tenth, a commission of experts would be created to evaluate new agrarian legislation. No new rural reserve zones would be created, and nothing in the agreement would affect the right to have private property. The concern of the "No" forces was for rural reserve zones to be set up by proper authorities and for their activation not to depend exclusively on the communities. The new agreement stated that the relevant government agency would work with them in accordance with current regulations.

Despite all these changes, some "No" leaders were disappointed because of the process through which the changes were made. Despite what Álvaro Uribe had said, they had expected to be part of these new conversations in Havana. However, none were invited to participate, leading one of them to say to me that they were very disappointed with the process and that there had been no meaningful changes.[28] Political analyst Eduardo Pizarro described their perspective: "While the leaders of the 'No' had the expectation of carrying out a second round of talks to refine the agreements (what they called a 'national agreement for peace') suddenly the government announced that it had already reached a final, definitive, and unmodifiable agreement with the FARC." Pizarro believed that not negotiating with the "No" left the country even more split.[29]

How Would the Second Final Agreement Be Approved?

On November 2, President Santos announced that there were alternatives for the approval of the second final agreement, adding, "As head of state, I must choose the path that least divides the country when it comes to endorsing a new agreement. When we have the new agreement, depending on the extent of the consensus, we will determine which path we take."[30] By the middle of the month the president and the principal political party leaders, with consent of the FARC, had decided that the new final agreement could be approved by Congress instead of through another plebiscite.

On November 24, 2016, the government and the FARC signed the second final agreement in the Teatro Colón in Bogotá. Using his presidential discretion and with apparent approval of the FARC representatives, President Santos decided that the people would approve the second agreement through their elected representatives in Congress. On the same day, the Santos administration sent the text of the agreement to the Senate. The Senate approved the agreement on November 29 and the Chamber on the following day. On December 1 the two sides, through a joint communiqué, declared that it was D-Day, that is, day 1 when the agreement began to be enforced.

CONCLUSION

Semana magazine captured the Colombian mood when the second final agreement was announced, entitling its article "The New Agreement Is Not Going to Satisfy Everyone." After the announcement of the agreement on November 14, some celebrated, while others responded with caution. Of special note was the almost immediate approval of the agreement by the government of the United States with National Security Advisor Susan Rice sending congratulations. Secretary of State John Kerry stated, "After fifty-two years of war, no peace agreement can satisfy everyone in every detail, but it is an important step forward in Colombia's path towards a just and lasting peace."[31]

Indeed, the different comments from prominent Colombians substantiated Kerry's statement. Alianza Verde party senator Jorge Iván Ospina tweeted, "Do not tell me now that the adjustments made are not enough. This would lead to deterioration and a loss of a unique opportunity." Former Bogotá mayor and presidential candidate Antanas Mockus posted on social media his opinion: "Living in Colombia in 2016 is a privilege. At last we are finding a way to solve this difficult problem." Polo Democrático senator Iván Cepeda added, "Notwithstanding its changes, the new agreement preserves the essential bases of the one that was signed on September 26 in Cartagena, defends the rights of the people, and maintains the spirit of not being an act of submission but a true peace agreement." At that time, some of the "No" leaders, including Andrés Pastrana and Marta Lucía Ramírez, were more cautious. Álvaro Uribe asked for time to study the agreement before making a statement.[32]

Not surprisingly, the leaders of the "No" were not pleased with this second final agreement. Some thought that a second renegotiation might be possible. Some evangelical pastors immediately expressed their dismay. One of the "No" leaders, Centro Democrático member Rafael Nieto Loaiza, concluded that there really were no differences between the first and the second final agreements. As he wrote in the Medellín newspaper *El Colombiano*, "It is not then a matter of whether many or a few quantitative changes were made in the text. It is plainly and simply not a new agreement because 'the structure of the agreement,' 'the fundamental pillars,' remained intact. When there's a confession, you need no proof, we lawyers say. By not negotiating a new agreement, Santos lost the golden opportunity to, on the one hand, put an end to the social and political polarization that he has led us to since the 2014 campaign, where he divided the country between 'friends' and 'enemies' of peace, and, on the other, to come to a great national agreement that would ensure, truly, the sustainability of the pact with the guerrillas."[33]

The Christian Covenant for Peace, a coalition of evangelical churches established ten days after the plebiscite, was likewise displeased, issuing its first objections even before it had studied the entire second final agreement. In a communiqué Claudia Castellanos, Eduardo Cañas, Héctor Pardo, and Jhon Milton Rodríguez said, "Although some modifications have been made in terms of language, structurally it has the same aspect. We suggest that if the objective of implementing the gender approach is the recognition of women's rights, the term 'women's rights approach' should be used."[34]

In the changes in the second final agreement, neither the government nor the FARC nor the "No" forces got all the changes that they wanted. The most important change was that the peace agreement did not become part of the constitution. This was a clear victory of the "No" groups but a loss to the FARC. This meant that the guerrilla group would demobilize and disarm under the assumption that the Colombian government would later approve the stipulations of the agreement through its regular processes. In late 2017, as Congress began its debates to implement the agreement, a political scientist noted, "If the agreement had become a part of the constitution, the debate now going on in Congress would have been different."[35] A sociologist said something very similar in an interview.[36] A leader of a women's group added, "In the current debate in Congress, often the opponents to the proposals of the government say, 'We won the plebiscite.'"[37] The three individuals agreed that although the second final agreement was approved by Congress without a national debate, that did not mean that its implementation would proceed without difficulties.

PART FOUR

Conclusions

I DIVIDE THIS FINAL PART of the book into two topics. The first, in chapter 8, is an analysis of why the government under Juan Manuel Santos was successful in negotiating a peace agreement with the FARC after so many of his predecessors had failed. Given the complexity of the country and of the conflict that had lasted more than fifty years, the explanation combines many factors. The last chapter of the book has my tentative conclusions after a year of the implementation of the second final agreement. I point out that, very importantly, the homicide rate in Colombia was at the lowest point in decades a year into the implementation. However, I also analyze the difficulties in implementing the agreement, especially after the election as president of Iván Duque, the candidate of the Centro Democrático of Álvaro Uribe Vélez.

CHAPTER EIGHT

The Reasons an Agreement
with the FARC Was Reached

IN THIS CHAPTER I ANALYZE reasons that it was possible for the government and the FARC to reach a peace agreement. After so many peace processes that failed with the FARC, why did this one lead to an agreement and even a second agreement after the "No" vote victory in the plebiscite? Using the terms of the theoretical literature cited in the introduction, I divide this question into two subquestions: Why was there a "mutually hurting stalemate" this time? Why was the moment "ripe" for the negotiations during the Santos presidency when it had not been in previous dialogues?

THE REASONS THAT AN AGREEMENT WITH THE FARC WAS POSSIBLE

As in most matters in the social world, no one single factor explains the breakthrough. Before I went to Bogotá in October 2017, I had some explanations in mind. However, I have always found that I can learn more from interviews in which Colombians analyze their own country. In the interviews, I asked the following open-ended question to scholars and government officials: Why was it possible for the Santos administration to reach an agreement with the FARC when other presidents had been unsuccessful? Some respondents gave only one or two reasons, but others had multiple explanations. I had expected some of the responses, but the people I interviewed also had ideas I had not anticipated.

I consulted recent publications by Colombian scholars. Eduardo Pizarro, in his book *Cambiar el futuro*, gave five reasons for the Santos success: the weakening of the FARC, the government now recognizing the guerrilla group as a "belligerent force," public opinion favoring another attempt eight years after the Pastrana failure, each side recognizing that it could not defeat the other, and each side wanting to find a way to get out of a mutually hurting stalemate.[1] A sociologist I interviewed highlighted some other factors, saying, "There are four reasons for the success of the peace process this time: the change of military balance, better negotiators, that the negotiations were held in Cuba, and the improvement in relations with Chávez in Venezuela."[2]

A definitive analysis appeared in late July 2018 when Sergio Jaramillo published an article in *El Tiempo* called "What Made Peace with the FARC Possible."[3] Jaramillo was high commissioner for peace, one of the government's negotiators in Havana, and considered to be the brains behind the peace process. Given his importance in the negotiations, below I organize the reasons for the success as Jaramillo did and supplement his arguments with information from my interviews and other written sources.

The Change in Objective Conditions

Sergio Jaramillo divided the reasons for the success of the negotiations into two parts, saying, "There are two complementary ways of seeing the problem. The first is: what conditions changed that made the negotiations possible?" The second is "to understand the peace process as the construction of a space that allows changing the mix of interests, so that cooperation prevails over confrontation."[4] Put in different terms, the first way is by looking at the changes in the objective conditions. The second way encompasses a number of decisions made in the context of those changes.

The necessary precondition for success was the change in the military balance of power. High Commissioner for Peace Jaramillo stated this in his newspaper op-ed article, as did President Juan Manuel Santos and almost all of the experts whom I interviewed. Statistics back up this argument. As I pointed out in chapter 3, during the Uribe years the total number of troops in the armed forces and police increased from 291,316 to 431,900, a rise of 48 percent. At the same time, the estimated number of FARC combatants fell from 24,000 to 8,000, a loss of two-thirds. The armed forces also improved because of better weapons and communications equipment. The new troops, weapons, and communications equipment came from Plan Colombia, and their effect was to lessen the importance of the country's geographic barriers. Yet the military was not able to defeat the FARC, and in its much weaker position, the guerrilla group had no realistic chance of winning. As I argued in the conclusion of chapter 3, a major argument of this book is that the Santos peace process led to an agreement with the FARC because the military balance of power had changed. Because of this new situation, as I demonstrated in previous chapters, there was a change in the nature of the negotiations. No longer, as in earlier ones, did one side "freeze" the proceedings. Now both sides demonstrated that they wanted the negotiations to succeed. Both sides feared failure for which they would be held responsible. They took actions, issued positive statements, and made goodwill gestures.

Even the most difficult incident during the negotiations showed the fear of failure on each side. As I described in chapter 4, on November 15, 2014, President Santos suspended the peace dialogues with the FARC after FARC troops kidnapped general Rubén Darío Alzate Mora, commander of the Fuerza de Tarea Conjunta Titán in the Chocó department. The president ordered the negotiating team not to return to Havana for the next round of talks. The FARC leadership temporarily denied the seizure and called for the president not to be hasty. There was no freezing, and the talks began again soon after the FARC released the general.

The change in the military balance of power also had two positive externalities. After the paramilitary forces demobilized, victims' organizations could take a more active role in the negotiations. The demobilization of the paramilitary groups during the Uribe presidency removed a complication that other presidents had experienced. One of the reasons that this took place was that the Colombian military had become strong enough to control the Marxist guerrillas without paramilitary help. The difficulty that the paramilitary groups caused for the government in negotiations was most graphically shown on January 7, 1999, when FARC leader Manuel Marulanda did not appear for the ceremony inaugurating the Andrés Pastrana negotiations, claiming that a paramilitary group planned to assassinate him there.[5] The problem caused by the presence of the paramilitary groups was seen throughout the earlier negotiations, most commonly when the FARC equated paramilitary actions with actions of the Colombian military. That interpretation was correct at times. Even though alleged paramilitary actions were still a concern for the FARC during the Santos negotiations, at no point did they lead to a termination of the talks.

A second positive externality of the different military balance of power was that organized victims' groups could take part in the peace process. Previously, they feared that they would be victims of paramilitary groups.

Decisions Made

While the change in the military balance of power was the sine qua non of the peace process, it was not enough. Wise decisions also made the achievement possible. Sergio Jaramillo reported ten decisions made that were important for the success.[6]

As Jaramillo said, "The first step was, simply, to recognize that there was a window of opportunity for peace, and above all, to recognize the conflict. That was what President Santos did in 2010." In chapter 3, I described how this happened in the Santos administration and in the FARC with leaders of both sides realizing that the time was right for negotiations.

Colombian historian and Jesuit priest Fernán González González explained the decision this way: "This led one to think that both this guerrilla leader and the president were reaching a stage of realism, based on the awareness of their strengths and weaknesses. . . . Santos would have decided that, despite the political collapse and military setback of the FARC, this group had endured a major military offense without falling apart and had already begun to open the door to a possible negotiation. For his part, Timochenko would be aware that the FARC was no longer able to recover the strength they had achieved in the late 1990s and that the only possibility left was simple resistance in order to move gradually closer to a negotiation."[7]

According to Jaramillo, the second-most important decision leading to success was constructing a suitable environment with international participation. This began with the normalization of relations with Venezuelan president Hugo Chávez. He had played a role in negotiations between the FARC and the Colombian government during Álvaro Uribe's second term. FARC leaders had long found Venezuela to be a safe haven. Chávez supported the FARC because he thought he might need their guerrilla expertise when the United States invaded his country. When newly elected, President Santos met with Chávez and called him "my new best friend."[8] In addition, by the time of the Santos negotiations, Chávez had decided that Venezuela did not face danger from the United States. Therefore, the Venezuelan president could help in the peace process. After the death of Chávez in 2013, Nicolás Maduro continued this assistance.

In addition to Venezuela, the Santos administration decided to get the international support necessary for the tasks that had to be done, inviting other countries, mainly those in the region, to play a part in the peace process. The first and the primary countries of support were Cuba and Norway, who were the guarantors of the negotiation, with Cuba as host. Later Chile and Venezuela became supporters. Jaramillo mentioned other international actors, including the United Nations and the European Union.

Jaramillo gave special credit to the United States. As he stated,

A separate chapter is the United States. President Obama strongly supported the process. His government did not interfere in any way, and when by the end of 2014 everything indicated that a more active role for the United States was desirable, at the request of President Santos, Secretary of State John Kerry—who could not have demonstrated a greater commitment to the process—quickly dispatched Bernie Aronson as special envoy to Havana. A retired diplomat, very patient and very discerning, who helped a lot to get the FARC to understand Washington's point of view, and vice versa.

Unfortunately, with the change of government in the United States, the attitude also changed. Which proves once again that you cannot miss windows of opportunity. With the current international context, the negotiation would have been much more difficult, or perhaps impossible.

A sociologist interviewed agreed with this point, emphasizing the importance of the negotiations being held in Cuba and the change in relations with Chávez in Venezuela.[9]

Cuba provided a suitable environment for the negotiations. The FARC delegates felt safe there. At the same time, Cuba was trying to improve relations with the United States, and the Obama administration favored the peace process. Having the negotiations in Havana was possible because the FARC leadership had changed its position on the issue. After the negotiations with the Barco and Gaviria administrations in the late 1980s and early 1990s, the FARC leaders had consistently insisted that any talks with the government take place in a demilitarized zone in Colombia. That had occurred during the Pastrana negotiations, but during his presidency, Álvaro Uribe would not consider such a zone. In the Santos negotiations, the guerrilla group accepted a foreign location for the preliminary talks.

The third decision that Jaramillo mentioned was that the conversations were secret and that the two sides agreed to a framework for the negotiations before they became public. Secrecy alongside an agreed-upon agenda was an advantage for several reasons. Maintaining the confidentiality of the talks was easier, and serious discussion could take place without pressure from public opinion and without the temptation of using the media to please a constituency. The secret conversations gave a necessary dignity to the peace process, and the framework agreement of August 26, 2012, was a contract that established the agenda and the terms and vision of the peace process.

The fourth decision leading to success of the talks was to create a narrative that gave direction to the peace process, establishing clear limits to the negotiation and a space within which the two sides could live with rules and processes. The related fifth decision was to establish a methodology capable of "containing" the process, especially in its public phase. As Jaramillo stated, "We argued and fought over almost every word we agreed upon with the FARC, and yet we managed to jointly draft the three hundred pages of the agreement."

The organization of a credible and effective negotiation team was the sixth decision, as I pointed out in the conclusion to chapter 3. I have emphasized the contributions of individuals from the government, the FARC, and the international community who played important roles in the peace process. Each contributed in his or her own way and, although it is a counterfactual argument, the process would have suffered—and perhaps failed—without their participation. Their names appear in appendix 1.

In addition to the presence of those individuals, the governmental negotiating team was better during the Santos negotiations because of the inclusion of military officers. A historian explained, "It was very important that military officials were in the negotiations. When FARC negotiators wanted to talk about something difficult that was going on, many times they went to General Flórez instead of Jaramillo or de la Calle."[10] In addition, another historian pointed out that the army's role was different this time: "They did not oppose the peace process, as they had before. It also was very intelligent to have military representatives at the table. The military was led by a different generation, not worried about being prosecuted for crimes committed years before."[11]

These positive factors did not mean that the role was easy for the officers. As one respondent who was present in Havana when General Javier Alberto Flórez arrived at the negotiations said, "I saw General Flórez when he was going to enter into negotiations for the first time. The general had received emails from other generals, accusing him of being a traitor. He had a very stern face. I encouraged him to enter. It was the first time in seventy years that a general had negotiated with guerrillas."[12]

Yet it was not always easy for members of the military to sit with FARC leaders. Humberto de la Calle reported that, when in February 2014 he told Generals Jorge Enrique Mora and Óscar Naranjo that Fabián Rodríguez would be joining the FARC negotiating team, General Naranjo expressed no concern. General Mora reacted negatively, saying, "I'm not going to sit down with a narco at the table. I announce my withdrawal from the delegation."[13] Mora did remain in the delegation, however.

In a list of outstanding negotiators, Jaramillo also included people who were in the negotiations at different times: Frank Pearl, Luis Carlos Villegas, Nigeria Rentería, María Paulina Riveros, Gonzalo Restrepo, Roy Barreras, María Ángela Holguín, Rafael Pardo, and Juan Fernando Cristo. This team gave strength to the government. Jaramillo described how they interacted: "Most often, our internal discussions were no less intense than discussions with the FARC. But precisely because all the proposals that we brought to the table passed through the filter of a strong debate between people of very different experiences and opinions, the proposals that the government presented were always solid and, above all, unified. At the table we spoke with one voice." A member of the government's negotiation team said that he thought that the members of the Colombian military on the government's team had fewer conflicts with the FARC negotiators than they did with the civilian members of the government's team.[14]

In addition, there were changes in the FARC negotiation team that led to the agreement. Circumstances made them different. They were of a different generation. As a historian pointed out, after 1985 more and more leaders had connections to the drug trade. He added, "Historically, FARC leadership turned over every ten years, more or less. The current leadership saw this as their opportunity before new leaders replaced them."[15] A sociologist gave the same information in slightly different terms: "The FARC had a new generation of leaders, from universities instead of campesinos. The campesino leadership had the 'prolonged war' idea."[16] That guerrilla war paradigm, based on the Chinese Revolution more than on the Cuban one, was carried out on the premise that a long war would eventually wear down the official opposition. Jaramillo also had good things to say about the FARC negotiators: "For his part, Timochenko, the FARC commander, very intelligently promoted the presence at the table of the members of the secretariat and, above all, of the main regional commanders of the FARC."

In addition, the government's strategy for negotiations was better than in previous cases. As I pointed out in chapter 3, the government had a definite plan. Later decisions were also important, including the idea of specialized commissions and subcommissions to consider specific matters and then refer their conclusions to the central negotiation table. This proved to be an efficient way to handle very controversial matters such as demobilization, disarmament, and the transitional justice system.

The seventh decision, according to Jaramillo, was giving victims a central place in the agreement. Ironically, although the talks were not in their country, more Colombian groups participated. In addition to victims' organizations already mentioned, women and LGBTI groups took part. The final agreement, as a result, was the first peace agreement in the world that included women as victims. People who had been harmed in the conflict traveled to Havana to present their stories and demands. As a historian pointed out, "The role of the victims was important. They were more organized than before. Their presence at the table was symbolic, and this was new. The Law of Victims was passed before the negotiations began."[17] The victims' organizations were less threatened and became more powerful after the paramilitary demobilization.

The eighth decision was creating an implementation model that was based on participation. The idea was that the only guarantee of a stable and lasting peace was through the strengthening of institutions to take care of social conflicts and to protect the rights of citizens. The question was how to do this given previous failures in Colombia.

The ninth decision was to offer the FARC guarantees to disarm beyond UN participation. The guarantees were political ones, including seats in Congress and the political party to be formed by the insurgents; security ones, including the training of FARC troops to be part of forces protecting politicians; juridical ones, including the fast track to pass the reforms; and socioeconomic ones, including a monthly payment to demobilized troops that was greater than current unemployment compensation.

The final decision, according to Jaramillo, was having a popular vote on the agreement. As he stated, "There was an inherent tension between ending a war, which clearly does not require a vote, and other parts of the agreement, such as comprehensive rural reform, which we believe needed democratic legitimation."

Other Reasons for the Success

In comparison with previous peace processes, other factors in the success of the Santos negotiations were Uribe's opposition, the lack of unity within the FARC, and the relative lack of importance President Santos believed the success of the process would hold in determining his place in history. All these factors contrasted with previous negotiations.

Álvaro Uribe opposed the Santos peace process from its beginning. During the bargaining between the FARC and the government, this opposition made the position of the Santos administration stronger, especially during the 2014 presidential campaign. When it appeared that the Centro Democrático candidate might win, the FARC were more willing to compromise.

This conclusion might seem counterintuitive since opposition in earlier negotiations made success less likely. However, it was different in this case because of the change in the balance of power. When the government was relatively weak and the FARC relatively strong, as in the Pastrana negotiations, opposition to the government from the military or civilians made it weaker. Now that the government was stronger, organized opposition, especially when it could lead to the election of a president opposed to negotiations, made the Santos-led government stronger. Yet, while this opposition might have encouraged the government and the FARC to arrive at an agreement, it made the implementation of the agreement difficult.

In prior negotiations the lack of unity within the FARC had made an agreement less likely. However, in this case the guerrilla group was even more divided, as mentioned by a Colombian sociologist.[18] During the peace process, the group tried to minimize internal divisions by bringing to Havana negotiators representing different groups. Yet, with the FARC's relatively weaker bargaining position, lack of unity made success of the talks more likely. It also led to some FARC fronts not accepting the agreement.

Finally, although at times Juan Manuel Santos seemed close to making too much of his prestige depend on the success of the process, he never did so to the extent that Andrés Pastrana had. Other things equal, a bargainer is stronger when it appears that success or failure is not important to him or her. Santos at times was a strong negotiator when he threatened to end the negotiations. Of course, that was only possible given the relative weakness of the FARC.

CHAPTER NINE

Tentative Conclusions about the Implementation of the Agreement

THIS FINAL CHAPTER CONSIDERS HOW well the agreement with the FARC was being implemented until August 2018. While the Santos administration should be congratulated for reaching an agreement to end the guerrilla conflict that had lasted over half a century, the question then became how much of the agreement would be carried out by his administration in its waning months and by the next administration.

Colombia has a long tradition of not implementing its agreements, laws, and constitutions, beginning with the Spanish colonial government system that appeared to be centralized but in fact functioned poorly. In theory, political authority in the Iberian colonies came from the king. The Council of the Indies issued rules for the colonies, which viceroys, audiencias, and cabildos, none of whom were selected democratically, were to carry out the regulations. What on paper was an efficient, centralized bureaucracy, in practice functioned under the policy of "I obey, but do not comply." This phrase, historian John Phelan argued, reflected a centralization of authority among the viceroys and governors that existed in theory but was not carried out in reality.[1] "Obeying" but not "complying" has been a constant theme in Colombia during its entire history. Most recently, the provisions of the Constitution of 1991 and of the Law and Justice and Peace of 2005 have never been completely implemented.

In addition to that noncompliance characteristic, throughout this book it has been obvious that President Juan Manuel Santos was negotiating with actors in the Colombian political establishment and especially with Álvaro Uribe Vélez at the same time as the government was negotiating with the FARC. While this dual bargaining was apparent from the beginning, as more details of the tentative agreement became known, so did the extent of opposition to it. The victory of the "No" vote in the October 2016 plebiscite showed that, at least at that moment, Santos had succeeded with the guerrillas but was losing with a slight majority of the Colombian people. Although Congress did approve the second final agreement, the opposition forces did not disappear.

In the first two weeks of December 2016, the application of the second final agreement began well. Congress began its consideration of the amnesty law. The FARC announced that it would continue a final march to the transitional zones. The government signed the first pardons. Six FARC members were to become members of the two houses of Congress. The FARC announced the founding of its new party. In addition, President Santos later announced in his New Year's speech that the 2017 homicide rate (24 per 100,000 people) was the lowest in forty-two years.[2]

PROBLEMS OF IMPLEMENTATION

While the aforementioned actions might have been reason for optimism about the implementation of the agreement, it soon became evident that all was not going well. Problems emerged in the FARC demobilization and in the implementation of the treaty by Congress and the judicial system. This led to the following analysis in *Semana* at the end of 2017: "Once again peace is slipping from our grasp, without us even noticing it. Or maybe it is that since the 'Sí' lost the plebiscite, the possibility of a stable and lasting peace was already a chimera impossible to sustain over time, and only now has that truth suddenly come to light. The truth is that one year and three months after the defeat of the plebiscite, all attempts to re-legitimize the peace agreement have been unsuccessful: neither the inclusion of 176 proposals made by the 'No' nor the renegotiation that the FARC accepted, in which they gave up almost everything that had been agreed on in the conclave at the end of July, served to give legitimacy to the peace agreement."[3] From the start, two kinds of difficulties occurred: in the demobilization of the FARC troops and in the implementation of the agreement within the national government.

Difficulties in the Demobilization

Problems in demobilization came from both sides. On one side, some of the FARC troops refused to abide by the agreement. On the other, the government did not have the zones ready for the demobilized troops on time.

The first problem appeared on December 13, 2016, when the FARC leadership expelled five leaders of fronts that had refused to accept the peace agreement. As the central leadership stated on its webpage, "We call on the fighters, who, under false pretenses, have been led to embark on a path of adventure without a future, to step back from the mistaken decision made by their immediate leaders and return to the ranks of the FARC-EP where they will be welcomed again by their comrades."[4]

A number of problems appeared because the government did not carry out what it had promised for the demobilization. First, the government failed to have some of the placement zones ready when the demobilized FARC members arrived. These zones lacked promised dwellings and water supplies. While the agreement was that the demobilized guerrilla troops would be in the twenty-three Transitional Local Normalization Zones and the eight Transitional Normalization Spots by the end of 2016, that was not possible because the territories were not ready. The government moved the deadline for the areas to January 10. Negotiator Sergio Jaramillo summarized the situation in this way: "In addition, the logistical problems in the twenty-six remote areas include everything: the roads are in terrible condition; people do not always want to rent their land for a FARC camp, or they ask for a fortune; there is not enough water, etc. That's the reality."[5] Nevertheless, optimistically, the government projected that this would not prevent the verification of the bilateral cease-fire by the United Nations.

The first tweet of Timochenko of 2017 made it clear that, in his opinion, the FARC was not responsible for this problem: "While the @FARC_EPueblo are strictly complying with what was agreed, the government is not providing infrastructure to the #ZonasVeredales." More specifically, he spelled out that one zone had no water, another had no water or water pipes, and there were three where the government had not constructed anything. He concluded, "If the government does not immediately install the necessary infrastructure, it is necessary to reframe the date of arrival of the @FARC_EPueblo to #ZonasVeredales." Carlos Córdoba, government manager of the zones, was more optimistic, saying, "We have made a gigantic effort to reach each of these areas, to expedite the installation of the necessary structures so that the people of the FARC will have decent conditions for the duration of their stay."[6] By the end of January, only 40 percent of the guerrilla fighters were in the zones.

It was at the end of that month that the last great FARC march took place. President Santos proclaimed, "How long had we dreamed about what we are seeing now? That which today is a reality seemed impossible, seemed like a dream."[7] On February 8, 6,300 FARC members were in the zones.

Disarmament was the second difficulty, coming as a result of the first: in early February the representatives of the United Nations voiced their concern that the FARC might delay the laying down of arms because of the delay in the zones. One of the principal points was that the containers for the arms had not arrived. In reply to that, General Javier Flórez said, "Although the containers are not here, there are some special crates in which to deposit the weaponry." These, he said, could be placed under UN security.[8] The surrender of weapons was to begin on March 1, but the FARC acted early and turned over 322 arms on February 28. Yet the process did not go as well as expected. Álvaro Sierra wrote in *El Tiempo*, "Today is D-Day+100 of the timetable agreed to. While everyone expected an oiled and well-prepared process because there were months to do it, the government and the FARC are engaged in mutual public recriminations for delays and conspicuous breaches in the schedule they agreed upon."[9]

The disarmament was supposed to finish by the end of May 2017. However, it was only on June 27 that the United Nations in a communiqué stated, "As of today (Monday), the mission has stored all the registered individual weapons of the FARC: 7,132 weapons, except those that, in accordance with the road map, will serve to provide security for the 26 camps."[10]

A third difficulty coming with the FARC demobilization was what organizations would rule in areas where the guerrilla group had been the de facto government. The government said that it intended to occupy those areas with sixty-five thousand members of the armed forces and police in a program called the Victory Plan of the Army and the Safe and Peaceful Communities Plan of the National Police. Nevertheless, there were alarms as early as February when in some areas other groups arrived before the governmental forces did. It was estimated that the FARC had been in 242 municipalities, and it was reported that people in many areas were concerned about which force would arrive first.

During 2017, perhaps the most notable instance of this vacuum of power occurred on November 27 when thirteen people were killed in the southwestern department of Nariño, long a center of the illicit drug trade. This came after an apparent confrontation between the Comuneros del Sur faction of the Ejército de Liberación Nacional (ELN) and dissidents from the 29th Front of the FARC. As Héctor Silva Ávalos and Ángela Olaya stated in an InSight Crime article, "The massacre has revealed the ticking time bomb that threatens this part of the country, marked both by the absence of the state and the efforts of illegal armed groups to take control of its key drug trafficking economy." The authors attributed the causes of the massacre to failures in the implementation of the FARC peace agreement, especially in the construction of infrastructure and secure conditions for communities and ex-guerrillas, and stated that the incident showed "how acute post-conflict challenges have opened up possibilities for other actors to recycle the region's illegal economies."[11]

At the end of February 2017 President Santos had ordered an accelerated rate of public force occupation of former FARC territories. He said, "I have instructed the minister of defense to accelerate and strengthen the fulfillment of the plan for occupation and consolidation in the territories where the FARC were present, to guarantee the tranquility of the inhabitants."[12] The Nariño case in November, however, shows that this policy was not completely effective.

A final problem in the implementation was protection of former FARC members, especially if they were electoral candidates. In mid-January 2018 the FARC website reported that "more than thirty" had been killed.[13] The fear was that FARC candidates would be assassinated as Unión Patriótica ones had been after the Betancur peace agreement.

Difficulties in Congress and the Judiciary

In 2017 Congress held extra sessions to consider the Special Jurisdiction for Peace (Jurisdicción Especial para la Paz, JEP). In March as the Senate anticipated its final vote, Minister of Defense Luis Carlos Villegas said, "It is the most important legislation of the package completed because it is for the implementation of mechanisms of justice that will allow for ending the dispute among the people who participated in the conflict."[14] At the beginning of the session, it was difficult to obtain a quorum because members of Uribe's Centro Democrático party did not attend. This was a way of blocking the legislation without voting against it. However, the call of President Santos to his Unidad Nacional coalition led to a final vote with sixty-one in favor and two against in the Senate. The principal debates had been about the judgment of military personnel, the treatment of civilians, the participation of former FARC members in politics, and the investigation of matters such as the drug trade.

In mid-November the Constitutional Court made its decision about the JEP. While in general the court found the law to be constitutional, it did make ten changes in it.[15] The most important were as follows:

> Former guerrillas could participate in politics, but the court could later decide that they could not continue given the crimes for which they had been convicted.

> Civilians could only be judged in the system if they chose to be. It was not mandatory.

> The same was the case for state agents who were not part of the armed forces.

Throughout the year, many of the difficulties in Congress came from the constant opposition of Senator Álvaro Uribe and his Centro Democrático party. In February José Obdulio Gaviria, a CD senator, said that, if his party won the 2018 presidential election, it would change the peace agreement. The same month, Uribe said that his party would go out into the streets to get signatures to support its position against the peace agreement.

As early as February 2017, in a communiqué the FARC explained failures and anticipated others. According to the leaders of the former guerrilla group, a bureaucratic labyrinth had appeared in the implementation of the agreement. The FARC noted how it had previously shown how that bureaucratic labyrinth had delayed the transitional zones and how the stuttering and lies of government officials had delayed the implementation. The communiqué concluded, "Thinking in good faith and for the sake of discussion, let us admit that it is indeed about that, about the disgraceful reality of a state which, after putting a seal on the most serious commitments, is unable to implement them in an efficient manner due to the obstruction and incompetence of its agents."[16] It was as if, for the first time, the FARC were learning about democracy, Colombian style. It also seemed that, one more time, the Colombian government was behaving in a way that came from its Spanish colonial heritage—making many formal rules but later not effectively implementing them.

The process of granting amnesty and conditional liberty to the demobilized FARC troops was slow also. Spanish jurist Enrique Santiago, advisor to the FARC, said in mid-February that, with a few exceptions, the judges and prosecutors were not granting amnesty or giving conditional liberty as called for in the Law of Amnesty. He added, "Without application of the amnesty and without the release of those members or collaborators of the FARC who have such right under the final agreement, it is irresponsible to intend to require the surrender of weapons."[17]

Despite the difficulties, some believed that there was much to be optimistic about. As the leader of a women's group said in an interview, "We should not expect that everything in the agreement will be put into effect at once. It would be better to put a long timeline on it, perhaps ten years. So, I will be happy if 10 percent of the agreement can be implemented over each of the next ten years."[18] In early January 2018, Jean Arnault, chief of the UN Mission in Colombia, gave a report on the last three months of 2017. He drew attention to the necessity of increasing the efforts to guarantee the transition of former guerrillas to civilian life and stressed the importance that the government have a presence in all parts of the country, saying, "The control of the territory by the state is inseparable from the presence of institutions." He added that many FARC members had shown that they were ready and able to work in agriculture, environmental protection, and crop substitution. He continued, "The president has taken the important step of recognizing the need for access to land ownership as an important incentive for reintegration, and a basic element of many reintegration processes."[19]

As 2018 began, it was clear that the future of the Santos-FARC peace agreement depended on the elections. Congressional elections were to be March 11. The first round of presidential elections was to be May 27, and if no candidate received a majority of the vote, a second round would be on June 17. The FARC would participate, having changed the name of its party to the Common Alternative Revolutionary Force (Fuerza Alternativa Revolucionaria del

Común, FARC). The National Electoral Council recognized it on October 31, 2017. As a result, the article modifying the acronym of the party ("la FARC") was different from that of the guerrilla group ("las FARC").

It seemed clear that the future of the peace agreement depended on the results of these elections. If a Centro Democrático president, or someone in an alliance with the Uribe party won, he or she would attempt to change the agreement. If a candidate who supported the agreement won, she or he would try to continue with the implementation.

A lengthy analysis of this came in an email from one political scientist whom I had interviewed: "Hypothesis #1: Likelihood of success of the peace agreement is directly related to who wins the presidential elections in 2018. (If the candidates from the right—Uribe's appointed candidate or Vargas Lleras— win, the agreement will be in trouble; if the center-left coalition candidate wins, anyone from de la Calle to Fajardo, the peace agreement's chances will improve.) The caveat is whether the electoral results for the FARC presidential candidate will determine or not the peace agreement's legitimacy. Even de la Calle in an interview with the Caracol TV news director tonight said, 'People don't like the FARC; they committed heinous crimes.'"[20]

In the first eight months of 2018, the overall level of violence continued to be historically low in Colombia as a whole. However, that was not the case in all of the country. One report was that, of the 242 municipalities in which the FARC had operated before the peace agreement was signed, insecurity persisted in 78 because of the presence of other armed groups.[21] To some degree, this violence came from the assassination of civil rights leaders in areas in which the FARC had dominated. In May the United Nations reported that 261 leaders had been murdered in the two years since the peace agreement became effective, as compared to 35 cases in 2013.[22]

On a positive note, the Special Jurisdiction for Peace began its processes in the second week of January 2018. In July the tribunal called for thirty-one former members of the FARC leadership to be tried for kidnapping. Later the same month, retired army colonel Juan Carlos Barrera appeared before the JEP. In 2008 President Uribe had removed Barrera and twenty-six other army officers from active service for their roles in the false positives (described in chapter 2). Generals Mario Montoya Uribe and William Torres Escalante also appeared before the high tribunal.

Yet, overall, little doubt remained by mid-2018 that the implementation of the peace agreement had difficulties. The analysts in *Semana* magazine stated that there were five issues that "have the peace process with the FARC either on the brink of the abyss or of success—if they are corrected."[23] The five issues were as follows:

1. Reincorporation. "Although the government has achieved important objectives such as the certification of the members of the FARC, the opening of savings accounts, access to subsidies and affiliation to the health system, it fell short" in other long-term projects meant to ensure ex-combatants a dignified life, making the agreement's future uncertain.

2. Substitution of illegal coca crops. Eleven rural districts linked to the project received a promised monthly allowance during the first year, but there was no support for short-cycle projects that would have provided a quick income and improved their quality of life.

3. The legitimacy of the JEP. There were delays in the normative architecture. Only fifteen days before the first electoral round, still missing were the Constitutional Court's review of the statutory law and congressional approval of the procedural rules.

4. Rural reform. "Although solving the agrarian problem is essential to building a stable and lasting peace, the issue seems to be closer to sinking than to surfacing. The comprehensive proposal of rural development with emphasis on the territory, aimed at overcoming the poverty and inequality gap, hangs in the balance." Rural reform was "on low heat" and showed signs of repeating past failures.

5. Deadly blow to politics. The image of the Fuerza Alternativa Revolucionaria del Común failed in its first electoral contest. "The political landing of the FARC, one of the points that had made the most progress during the implementation, lost momentum in the last month."

THE ELECTION OF IVÁN DUQUE

Just as Colombian democracy affected the peace accords with the FARC, as seen in the October 2016 plebiscite and the slowness of Congress in the 2017 implementation, the same was the case in the 2018 elections. In them, the Centro Democrático became the political party with the largest number of seats in Congress, and its candidate, Iván Duque, won the presidential election.

Congressional elections in Colombia are by the proportional representation system. Each of the thirty-two departments has a number of seats based on its population. The entire nation is the electoral district for the election of the 100 members of the Senate, meaning that a party only has to receive 1 percent of the national vote to elect one senator.

In the March 11 congressional elections, the Centro Democrático won the largest number of seats in each house of the legislative body, with 19 of the 100 seats in the Senate and 33 of the 172 seats in the Chamber of Representatives. The Cambio Radical party won 15 seats in the upper house and 20 in the lower house, while three parties lost seats. The Partido de la U fell from 21 senators to 14 and from 27 representatives to 25 in the lower house. However, the Partido de la U, together with the traditional Liberal and Conservative Parties, still won 45 percent of the congressional seats. The parties on the left, Alianza Verde, Polo Democrático, and Docencia, won 20 percent of the vote. Alianza Verde went from 5 seats in the Senate to 15 and from 6 to 9 in the Chamber. As the new Congress met and coalitions were formed, President Duque had majority support in the Senate and more support in the lower house than the organized opposition against him.

For years Colombians had wondered how the FARC would do if it could offer electoral candidates. The 2018 congressional elections gave the first information. In elections that were relatively free from violence, candidates of the FARC party gained less than 0.5 percent of the vote, winning no seats in either house of Congress. According to the terms of the peace agreement, however, the FARC party has five members in each house of Congress.

Six candidates vied in the May 27 first round of the presidential election. After the candidates of the center of the ideological spectrum failed to form a coalition behind one candidate, Iván Duque of the Centro Democrático was first in the balloting with 39 percent of the vote while former M-19 member and former mayor of Bogotá Gustavo Petro came in second with 25 percent. As a result, the second round was between a candidate whose party was the most critical of the peace process and another whose party and background supported it.

The parties of the losing candidates immediately began lining up behind the two candidates for the June 17 second round. Petro and Duque had radically different proposals. On election day, Duque received 10,373,080 votes (54 percent) to Petro's 8,034,189 votes (42 percent). Not only did the Centro Democrático candidate win the overall vote, but he came in first in twenty-four of the thirty-two departments and nineteen of the thirty-two departmental capital cities.

Iván Duque became the youngest president in recent Colombian history, turning forty-two only six days before his August 7 inauguration. Born in Bogotá, Duque obtained a law degree from Sergio Arboleda University, a master's degree in economic law from American University, and another in management and public policy at Georgetown University. He worked in the Inter-American Development Bank and served one term as a senator from 2014 to 2018. He coordinated the activities of Álvaro Uribe in Washington soon after Uribe's presidency ended. The former president hand-picked Duque to be the Centro Democrático presidential candidate.

After the first round of the presidential election, attempting to downplay fears that he would dramatically change the agreement with the FARC, Duque told supporters, "We don't want to tear up the accord." Instead, he said he planned to improve the accord to achieve "peace with justice."[24] After winning the second round in June, the president-elect said that former FARC members who had been found guilty of crimes against humanity should not hold seats in Congress. While not against the Special Jurisdiction for Peace, he believed that proportional punishments, truth, justice, and reparation were needed. He added, "If we have a member of Congress convicted of crimes against humanity, how will the victims feel? If they are prosecuted, they must leave Congress and have the FARC assign someone else." Congressional members of the Centro Democrático, at about the same time, said that they intended to offer proposals to adjust the peace agreement.[25]

In his inaugural address, Duque invited all to "create a great pact for Colombia, to build a country, to build a future, and to put the things that unite us above our differences." Later he stated, "Today a new generation reaches the presidency of Colombia, motivated by service and not by the vain exercise of power, committed to the future and without anchors or prejudices of the past, inspired by social justice and security as the foundation of our freedoms, and dedicated to promoting understanding, teamwork, and consensus building." He added that his plan was "to govern Colombia with unwavering values and principles, overcoming the divisions of left and right, overcoming with grassroots dialogue the prickly feelings that invite social division. I want to govern Colombia in the spirit of building and never destroying." The new president concluded, "Let us Colombians work for progress! Let us work for development, let us work with hope, with joy, and for the collective happiness!"[26]

At this writing, it is far from clear what the effect of the Duque presidency is going to be on the FARC peace agreement and its implementation. As shown above, the Centro Democrático is a minority party in Congress and coalitions with other parties will be necessary for any success. Some of Duque's statements, both during the campaign and after his election, presented his ideas. How many of them he will be able to carry out remains to be seen.

Writing in *Semana*, journalist María Jimena Duzán left no doubt what direction she thought the Duque presidency would take. She wrote, "We have been notified: The Uribistas are going to come to power with the intention of tearing down what Santos constructed with the peace agreement and are determined to stop all that remains to be implemented." Later she added, "For Uribe's followers, that peace is a peace with impunity that pierces our rule of law, but at the same time they have opposed without blushing the military going to tell the truth to the JEP."[27]

FINAL WORDS

What will Colombia be like twenty-five years from now? Will the peace agreement, as in El Salvador, bring a much-needed cease-fire but little else? Or will the other changes called for in the agreement really take place? One of the key questions concerns the source of the money that is needed for the reforms. As political scientist Fernando Cepeda Ulloa wrote in September 2018, "Neither in last year or in this one or next year will there be a budget to finance the generous compromises in the final peace agreement."[28]

After more than fifty years studying Colombia, I've learned not to predict. In the past, whether in the case of the new constitution of 1991, the end of the Medellín and Cali drug cartels in the 1990s, or the paramilitary demobilization of the first decade of the new millennium, the results have not been what either Colombian politicians and academic experts or I had expected.

Some people have argued that the magical realism of Nobel laureate Gabriel García Márquez was not fiction but a description of his country. Colombian lawyer, university professor, and columnist Francisco Barbosa did not go that far but said, "There is no room for close comparisons with other realities; Colombia's is special. A country that for a large part of its history has been characterized by the partial building of institutions, forgetting part of its rural territories; an obvious lack of respect for life, but a deep love for speeches; a strong conviction for the defense of family values, but a disapproval of difference; a pure love for form but a familiar disdain for substance; a pride in our present but a deliberate forgetfulness of our past; an admiration for foreign rules and a constant derision of our own."[29]

While Barbosa's argument does have some validity, comparative analysis does also. Just as the two sides, in their peacemaking negotiations used experiences from other countries, Colombian leaders might look elsewhere for successes and failures in peace building. In her book about El Salvador twenty-five years after its peace treaty, Christine J. Wade describes "captured peace." She shows how "those in power seek to preserve their own interests at the expense of their professed commitment to peacebuilding," Wade concludes that, even after a treaty negotiated with international assistance, a meaningful transitional justice process was absent. One political party was using war narrative in the course of everyday politics, civil society was often viewed as a threat to the status quo, and application of economic policies favored the elites. The result was that "economic policies failed to reduce inequality, promote development, or generate sufficient employment opportunities."[30]

Given these results, it is of little wonder that almost 50 percent of the respondents in a public opinion poll twenty years after the treaty signing in El Salvador said that little or none of the peace accords had been fulfilled, and only 35 percent said that things were better since the signing of the accords.[31] One might hope that in Colombia in 2041, twenty-five years after the 2016 Second Final Agreement, peace building will have brought improvements.

Nevertheless, it seems fitting to end this book with some notes of optimism, as voiced by former Spanish president Felipe González and Colombian journalist María Jimena Duzán. González stated, "The peace agreement is not perfect, but it is the best thing that has happened in Colombia in the last 50 years."[32] Responding to criticisms of the peace process by Tomás Carrasquilla, the first minister of finance in the Duque administration, María Jimena Duzán wrote, "I cannot agree less with the minister. To say that the demobilization of the FARC was not positive for the country is to deny the thousands of lives that have been saved since these guerrillas silenced their rifles.—Homicide rates are the lowest of the last 42 years.—And although it is true that violence did not vanish from the country and that there are factions that have rearmed themselves, the armed struggle in Colombia was finally banished from our cosmogony [view of the universe]. And its burial began on the day that the FARC silenced their rifles, and it concluded when they were defeated at the polls in the past legislative elections."[33]

The unanswered question is, will the Duque administration seize this window of opportunity to implement the agreement, as the Santos administration did to negotiate it? As a result, will the Santos agreement with the FARC be like the Uribe agreement with the paramilitary groups, pretty on paper but with few concrete results other than the cease-fire? In the Uribe case, I concluded that it was positive that at least not as many people were being killed by the paramilitary groups.[34]

At this point, at least not as many people are being killed as they were during the conflict with the FARC. In early 2019 my wife and I took a two-week bus trip through parts of Colombia that had been devastated by the violence. This church-sponsored trip, which included two FARC demobilization areas, would not have been possible if the Santos-FARC agreement had not been signed. Some scholar in the future will determine whether the more peaceful country continues in the years that come and whether anything else will come from the negotiations of President Juan Manuel Santos with the Fuerzas Armadas Revolucionarias de Colombia.

Appendix 1

Participants in the Peace Process

Álvaro Uribe Vélez (1952–), president 2002–2010, critic of the peace process as leader of the Centro Democrático party

Juan Manuel Santos (1951–), minister of defense during the Uribe presidency, president during negotiations

Sergio Jaramillo (1966–), served under Santos in the Ministry of Defense, high commissioner for peace, brains behind the peace process

Enrique Santos (1945–), president's brother, journalist and writer, key in secret negotiations

Pablo Catatumbo (Jorge Torres Victoria, 1953–), member of FARC high command, FARC spokesperson

Bill Ury (1952–), Harvard professor, bargaining expert, assisted government

Alfonso Cano (Guillermo León Sáenz Vargas, 1948–2011), FARC commander, favored peace process, killed in 2011 before it began

Timochenko (Rodrigo Londoño Echeverri, 1959–), FARC commander after 2011

Humberto de la Calle (1946–), vice president 1994–1997, government's chief negotiator

Rodrigo Granda (Ricardo González, 1950–), FARC foreign minister, FARC negotiator

Iván Márquez (Luciano Marín Arango, 1955–), member of FARC high command, FARC negotiator

Álvaro Leyva (1942–), Conservative Party politician, served as FARC member of the judicial commission

Carlos Antonio Lozada (Julián Gallo Cubillos, 1961–), member of FARC high command, FARC negotiator

Bernard Aronson (1946–), US assistant secretary of state for inter-American affairs 1989–1993, US special envoy named by President Obama

Appendix 2

Chronology of the Peace Agreement

2010

August 7	Juan Manuel Santos is inaugurated as president.
September	Santos tells his brother talks have begun.

2011

January	First secret contact occurs in the Cesar department.
July 15–16	Second secret contact occurs on the Venezuelan island of La Orchila
July 20–21	Third secret contact occurs on La Orchila.

2012

January 22–23	Fourth secret contact occurs in Barinas, Venezuela.
February 23	Secret talks begin in Havana.
August 27	General Agreement of Havana for the End of Armed Conflict in Colombia is announced.
October 16–17	Formal installation of the dialogue table occurs in Oslo, Norway.
November 15	Dialogue begins in Havana.

2013

May 26	First agreement, "Towards a New Colombian Countryside: Comprehensive Rural Reform," is announced.
November 6	Agreement on political participation is announced.

2014

May 15	Agreement about drug trade is announced.
August 16	First group of victims testify.

2015

June 3	Agreement is reached to set up a truth commission.
September 23	Joint communiqué announces Special Jurisdiction for Peace.
September 23	Santos and Timochenko agree on March 23, 2016, as the deadline to sign the final agreement.
December 15	Government and FARC negotiators release "Full Agreement on Victims."

2016

January 19	Decision is reached to create tripartite mechanism of monitoring and verification of agreement.

June 22	Government and FARC negotiators announce an agreement on the end of the conflict.
August 5	Government and FARC negotiators establish planning and execution phases, define operation of 23 Transitional Local Normalization Zones and 8 Transitional Normalization Spots, and itemize specific procedures and a timeline to be developed during the cease-fire and laying down of arms.
August 12	Government and FARC negotiators announce an agreement on a mechanism for selection of the judges of the Special Jurisdiction for Peace.
August 24	Government and FARC negotiators announce that they have reached final agreement.
September 26	Final agreement is signed in Cartagena.
October 2	Agreement is defeated in a plebiscite.
October 5	Santos meets with Uribe and then with other "No" leaders.
November 3	The government and the FARC begin negotiation of second final agreement.
November 14	Government and FARC negotiators reach agreement.
November 24	The government and the FARC sign the second final agreement.
November 29	Senate approves the second final agreement.
November 30	Chamber approves the second final agreement.
December 1	The government and the FARC declare the first day of the implementation of the agreement (D-Day).

Notes

Introduction

1. Harvey F. Kline, *Showing Teeth to the Dragons: State-Building by Colombian President Álvaro Uribe Vélez, 2002–2006* (Tuscaloosa: University of Alabama Press, 2009), chap. 3.

2. Interview 14, historian, October 27, 2017. In all interviews for this book, I explained the project and promised that I would not use the name of the interviewee or describe him or her in such a way that would allow identification. I think that this method leads to more honest responses. For more on the interviews informing this research, see the selected bibliography.

3. Eduardo Pizarro, *Una democracia asediada: Balance y perspectivas del conflicto armado en Colombia* (Bogotá: Grupo Editorial Norma, 2004), 46. All Spanish translations in this book were done by Dorothy Kline, MA in Spanish, who lived in Colombia for over four years and was a college and high school teacher of Spanish for over twenty years.

4. Charles Tilly, "Reflections on the History of European State-Making," in *The Formation of National States in Western Europe*, ed. Charles Tilly (Princeton, NJ: Princeton University Press, 1975), 6.

5. Francis Fukuyama, *State-Building: Governance and World Order in the 21st Century* (Ithaca, NY: Cornell University Press, 2004), 6.

6. I. William Zartman, "Ripeness," Beyond Intractability, August 2003, http://www.beyondintractability.org.

Chapter 1

1. The historical circumstances leading to these patterns are described in Harvey F. Kline, *Colombia: Democracy under Assault* (Boulder, CO: Westview, 1995), 30–34.

2. Alfonso López Michelsen, "Del origen de la violencia en Colombia," *El Tiempo*, July 14, 1991.

3. Since the word "peasant" has European implications that do not apply in Colombia, I prefer to use the Spanish word *campesino*, which simply means someone who lives in the country (*campo*) and usually refers only to the poor there, no matter what their land tenure status is.

4. Fabio Zambrano Pantoja, "Contradicciones del sistema político colombiano," *Análisis: Conflicto social y violencia en Colombia*, no. 1 (1988), 23, emphasis in the original.

5. Eduardo Santa, *Sociología política de Colombia* (Bogotá: Tercer Mundo, 1964), 44–48.

6. Marco Palacios, *Between Legitimacy and Violence: A History of Colombia, 1875–2002* (Durham, NC: Duke University Press, 2007), 127–28.

7. Palacios, *Between Legitimacy and Violence*, 168.

8. Michael J. LaRosa and Germán R. Mejía, *Colombia: A Concise Contemporary History* (Lanham, MD: Rowman & Littlefield Publishers, 2012), 95.

9. Interview 1, sociologist, May 24, 1994.

10. LaRosa and Mejía, *Colombia*, 79.

11. Harvey F. Kline, "The National Front: Historical Perspective and Overview," in *Politics of Compromise: Coalition Government in Colombia*, ed. R. Albert Berry, Ronald G. Hellman, and Mauricio Solaún (New Brunswick, NJ: Transaction Books, 1980), 68–69.

12. Palacios, *Between Legitimacy and Violence*, 153.

13. The term "consociational" was first used by Arend Lijphart, "Consociational Democracy," *World Politics* 21 (1969): 207–25, and was skillfully applied to the Colombian case by Jonathan Hartlyn, *The Politics of Coalition Rule in Colombia* (Cambridge: Cambridge University Press, 1988).

14. Francisco Leal Buitrago, "Defensa y seguridad nacional en Colombia, 1958–1993," in *Orden mundial y seguridad: Nuevos desafíos para Colombia y América Latina*, ed. Francisco Leal Buitrago, Juan Gabriel Tokatlian, and Rafael Pardo Rueda (Bogotá: Tercer Mundo Editores, 1994), 132.

15. Palacios, *Between Legitimacy and Violence*, 169.

16. On *foco* strategy, see Dictionary of Revolutionary Marxism, s.v. "foco theory," http://www.massline.org/Dictionary/index.htm.

17. Eduardo Pizarro, "Revolutionary Guerrilla Groups in Colombia," in *Violence in Colombia: The Contemporary Crisis in Historical Perspective*, ed. Charles Bergquist, Ricardo Peñaranda, and Gonzalo Sánchez (Wilmington, DE: Scholarly Resources Books, 1992), 177.

18. Alejandro Reyes Posada, *Guerreros y campesinos: Despojo y restitución de tierras en Colombia* (Bogotá: Editorial Planeta Colombiana, 2016), 17–18.

19. Geoffrey Ramsey, "FARC 'earns $2.4 to $3.5 billion' from drugs, says Colombian government," InSight Crime, October 24, 2012, https://www.insightcrime.org.

20. Philip Mauceri, "States, Elites, and the Responses to Insurgency," in *Politics in the Andes: Identity, Conflict, Reform*, ed. Jo-Marie Burt and Philip Mauceri (Pittsburgh, PA: University of Pittsburgh Press, 2004), 154–55.

21. "Pura Sangre: Después de los sucesos de Mejor Esquina, siguen las masacres en varias regiones del país," *Semana*, May 17, 1988, 26.

22. Armando Neira, "Aparece el MAS," ColombiaLink, December 2, 1981, http://www.colombianlink.com.

23. Palacios, *Between Legitimacy and Violence*, 243.

24. Ley 35 de 1982 (noviembre 19), "Por la cual se decreta una amnistía y se dictan normas tendientes al restablecimiento y preservación de la paz," Ministerio de Justicia y del Derecho, http://www.suin-juriscol.gov.co.

25. Francisco Barbosa, *¿Justicia transicional o impunidad? La encrucijada de la paz en Colombia* (Bogotá: Ediciones B, 2017), 50.

26. Barbosa, *¿Justicia transicional o impunidad?*, 46.

27. Ana María Bejarano, "Estrategias de paz y apertura democrática: Un balance

de las administraciones Betancur y Barco," in *Al filo del caos: Crisis política en la Colombia de los años 80*, ed. Francisco Leal Buitrago and León Zamosc (Bogotá: Tercer Mundo Editores, 1990), 93–96.

28. "Historia del M-19," Caracol, November 2, 2005, http://www.caracol.com.co.

29. Bejarano, "Estrategias de paz y apertura democrática," 115.

30. Harvey F. Kline, *State Building and Conflict Resolution in Colombia, 1986–1994* (Tuscaloosa: University of Alabama Press, 1999), 111–17.

31. Harvey F. Kline, *Chronicle of a Failure Foretold: The Peace Process of Colombian President Andrés Pastrana* (Tuscaloosa: University of Alabama Press, 2007), 43–45.

32. Kline, *Chronicle of a Failure Foretold*, 41–43.

33. Eduardo Pizarro Leongómez, "Respuesta a 'Gabino': De las armas a la política," *El Tiempo*, September 10, 2007.

34. "Renuncia en comisión de Notables," *El Tiempo*, September 6, 2001, http://www.eltiempo.com.

35. Kline, *Chronicle of a Failure Foretold*, 71–74.

36. Kline, *Chronicle of a Failure Foretold*, 49–125.

37. "Las Farc ganan un billón de pesos al trimestre con el narcotráfico," *El Tiempo*, June 15, 2004, http://www.eltiempo.com.

38. Reyes Posada, *Guerreros y campesinos*, 23, 25.

39. "Acuerdo de comandantes del 30 de noviembre al 7 de diciembre de 1998," fondo Acuerdos de comandantes, Archivo Centro de Estudios Históricos del Ejército, folio 1, cited in Jorge Mauricio Cardona Angarita, "La Reestructuración del Ejército de Colombia 1998–2000, Estudio de Caso del Ataque en la Quebrada el Billar" (senior thesis, Pontificia Universidad Javeriana, Bogotá, 2015), 81.

40. Interview 28, member of the Colombian bargaining team, Skype, August 16, 2018.

41. Rafael Pardo Rueda, "The Prospects for Peace in Colombia: Lessons from Recent Experience" (Inter-American Dialogue Working Paper, July 2002), 4.

42. Pardo Rueda, "The Prospects for Peace in Colombia."

Chapter 2

1. Departamento Nacional de Planeación, Dirección de Justicia y Seguridad. *Cifras de violencia 1996–2002*, no. 1 (2002).

2. "Lo bueno y lo malo del programa de soldados campesinos, tres meses después de haber comenzado," *El Tiempo*, June 2, 2003, http://www.eltiempo.com.

3. "'En septiembre, todo el país tendrá Policía', asegura el general Teodoro Campo," *El Tiempo*, January 22, 2003, http://www.eltiempo.com.

4. "Manifiesto Democrático—100 Puntos Álvaro Uribe Vélez," https://www.mineducacion.gov.co. For more detail about the eight years that Uribe was president, see Harvey F. Kline, *Showing Teeth to the Dragons: State-Building by Colombian President Álvaro Uribe Vélez, 2002–2006* (Tuscaloosa: University of Alabama Press, 2009), 252; and Harvey F. Kline, *Fighting Monsters in the Abyss: The Second Administration of Álvaro Uribe Vélez, 2006–2010.* (Tuscaloosa: University of Alabama Press, 2015), 252.

5. "Diálogo con terrorismo no funciona: Presidente Uribe," Presidencia de la Re-

pública, Centro de Noticias del Estado, December 26, 2002, http://historico.presidencia.gov.co.

6. "Una propuesta para pensar," *El Tiempo*, May 31, 2003, https://www.eltiempo.com.

7. "Extradición divide debate sobre ley de alternatividad penal para facilitar negociaciones," *El Tiempo*, March 23, 2004, https://www.eltiempo.com.

8. Bibiana Mercado, "El dilema entre juzgar o perdonar delitos atroces," *El Tiempo*, June 1, 2003, https://www.eltiempo.com.

9. Élber Gutiérrez and Javier Héndez, "Gobierno ofrece indulto a guerrilla y 'paras,'" *El Espectador*, September 8, 2002. For additional information about the approval of the Law of Justice and Peace, see Kline, *Showing Teeth to the Dragons*, chap. 3.

10. "Ley 975 de 2005," Diario Oficial, 45.980, July 25, 2005, http://www.cepal.org.

11. Interview 2, private foundation official, June 28, 2004.

12. Germán Giraldo Restrepo and Gabriel Marcella, "Transforming the Colombian Army during the War on Terrorism" (USAWC Strategy Research Project, March 15, 2006), www.dtic.mil.

13. "Colombia, A Positive Country," Presidencia de la República, Servicio de Noticias del Estado (SNE), October 30, 2006, last accessed October 30, 2007, http://www.presidencia.gov.co.

14. "Red de cooperación ciudadana es diferente a red de informantes," Presidencia de la República, SNE, September 9, 2002, http://www.presidencia.gov.co.

15. "En 2005 gobierno pagó $7.716 millones en recompensas," Presidencia de la República, SNE, December 28, 2005, last accessed October 30, 2007, http://www.presidencia.gov.co.

16. For more details, see Kline, *Showing Teeth to the Dragons*, 45–48.

17. Ministerio de Defensa, *Logros de la Política de Consolidación de la Seguridad Democrática—PCSD*, June, 2010; Ministerio de Defensa Nacional, *Logros de la Política Integral de Defensa y Seguridad para la Prosperidad*, March 2011.

18. Interview 6, sociologist, October 23, 2017.

19. "Los 'Urabeños', la banda criminal que más tiene integrantes," *El Tiempo*, September 25, 2012, http://www.eltiempo.com.

20. "Falso positivo ocurrido en 1990," *El Tiempo*, May 22, 2013, http://www.eltiempo.com.

21. Sergio Jaramillo, "Lo que hizo posible la paz con las Farc," *El Tiempo*, July 24, 2018, https://m.eltiempo.com.

22. María Jimena Duzán, *Santos: Paradojas de la paz y del poder* (Bogotá: Penguin Random House, 2018), 73–74.

23. Interview 15, sociologist, October 30, 2017.

24. Interview 16b, sociologist, email, November 6, 2017.

25. Interview 10, political scientist, October 25, 2017.

26. Interview 13, economist, October 27, 2017.

27. Interview 17a, sociologist, November 2, 2017.

28. Francisco Barbosa, *¿Justicia transicional o impunidad?* (Bogotá: Ediciones B, 2017), 262.

29. Interview 25, sociologist and journalist, telephone, November 15, 2017.

30. Interview 28, member of governmental negotiation team, Skype, August 16, 2018.

31. For more detail about the operation, see Kline, *Fighting Monsters in the Abyss*, 96–97.

32. "Operación Jaque fue determinante en la búsqueda de la paz: Presidente Santos," Presidencia de la República, July 29, 2018, http://es.presidencia.gov.co.

33. "De la guerrilla robusta del Caguán a las Farc acorraladas de hoy," *El Tiempo* September 2, 2012, 4.

34. Alejandro Reyes Posada, *Guerreros y campesinos: Despojo y restitución de tierras en Colombia* (Bogotá: Editorial Planeta Colombiana, 2016), 31.

35. Reyes Posada, *Guerreros y campesinos*, 30.

Chapter 3

1. Harvey F. Kline, *Fighting Monsters in the Abyss: The Second Administration of Colombian President Álvaro Uribe Vélez, 2006–2010* (Tuscaloosa: University of Alabama Press, 2015), 175.

2. "Juan Manuel Santos renunció al Mindefensa," *El Espectador*, May 18, 2009, https://www.elespectador.com.

3. "De la guerrilla robusta del Caguán a las Farc acorraladas de hoy," *El Tiempo* September 2, 2012, 4.

4. María Jimena Duzán, *Santos: Paradojas de la paz y del poder* (Bogotá: Penguin Random House, 2018), 84.

5. Interview 15, sociologist, October 30, 2017.

6. Eduardo Pizarro, *Cambiar el futuro: Historia de los procesos de paz en Colombia (1981–2016)* (Bogotá: Penguin Random House Grupo Editorial, 2017), 268.

7. "Juan Santos Sworn in as Colombia's 59th President," CTV News, August 7, 2010, http://www.ctvnews.ca.

8. Sergio Jaramillo, "Lo que hizo posible la paz con las Farc," *El Tiempo*, July 24, 2018, http://www.eltiempo.com.

9. Interview 15, sociologist, October 30, 2017.

10. Fernán E. González González, *Poder y violencia en Colombia*, 5th ed. (Bogotá: Odecofi-Cinep, 2016), 488.

11. Interview 26, political analyst and leader of victims' group, November 17, 2017.

12. "Santos dice que Chávez es su nuevo mejor amigo," *Semana*, November 8, 2010, https://www.semana.com.

13. Interview 16b, sociologist, email, November 6, 2017.

14. Enrique Santos Calderón, *Así empezó todo: El primer cara a cara secreto entre el gobierno y las FARC en la Habana* (Bogotá: Intermedio Editores, 2014), 21.

15. Interview 17b, sociologist, email, January 17, 2018.

16. Duzán, *Santos*, 101.

17. Humberto de la Calle, "Paz y justicia no son agua y aceite," chap. 4 in *Revelaciones al final de una guerra: Testimonio del jefe negociador del gobierno colombiano en la Habana* (Bogotá: Penguin Random House Grupo Editorial, 2019), Kindle.

18. Duzán, *Santos*, 105–6.

19. Duzán, *Santos*, 106–7.

20. Jaramillo, "Lo que hizo posible la paz con las Farc," *El Tiempo*, July 24, 2018.

21. "'Hasta la tumba por la paz' dice el presidente Santos,'" *El Tiempo*, June 16, 2015, https://www.eltiempo.com.

22. Interview 15, sociologist, October 30, 2017.

23. Jaramillo, "Lo que hizo posible la paz con las Farc," *El Tiempo*, July 24, 2018.

24. Duzán, *Santos*, 100–101.

25. "Santos condiciona eventual diálogo de paz con Farc," *El Tiempo*, January 26, 2011, https://www.eltiempo.com.

26. González González, *Poder y violencia en Colombia*, 484.

27. Jaramillo, "Lo que hizo posible la paz con las Farc," *El Tiempo*, July 24, 2018.

28. Santos Calderón, *Así empezó todo*, 26.

29. Interview 16a, sociologist, November 1, 2017.

30. Interview 16b, sociologist, email, November 6, 2017.

31. Jaramillo, "Lo que hizo posible la paz con las Farc," *El Tiempo*, July 24, 2018.

32. De la Calle, "Cómo terminamos la guerra," chap. 8 in *Revelaciones*.

33. Santos Calderón, *Así empezó todo*, 25.

34. Interview 17b, sociologist, email, January 17, 2018.

35. Peter Beaumont, "Fidel Castro and Hugo Chávez Played Role in Colombia's Peace Talks with Farc," *The Guardian*, October 13, 2012, https://www.theguardian.com.

36. Jaramillo, "Lo que hizo posible la paz con las Farc," *El Tiempo*, July 24, 2018.

37. Duzán, *Santos*, 91–92.

38. Duzán, *Santos*, 92.

39. Interview 15, sociologist, October 30, 2017.

40. Interview 6, sociologist, October 23, 2017.

41. Interview 9, political scientist, October 25, 2017.

42. Interview 12, historian, October 26, 2017.

43. Interview 17a, sociologist, November 2, 2017.

44. Duzán, *Santos*, 109.

45. Duzán, *Santos*, 110.

46. Duzán, *Santos*, 111–12.

47. Duzán, *Santos*, 112.

48. "Santos planteó condiciones para 'siquiera pensar' en diálogo con Farc," *El Tiempo*, February 8, 2011, https://www.eltiempo.com.

49. The agenda and operating rules contained within the General Agreement and included in the text are from "General Agreement for the Termination of the Conflict and the Construction of a Stable and Lasting Peace," issued by the peace delegations of the Colombian Government and FARC-EP, http://farc-epeace.org. Minor adjustments were made to facilitate reading.

50. "El 74,2% respalda diálogo: Encuesta," *El Tiempo*, August 25, 2012, https://www.eltiempo.com.

51. Santos Calderón, *Así empezó todo*, 47–48.

52. Alejandro Reyes Posada, *Guerreros y campesinos: Despojo y restitución de tierras en Colombia* (Bogotá: Editorial Planeta Colombiana, 2016), 394, 397.

53. Interview 9, political scientist, October 25, 2017.

54. Interview 15, sociologist, October 30, 2017.

55. Reyes Posada, *Guerreros y campesinos*, 30, 32.

56. Nicole Summers, "Colombia's Victims' Law: Transitional Justice in a Time of Violent Conflict?," *Harvard Human Rights Journal* 25 (2009): 225–26.

57. Reyes Posada, *Guerreros y campesinos*, 383–84.

58. De la Calle, "La verdad como estrategia," chap. 2 in *Revelaciones*.

59. De la Calle, "La verdad como estrategia," chap. 2 in *Revelaciones*.

60. González González, *Poder y violencia en Colombia*, 490.

61. "Delegados de Farc se contradicen sobre secuestrados en su poder," *El Tiempo*, December 3, 2012, https://www.eltiempo.com.

62. "Proceso de paz: Se reanudan las mesas de negociación entre Gobierno y Farc," *El Tiempo*, December 5, 2012, https://www.eltiempo.com.

63. De la Calle, "Tomar el conflicto por sus cuernos: Tierra y cultivos ilícitos," chap. 6 in *Revelaciones*.

64. "World Urbanization Prospects: The 2018 Revision," United Nations, Department of Economic and Social Affairs, Population Division, https://population.un.org.

65. "Farc dicen que seguirán secuestrando a militares y policías," *El Tiempo*, January 30, 2013, https://www.eltiempo.com.

66. "De la Calle les habla duro a las FARC," *Semana*, January 30, 2013, https://www.semana.com.

67. "Proceso de paz: Farc piden tierras para campesinos," *El Tiempo*, February 9, 2013, https://www.eltiempo.com.

68. Marisol Gómez, "Farc proponen ocho puntos para el uso de la tierra," *El Tiempo*, February 6, 2013, https://www.eltiempo.com.

69. De la Calle, "Tomar el conflicto por sus cuernos," chap. 6 in *Revelaciones*.

70. "Fedegán opina de propuestas agrarias en proceso de paz," *El Tiempo*, February 24, 2013, https://www.eltiempo.com.

71. Marisol Gómez Giraldo, "Conozca los pilares de la reforma agraria que se 'cocina' en Colombia," *El Tiempo*, February 23, 2013, https://www.eltiempo.com.

72. Jaramillo, "Lo que hizo posible la paz con las Farc," *El Tiempo*, July 24, 2018.

73. "Las FARC exigen una 'reforma agraria profunda,'" *Semana*, April 24, 2013, https://www.semana.com.

74. Summary and discussion of the agreement on a comprehensive agricultural development policy draws on Joint Communiqué, Havana. May 26, 2013, issued by the peace delegations of the Colombian Government and FARC-EP, http://www.altocomisionadoparalapaz.gov.co.

75. Marisol Gómez Giraldo, "Redistribuirán tres millones de hectáreas a 250 mil campesinos," *El Tiempo*, May 18, 2013, https://www.eltiempo.com.

76. Marisol Gómez Giraldo, "'No vamos contra minería ni inversión extranjera si se regulan': Farc," *El Tiempo*, May 20, 2013, https://www.eltiempo.com.

77. "'Celebramos este paso fundamental en La Habana': Santos," *El Tiempo*, May 26, 2013, https://www.eltiempo.com.

78. De la Calle, "No es el momento de las armas," chap. 5 in *Revelaciones*.

79. De la Calle, "Paz y justicia no son agua y aceite," chap. 4 in *Revelaciones*.

80. De la Calle, "Paz y justicia no son agua y aceite," chap. 4 in *Revelaciones*.

81. Summary and discussion of the FARC's ten-point proposal on political participation draws on "Las 10 propuestas de las Farc para la participación política," *El Tiempo*, June 19, 2013, https://www.eltiempo.com.

82. Milagros López de Guereño, "Farc proponen sustituir la Cámara de Representantes," *El Tiempo*, June 20, 2013, https://www.eltiempo.com.

83. "Semana clave en los diálogos de paz con las Farc," *El Tiempo*, June 22, 2013, https://www.eltiempo.com.

84. "Propuesta de Farc llevaría a 'constituyente contrarrevolucionaria,'" *El Tiempo*, June 19, 2013, https://www.eltiempo.com.

85. "De la Calle: 'Este es un acuerdo a tres bandas,'" *Semana*, November 6, 2013, https://www.semana.com.

86. Summary and discussion of the agreement on political rights draws on Joint Communiqué, Havana, November 6, 2013, issued by the peace delegations of the Colombian Government and FARC-EP, https://www.mesadeconversaciones.com.co.

87. Pizarro, *Cambiar el futuro*, 385.

88. Diego Alarcón, "'En 2013, la mesa de La Habana casi se levanta', Henry Acosta," *El Tiempo*, September 11, 2016, https://www.eltiempo.com.

89. Summary and discussion of the FARC's ten-point proposal concerning illicit drugs draws on "Propuestas de las FARC sobre drogas ilícitas," *Semana*, December 2, 2013, https://www.semana.com.

90. "National Program for the Substitution of the Illicit Use of Coca, Poppy or Marijuana Crops," January 14, 2014, issued by the peace delegation of the FARC-EP, accessed March 26, 2018, http://farc-epeace.org.

91. De la Calle, "No es el momento de las armas," chap. 5 in *Revelaciones*.

92. De la Calle, "No es el momento de las armas," chap. 5 in *Revelaciones*.

93. "'Nunca habíamos avanzado tanto' en negociaciones de paz: De la Calle," *El Tiempo*, December 21, 2013, https://www.eltiempo.com.

94. "Santos dice que proceso de paz se acaba si hay atentado contra una figura importante," *Semana*, January 22, 2014, https://www.semana.com.

95. De la Calle, "No es el momento de las armas," chap. 5 in *Revelaciones*.

96. "Paz: ¿escollo a la vista?," *Semana*, April 19, 2014, https://www.semana.com.

97. "Oposición quiere 'asustar' con 'versiones delirantes' sobre La Habana," *El Tiempo*, April 23, 2014, https://www.eltiempo.com.

98. "No somos una organización narcotraficante: Farc," *El Tiempo*, April 24, 2014, https://www.eltiempo.com.

99. "Colombia: Hacker Tried to Sabotage Peace Talks," Associated Press, May 6, 2014.

100. "Paso histórico cierra tercer punto de agenda de La Habana: Farc prometen 'romper relación con narcotráfico,' Gobierno priorizará sustitución de cultivos," *El Tiempo*, May 16, 2014, https://www.eltiempo.com.

101. Summary and discussion of the agreement on illicit drugs draws on "Entérese del proceso de paz," Oficina del Alto Comisionado para la Paz, June 2014, http://www.altocomisionadoparalapaz.gov.co.

102. "Paso histórico," *El Tiempo*, May 16, 2014.

103. María Isabel Rueda, "¿Llegó la hora?," *El Tiempo*, August 18, 2012, https://www.eltiempo.com.

104. León Valencia, "A diferencia del Caguán y Ralito," *Semana*, September 1, 2012, https://www.semana.com.

105. Rafael Nieto Loaiza, "El Clavo Ardiente," *El Colombiano*, September 2, 2012, https://www.elpais.com.co.

106. Óscar Iván Zuluaga, "La paz es la seguridad," *El Tiempo*, September 2, 2012, https://www.eltiempo.com.

107. William Zartman, "Ripeness," Beyond Intractability, August 2003, http://www.beyondintractability.org.

108. Gustavo Palomares, "Las Farc y la paz: 'Hurting Stalemate,'" *El Tiempo*, November 7, 2012, https://www.eltiempo.com.

109. "Uribe dice que el Gobierno está negociando con las FARC en Cuba," *Semana*, August 19, 2012, https://www.semana.com.

110. Óscar Iván Zuluaga, "Por qué me opongo a las negociaciones," *El Tiempo*, October, 28, 2012, https://www.eltiempo.com.

111. "¿Alguien espió a los negociadores de La Habana?," *Semana*, February 3, 2014, https://www.semana.com.

112. "Colombia Probes Reported Military Spying of Peace Negotiators," Reuters.com, February 4, 2014.

113. "Entrevista con el comandante del Ejército, general Juan Pablo Rodríguez," *El Tiempo*, January 31, 2014, https://www.eltiempo.com.

114. "Humberto de la Calle habla de los mitos sobre el proceso de paz," *El Tiempo*, January 22, 2014, https://www.eltiempo.com.

115. "Humberto de la Calle habla de los mitos sobre el proceso de paz," *El Tiempo*, January 22, 2014.

116. "Humberto de la Calle habla de los mitos sobre el proceso de paz," *El Tiempo*, January 22, 2014.

117. "Humberto de la Calle habla de los mitos sobre el proceso de paz," *El Tiempo*, January 22, 2014.

118. "Inconformismo genera tensión en la SAC," *Dinero*, March 10, 2014.

119. "Proceso de paz y sus retos con Centro Democrático," *Semana*, March 14, 2014, https://www.semana.com.

120. "Proceso de paz es 'una olla que comienza a oler mal': Pastrana," *El Tiempo*, March 27, 2014, https://www.eltiempo.com.

121. Interview 24, political scientist, November 14, 2017.

Chapter 4

1. Text from the FARC statement issued upon the signing of the agreement on illicit drugs is from "Statement FARC-EP on Partial Agreement Illicit Drugs," May 16, 2014, issued by the peace delegation of the FARC-EP, accessed March 27, 2018, http://farc-epeace.org. Minor adjustments were made to facilitate reading.

2. Medófilo Medina, "Las implicaciones de convocar a las víctimas en el proceso de paz: Análisis sobre cuáles son las consecuencias políticas de incluir a los más afectados del conflicto," *El Tiempo*, June 13, 2014, https://m.eltiempo.com.

3. "Víctimas, punto central en Cuba antes de segunda vuelta presidencial," *El Tiempo*, June 3, 2014, https://m.eltiempo.com.

4. Sergio Jaramillo, "Lo que hizo posible la paz con las Farc," *El Tiempo*, July 24, 2018, https://m.eltiempo.com.

5. Delegación de paz de las FARC-EP, "Una Nueva Colombia sí es posible: Los retos de la paz y los problemas que enfrenta el Proceso en el contexto de la campaña electoral," press conference, July 6, 2014, in *La biblioteca del proceso de paz con las FARC-EP* (Bogotá: Presidencia de la República, Oficina del Alto Comisionado para la Paz, 2018), vol. 5, pt. 1, pp. 1, 97, http://www.altocomisionadoparalapaz.gov.co.

6. The list is from "Statement of Principles for the Discussion of Item 5 of the Agenda: Victims," June 7, 2014, issued by the peace delegations of the Colombian Government and FARC-EP, http://www.altocomisionadoparalapaz.gov.co.

7. "Farc dice que responsabilidad por víctimas llega hasta la Presidencia," *El Tiempo*, July 19, 2014, https://m.eltiempo.com.

8. "Las fuerzas militares son las fuerzas é legítimas del estado: Declaración del gral (r) Jorge Enrique Mora Rangel," Equipo Paz Gobierno, June 5, 2014, http://equipopazgobierno.presidencia.gov.co.

9. Álvaro Sierra Restrepo, "Gobierno y FARC hablarán de cese al fuego y dejación de armas," *Semana*, August 5, 2014, https://www.semana.com.

10. "The Inauguration of the Historical Commission of the Conflict and Its Victims," August 21, 2014, issued by the peace delegation of the FARC-EP, accessed March 27, 2018, http://farc-epeace.org.

11. "Inauguration of the Historical Commission," August 21, 2014.

12. María Jimena Duzán, *Santos: Paradojas de la paz y del poder* (Bogotá: Penguin Random House, 2018), 116–18.

13. Duzán, *Santos*, 124.

14. Duzán, *Santos*, 126.

15. "Estos son los nuevos integrantes de la mesa en La Habana," *Semana*, July 27, 2015, https://www.semana.com.

16. María Isabel Rueda, "Ojalá sea la última vez: Es inaudito que, por quinta vez, las Farc nos impongan presidente," *El Tiempo*, June 14, 2014, https://m.eltiempo.com.

17. "La paz en aprietos," *Semana*, August 2, 2014, https://www.semana.com.

18. "La paz en aprietos," *Semana*, August 2, 2014.

19. Jorge Restrepo, "Cuánto delito aguanta un país," *El Tiempo*, July 18, 2014, https://m.eltiempo.com.

20. Juan Manuel Santos, "Intervención durante la posesión para el periodo presidencial 2014–2018," July 8, 2014, in *La biblioteca del proceso de paz con las FARC-EP*, vol. 5, pt. 1, pp. 146–47, http://www.altocomisionadoparalapaz.gov.co.

21. "Víctimas de las Farc viajarán a La Habana," *El Tiempo*, July 17, 2014, https://m.eltiempo.com.

22. The text of the list is from "Comprehensive Rights of Victims for Peace and National Reconciliation," September 3, 2014, issued by the peace delegation of the FARC-EP, accessed March 27, 2018, http://farc-epeace.org.

23. "Comprehensive Rights of Victims," September 3, 2014.

24. "Gobierno y Farc piden equilibrio en testimonios de víctimas," *El Tiempo*, August 5, 2014, https://www.eltiempo.com.

25. "Comunicado de la Delegación del Gobierno Nacional en la Mesa de Conversaciones en Cuba, a la opinión pública," July 29, 2014, issued by the peace delegation of the Colombian Government, http://wsp.presidencia.gov.co.

26. "Farc proponen crear fondo para la reparación integral de las víctimas," *El Tiempo*, September 7, 2014, https://m.eltiempo.com.

27. Interview 20, leader of women's group, November 8, 2017.

28. Interview 7, sociologist, October 23, 2017.

29. "Colombian LGBT groups endorse peace deal," *Washington Blade*, August 27, 2016, http://www.washingtonblade.com.

30. "FARC ratifican decisión de crear un movimiento político," *Semana*, February 7, 2015, https://www.semana.com.

31. "Farc propone reforma política y jurídica en Colombia durante diálogos," *El Tiempo*, December 13, 2014, https://m.eltiempo.com.

32. "Farc plantean reducción de las FF.MM. en un posconflicto," *El Tiempo*, December 12, 2014, https://m.eltiempo.com.

33. Daniel Valero, "Se busca seguir modelo de la gendarmeria de ese país," *El Tiempo*, January 25, 2015, https://m.eltiempo.com.

34. The list is based on information provided in Las delegaciones de paz del Gobierno Colombiano y las FARC-EP, "Finalización del Ciclo 32 de Conversaciones y los lineamientos y mandato de la Subcomisión Técnica del Punto 3," February 12, 2015, in *La biblioteca del proceso de paz con las FARC-EP*, vol. 5, pt. 1, pp. 487–90, http://www.altocomisionadoparalapaz.gov.co.

35. Daniel Valero, "Santos intercedería para evitar extradición de guerrilleros a EE. UU.," *El Tiempo*, March 1, 2015, https://m.eltiempo.com.

36. Interview 16a, sociologist, November 1, 2017.

37. "Países garantes piden esfuerzos para salvar proceso de paz en Colombia: Cuba y Noruega expresaron su preocupación por el recrudecimiento del conflicto en el país," *El Tiempo*, May 27, 2015, https://www.eltiempo.com.

38. "Santos: 'Los colombianos van a refrendar la paz,'" *Semana*, December 17, 2014, https://www.semana.com.

39. "Uribe propone 'congresito' para evaluar acuerdos de La Habana," *Semana*, December 29, 2014, https://www.semana.com.

40. "'Para los guerrilleros cero cárcel': Iván Márquez," *Semana*, February 23, 2015, https://www.semana.com.

41. "No habrá acuerdo que contemple un solo día de cárcel," *Semana*, March 3, 2015, https://www.semana.com.

42. "Comisión de alto nivel ya diseña justicia transicional de uniformados," *El Tiempo*, March 27, 2015, https://m.eltiempo.com.

43. Marisol Gómez Giraldo, "Forcejeo en La Habana," *El Tiempo*, April 11, 2015, https://www.eltiempo.com.

44. Delegación de paz de las FARC-EP, "Claves para agilizar el Proceso de Paz: Tres aspectos que dinamizarían el avance de las Conversaciones de Paz," May 21,

2015, in *La biblioteca del proceso de paz con las FARC-EP*, vol. 5, pt. 2, p. 195, http://www
.altocomisionadoparalapaz.gov.co.

45. "Proceso de paz: Las verdades incómodas del Gobierno y las FARC," *Semana*,
June 4, 2014, https://www.semana.com.

46. Las delegaciones de paz del Gobierno Colombiano y las FARC-EP, "Avances de
la discusión del Punto 5: Consideraciones generales a propósito de la Comisión para
el Esclarecimiento de la Verdad, la Convivencia y la No Repetición," June 4, 2015, in
La biblioteca del proceso de paz con las FARC-EP, vol. 5, pt. 2, pp. 225–36, http://www
.altocomisionadoparalapaz.gov.co.

47. Emma Rosser, "Colombian Government and FARC Rebels Announce Truth Commission in Event of Peace," Colombia Reports, June 4, 2015, http://colombiareports
.com.

48. Juan Forero and John Otis, "Colombia, FARC Guerrillas to Form Truth Commission," *Wall Street Journal*, June 4, 2015, https://www.wsj.com.

49. "¿Qué es lo que plantea el abogado de las Farc?," *Semana*, July 25, 2015, https://
www.semana.com.

50. "El histórico discurso del presidente Santos sobre el proceso de paz," *El Tiempo*,
September 23, 2015, https://www.eltiempo.com.

51. "Historic Agreement on Special Jurisdiction for Peace," September 24, 2015,
issued by the peace delegation of the FARC-EP, accessed March 27, 2018, http://farc
-epeace.org.

52. William Neuman, "Colombia's President Says Peace Talks Overcame Late Surprise," *New York Times*, September 25, 2015, https://www.nytimes.com.

53. Humberto de la Calle, "Declaración del jefe del equipo negociador, Humberto
de la Calle," October 2, 2015, http://www.altocomisionadoparalapaz.gov.co.

54. Joint Communiqué 60, "Regarding the Agreement for the Creation of a Special Jurisdiction for Peace," September 23, 2015, issued by the peace delegations of the
Colombian Government and FARC-EP, http://www.altocomisionadoparalapaz.gov.co.

55. Summary and discussion of points 2–10 of Memorandum 60 draws from Joint
Communiqué 60, September 23, 2015, http://www.altocomisionadoparalapaz.gov.co.

56. "Primeras diferencias entre Gobierno y FARC sobre acuerdo de justicia," *Semana*, September 29, 2015, https://www.semana.com.

57. "Primeras diferencias," *Semana*, September 29, 2015.

58. De la Calle, "Declaración," October 2, 2015.

59. De la Calle, "Declaración," October 2, 2015.

60. Delegación de paz de las FARC-EP, "Diez propuestas mínimas para garantizar
el fin del conflicto, la reconciliación nacional y la construcción de la paz estable y duradera," October 6, 2015, in *La biblioteca del proceso de paz con las FARC-EP*, 6:99–101,
http://www.altocomisionadoparalapaz.gov.co.

61. "'Se está avanzando en concentración de las FARC': Humberto de la Calle," *El
Tiempo*, October 28, 2015, https://www.eltiempo.com.

62. "Aclaración necesaria," December 3, 2015, issued by the peace delegation of
the FARC-EP, accessed March 27, 2015, www.pazfarc-ep.org.

63. "Peace Territories Should Become Laboratories of Reconciliation," December 1,

2015, issued by the peace delegation of the FARC-EP, accessed March 27, 2018, http:// farc-epeace.org.

64. "Octava propuesta sobre Fin del Conflicto, referida a 'Garantías de seguridad integral para la población en general y para el movimiento político en el que se transformen las FARC-EP,'" November 30, 2015, issued by the peace delegation of the FARC-EP, accessed March 27, 2015, http://www.pazfarc-ep.org.

65. "Octava propuesta sobre Fin del Conflicto," November 30, 2015, issued by the peace delegation of the FARC-EP.

66. See Harvey F. Kline, *Fighting Monsters in the Abyss: The Second Administration of Colombian President Álvaro Uribe Vélez, 2006–2010* (Tuscaloosa: University of Alabama Press, 2015), chap. 8.

67. "FARC Proposes Action Plan to Dismantle Paramilitary Structures," November 28, 2015, issued by the peace delegation of the FARC-EP, accessed March 27, 2018, http://FARC-epeace.org.

68. "FARC Proposes Action Plan to Dismantle Paramilitary Structures," November 28, 2015, issued by the peace delegation of the FARC-EP.

69. A copy of the agreement in English is available here: "Full Agreement on Victims," December 21, 2015, issued by the peace delegation of the FARC-EP, accessed March 27, 2018, http://farc-epeace.org. My summary of the agreement draws on this source.

70. Humberto de la Calle, "Declaración del jefe de la Delegación del Gobierno Nacional Humberto de la Calle," December 15, 2015, http://www.altocomisionadoparalapaz .gov.co. Capitalization in the original.

71. "Los 73 días cruciales para el proceso de paz," *El Tiempo*, January 9, 2016, https:// www.eltiempo.com.

72. "Fuerte choque de Germán Vargas y Carlos Holmes en Senado," *El Tiempo*, May 13, 2014, https://www.eltiempo.com.

73. Rafael Nieto Loaiza, "Reflexiones Sobre La Paz II," *El Colombiano*, May 25, 2014, http://www.elcolombiano.com.

74. "Óscar Iván Zuluaga se pronuncia sobre proceso de paz," *El Tiempo*, June 7, 2014, https://www.eltiempo.com.

75. "Santos: 'Colombia está aburrida de falsas acusaciones de Uribe,'" *Semana*, June 17, 2014, https://www.semana.com.

76. León Valencia, "No es cierto Uribe, no es cierto," *Semana*, July 5, 2014, https:// www.semana.com.

77. "Uribismo 'rechaza' la presencia de militares activos en La Habana," *El Tiempo*, August 21, 2014, https://www.eltiempo.com.

78. "Santos le exige a Uribe no 'sabotear' más el proceso," *Semana*, October 6, 2014, https://www.semana.com.

79. "'Afirmaciones del Centro Democrático son inexactas': Humberto de la Calle," *El Tiempo*, October 17, 2014, https://www.eltiempo.com.

80. "'Afirmaciones del Centro Democrático son inexactas': Humberto de la Calle," *El Tiempo*, October 17, 2014.

81. "Las respuestas del Gobierno a reparos del uribismo al proceso de paz," *El Tiempo*, October 22, 2014, https://www.eltiempo.com.

82. "Santos responde críticas del uribismo," *El Tiempo*, October 18, 2014, https://www.eltiempo.com.

83. Harvey F. Kline, *Chronicle of a Failure Foretold: The Peace Process of Colombian President Andrés Pastrana* (Tuscaloosa: University of Alabama Press, 2007), 123.

84. Presidencia de la República, "Declaración del presidente Juan Manuel Santos luego de la reunión este domingo en el Ministerio de Defensa," November 16, 2014, http://wp.presidencia.gov.co.

85. "FARC confirman que sí tienen al general Alzate," *Semana*, November 18, 2014, https://www.semana.com.

86. "The Peace Process Should Continue," November 18, 2014, issued by the peace delegation of the FARC-EP, accessed March 27, 2018, http://farc-epeace.org.

87. "Colombia: Agreement Is Reached to Release General Held by Rebels," *New York Times*, November 19, 2014, https://www.nytimes.com.

88. Marisol Gómez Giraldo, "Decisión de las Farc de liberar al oficial y otras cuatro personas, es señal de paz sin precedentes," *El Tiempo*, November 22, 2014, https://www.eltiempo.com.

89. "Editorial: Un año decisivo," *El Tiempo*, December 30, 2014, https://www.eltiempo.com.

90. "Farc proponen una comisión nacional para desmantelar paramilitarismo," *El Tiempo*, January 21, 2016, https://www.eltiempo.com.

91. Francisco Barbosa, "Proceso de paz en la Habana y cárcel para delitos atroces?," *El Tiempo*, November 17, 2014, https://www.eltiempo.com.

92. Álvaro Sierra Restrepo, "Las Farc y las víctimas: Sí, pero no," *El Tiempo*, November 6, 2014, https://www.eltiempo.com.

Chapter 5

1. "Cinco generales y un almirante viajan mañana a La Habana," *Semana*, March 1, 2015, https://www.semana.com.

2. Dag Nylander, Rita Sandberg, and Idun Tvedt, "Designing Peace: The Colombian Peace Process," Norwegian Centre for Conflict Resolution, April 4, 2018, https://noref.no.

3. "'No vamos a entregar el país': General (r) Mora Rangel," *Semana*, December 1, 2015, https://www.semana.com.

4. Marco León Calarcá, peace delegation of the FARC-EP, "Mixed Messages," FARC Communiqué, February 8, 2016, last accessed February 9, 2016, http://farc-epeace.org.

5. "Lo de La Guajira no fue un pequeño 'impasse': Comisionado de Paz," *El Tiempo*, February 23, 2016.

6. "Farc dicen que no se violaron protocolos en visita a La Guajira," *El Tiempo*, February 23, 2016, https://www.eltiempo.com.

7. "Las razones del Gobierno para no firmar aún el acuerdo final de paz," *El Tiempo*, March 23, 2016, https://www.eltiempo.com.

8. Humberto de la Calle, "Declaración del jefe de la delegación del Gobierno Humberto de la Calle," March 23, 2016, http://www.altocomisionadoparalapaz.gov.co.

9. Harvey F. Kline, *Chronicle of a Failure Foretold: The Peace Process of Colombian President Andrés Pastrana* (Tuscaloosa: University of Alabama Press, 2007), chap. 5.

10. "Farc dicen que lógica de la guerra no permitió firma el 23 de marzo," *El Tiempo*, March 24, 2016, https://www.eltiempo.com.

11. Marisol Gómez Giraldo, "La apuesta de las Farc que trancó las negociaciones," *El Tiempo*, March 26, 2016, https://www.eltiempo.com.

12. "Sin firma en La Habana, ¿y ahora qué?," *Semana*, March 26, 2016, https://www.semana.com.

13. "Sin firma en La Habana, ¿y ahora qué?," *Semana*, March 26, 2016.

14. Marta Ruiz, "Vamos a dejar hasta el último fusil," *Semana*, March 27, 2016, https://www.semana.com.

15. "Proceso de paz: Lo que hay, lo que falta y los cabos sueltos," *Semana*, March 22, 2016, https://www.semana.com.

16. "Expertos en justicia se integran a la mesa de diálogos en Cuba," *El País*, July 27, 2015, https://www.elpais.com.co.

17. "Proceso de paz: En la recta final," *Semana*, May 14, 2016, https://www.semana.com.

18. "Los seis pasos para blindar los acuerdos de La Habana," *Semana*, May 12, 2016, https://www.semana.com.

19. "Santos afirma que las Farc reconocen por primera vez la Constitución nacional," *El Heraldo*, May 13, 2016, https://www.elheraldo.co.

20. "Santos: 'Los colombianos van a refrendar la paz,'" *Semana*, December 17, 2014, https://www.semana.com.

21. Interview 8, political scientist, October 25, 2017.

22. Interview 27, writer and journalist, email, November 20, 2017.

23. Interview 16c, sociologist, email, April 12, 2018.

24. "Denuncian 'conejo' al plebiscito por la paz," *Semana*, May 18, 2016, https://www.semana.com.

25. Joint Communiqué 69, May 12, 2016, issued by the peace delegations of the Colombian Government and FARC-EP, http://www.altocomisionadoparalapaz.gov.co.

26. Susanne Jonas, *Of Centaurs and Doves: Guatemala's Peace Process* (Boulder, CO: Westview Press, 2000), chap. 8.

27. Joint Communiqué 72, May 25, 2016, issued by the peace delegations of the Colombian Government and FARC-EP, http://www.altocomisionadoparalapaz.gov.co.

28. "Las cuatro claves del comienzo del fin de la guerra," *El Tiempo*, June 22, 2016, https://www.eltiempo.com.

29. Interview 28, member of governmental negotiation team, Skype, August 16, 2018.

30. Joint Communiqué 75, June 22, 2016, issued by the peace delegations of the Colombian Government and FARC-EP, http://www.altocomisionadoparalapaz.gov.co.

31. "'Claro que haremos política, esa es nuestra misión de ser': Timochenko," *El Tiempo*, June 23, 2016, https://www.eltiempo.com.

32. Summary and discussion of the bilateral cease-fire and turning in of arms agreement draws on Joint Comminqué 76, June 22, 2016, issued by the peace delegations of the Colombian Government and FARC-EP, http://es.presidencia.gov.co.

33. "'En zonas de concentración el Estado rige plenamente': Mindefensa," *El Tiempo*, June 25, 2016, https://www.eltiempo.com.

34. Milagros López de Guereño, "'No habrá ningún despeje': Humberto de la Calle," *El Tiempo*, June 24, 2016, https://www.eltiempo.com.

35. Interview 20, leader of women's group, November 8, 2017.

36. Nick Miroff, "This U.S. Envoy Helped Colombia Forge Peace. His Departure Leaves a Vacuum," *Washington Post*, January 30, 2017, https://www.washingtonpost.com.

37. Sergio Gómez Maseri, "'Un triunfo amplio del sí ayudaría mucho a la paz': Bernie Aronson," *El Tiempo*, July 2, 2016, https://www.eltiempo.com.

38. "FARC renuncian a la extorsión y al reclutamiento," *Semana*, July 4, 2016, https://www.semana.com.

39. Acto Legislativo No. 1 de 2016, "Por medio del cual se establecen instrumentos jurídicos para facilitar y asegurar la implementación y el desarrollo normativo del acuerdo final para la terminación del conflicto y la construcción de una paz estable y duradera," July 7, 2016, http://es.presidencia.gov.co.

40. "Este es el frente de las Farc que amenaza con no desmovilizarse," *El Tiempo*, July 6, 2016, https://www.eltiempo.com.

41. "Jefes de Farc hablarán con frente que busca apartarse de proceso paz," *El Tiempo*, July 7, 2016, https://www.eltiempo.com.

42. "Santos a las FARC: El que no se desmovilice terminará en una tumba o en una cárcel," CNN Español, July 7, 2016, http://cnnespanol.cnn.com.

43. Joint Communiqué 82, July 24, 2016, issued by the peace delegations of the Colombian Government and FARC-EP, http://www.altocomisionadoparalapaz.gov.co.

44. "El debate del Gobierno y FARC sobre cuándo aplicar amnistía," *El Tiempo*, August 5, 2016, https://www.eltiempo.com.

45. "Todo listo para el fin de la guerra," *Semana*, August 6, 2016, https://www.semana.com.

46. Humberto de la Calle, "Declaración de Humberto de la Calle sobre los protocolos de cese al fuego y dejación de armas," August 5, 2016, http://www.altocomisionadoparalapaz.gov.co.

47. Joint Communiqué 88, "Mecanismo de selección de los magistrados de la Jurisdicción Especial para La Paz," August 12, 2016, issued by the peace delegations of the Colombian Government and FARC-EP, http://www.altocomisionadoparalapaz.gov.co.

48. José Marulanda, "'Si no hay amnistía, las Farc no ingresarán en zonas de ubicación,' FARC Marcos Calarcá," FARC Communiqué, August 20, 2016, last accessed August 23, 2016, http://farc-epeace.org.

49. "Los dos temas que tienen enredada la firma del acuerdo final," *Semana*, August 23, 2016, https://www.semana.com.

50. "'El país debe encarar debate de participación en política de las Farc.' Así lo señaló Humberto de la Calle," *El Tiempo*, August 16, 2016, https://www.eltiempo.com.

51. "¿Qué es lo más duro que viene después del acuerdo?," *Semana*, August 27, 2016, https://www.semana.com.

52. "¿Qué es lo más duro que viene después del acuerdo?," *Semana*, August 27, 2016.

53. "Preguntas y respuestas sobre el Acuerdo Final," August 24, 2016, Oficina del Alto Comisionado para la Paz, http://www.altocomisionadoparalapaz.gov.co.

54. Summary and discussion of the final agreement draws on "Acuerdo final para la terminación del conflicto y la construcción de una paz estable y duradera," August 24, 2016, issued by the peace delegations of the Colombian Government and FARC-EP, http://www.urnadecristal.gov.co.

Chapter 6

1. Alejandro Reyes Posada, *Guerreros y campesinos: Despojo y restitución de tierras en Colombia* (Bogotá: Editorial Planeta Colombiana, 2016), 401.

2. Interview 24, political scientist, November 14, 2017.

3. Acto Legislativo No. 1 de 2012, "Por medio del cual se establecen instrumentos jurídicos de justicia transicional en el marco del artículo 22 de la Constitución Política y se dictan otras disposiciones," July 31, 2012, http://wsp.presidencia.gov.co.

4. María Isabel Rueda, "Testigos de una refundación," *El Tiempo*, February 27, 2016, https://m.eltiempo.com.

5. Unless otherwise noted, the information and quotations in the paragraphs of this section are from these two sources: Andrés Pastrana, "'Se entregó el país en 72 horas': Andrés Pastrana," *El Tiempo*, February 28, 2016, https://m.eltiempo.com; "Refutan críticas de Andrés Pastrana a acuerdo con las Farc," *El Tiempo*, February 28, 2016, https://m.eltiempo.com.

6. "Proof Texting Definition," The Bible Study Site, http://www.biblestudy.org.

7. "Uribe recoge firmas en contra de acuerdos de paz con las FARC," *Semana*, June 4, 2016, https://www.semana.com.

8. "Santos acusó a Uribe de ofrecer más a las FARC," *Semana*, June 6, 2016, https://www.semana.com.

9. "Ésta es la carta de Santos a Uribe invitándolo a la reconciliación," *El Tiempo*, July 12, 2016, https://m.eltiempo.com.

10. Interview 24, political scientist, November 14, 2017.

11. Álvaro Uribe's thirteen tweeted objections to the final agreement as reported in "Impunidad, permisividad, falta de autoridad y de justicia y claudicación lo que hay en los acuerdos de La Habana," Centro Democrático, July 14, 2016, http://www.centrodemocratico.com.

12. "Cuatro interrogantes sobre el plebiscito," *Semana*, July 23, 2016, https://www.semana.com.

13. Interview 14, historian, October 27, 2017.

14. Interview 6, sociologist, October 23, 2017.

15. Interview 9, political scientist, October 25, 2017.

16. Sergio Jaramillo, "Lo que hizo posible la paz con las Farc," *El Tiempo*, July 24, 2018, https://m.eltiempo.com.

17. "Los motivos para rechazar lo acordado en La Habana con las Farc," *El Tiempo*, July 23, 2016, https://m.eltiempo.com.

18. "Pastrana tilda de 'golpe de Estado' el proceso de paz y rechaza el plebiscito," *Semana*, July 28, 2016, https://www.semana.com.

19. "'La consecuencia de que gane el "No" es la guerra': César Gaviria," *El Tiempo*, August 14, 2016, https://m.eltiempo.com.

20. Nicholas Casey, "Colombia and FARC Announce Deal to End the Americas' Longest War," *New York Times*, August 24, 2016, https://www.nytimes.com.

21. "Uribe dirá 'Sí' a la paz pidiendo a electores que voten 'No' al plebiscito," *Semana*, August 3, 2016, https://www.semana.com.

22. "Uribismo oficializa su decisión de votar por el 'No' en el plebiscito," *El Tiempo*, August 3, 2016, https://m.eltiempo.com.

23. "Uribismo le dice a Gaviria que acuerdos son 'impunidad disfrazada,'" *El Tiempo*, August 14, 2016, https://m.eltiempo.com.

24. "Los cinco sapos del acuerdo de La Habana," *Semana*, September 25, 2016, https://www.semana.com.

25. Interview 18, political scientist, November 6, 2017.

26. Eduardo Pizarro, *Cambiar el futuro: Historia de los procesos de paz en Colombia (1981–2016)* (Bogotá: Penguin Random House Grupo Editorial, 2017), 380.

27. "Plebiscito: Polarización entre 'fachos' y 'castro-chavistas,'" *Semana*, September 3, 2016, https://www.semana.com.

28. "Los caminos cruzados de Pastrana y Uribe, entre amores y odios," *Semana*, September 2, 2016, https://www.semana.com.

29. "Los cinco sapos del acuerdo de La Habana," *Semana*, September 24, 2016.

30. "Gina le agua el voto cristiano al Gobierno," *La Silla Vacía*, August 10, 2016. https://lasillavacia.com.

31. "Ideología de género, el caballo de batalla del No al plebiscite," *Semana*, September 9, 2016, https://www.semana.com.

32. "Ideología de género," *Semana*, September 9, 2016.

33. Alfredo Molano Jimeno and Marcela Osorio Granados, "Votos por oraciones," *El Espectador*, September 11, 2016, http://www.elespectador.com.

34. Molano and Osorio, "Votos por oraciones," *El Espectador*, September 11, 2016.

35. Interview 7, sociologist, October 23, 2017.

36. Interview 8, political scientist, October 25, 2017.

37. Interview 20, leader of women's group, November 8, 2017.

38. Interview 18, political scientist, November 6, 2017.

39. Interview 6, sociologist, October 23, 2017.

40. Interview 19, historian, November 8, 2017.

41. Interview 14, historian, October 27, 2017.

42. "Colombian Opposition to Peace Deal Feeds Off Gay Rights Backlash," *New York Times*, October 8, 2016, https://www.nytimes.com.

43. "Álvaro Uribe regaña a Vélez por revelar la estrategia del No," *Semana*, October 6, 2016, https://www.semana.com.

44. "La cuestionable estrategia de campaña del No," *El Espectador*, October 6, 2016, https://www.elespectador.com.

45. "FARC están preparadas para la guerra urbana si fracasa proceso de paz," *Semana*, June 6, 2016, https://www.semana.com.

46. "'Si el plebiscito no se aprueba volvemos a la guerra. Así de sencillo': Presidente Santos," Presidencia de la República, Servicio de Noticias del Estado (SNE), June 16, 2016, http://es.presidencia.gov.co.

47. "Por qué fracasaron las encuestas en el plebiscito por la paz en Colombia," *El Comercio*, October 3, 2016, https://www.elcomercio.com.

48. "De ganar el No, habría un desastre nacional" *Semana*, September 7, 2016, https://www.semana.com.

49. "Prefiero mil veces ver a los guerrilleros en el Congreso que reclutando niños: Presidente Santos," Presidencia de la República, SNE, September 2, 2016, http://es.presidencia.gov.co.

50. María Jimena Duzán, *Santos: Paradojas de la paz y del poder* (Bogotá: Penguin Random House, 2018), 11, 19.

51. "Polarización del país, reflejada en resultados del escrutinio," *El Tiempo*, October 2, 2016, https://m.eltiempo.com.

52. Francisco Barbosa, *¿Justicia transicional o impunidad?* (Bogotá: Ediciones B, 2017), 81.

53. Catalina Lobo-Guerrero, "'Déjenos transformar el país en un país desarrollado, y esa es mi sanción': Romaña," La Silla Vacía, September 20, 2016, http://lasillavacia.com.

54. Interview 26, political analyst and leader of victims' group, November 17, 2017.

55. Interview 16a, sociologist, November 1, 2017; interview 19, historian, November 8, 2017.

56. Interview 6, sociologist, October 23, 2017.

57. Vladimir Flórez, "Un plebiscito innecesario: Ningún mandatario en Colombia había sometido a votación acuerdo alguno alcanzado con insurgentes," *El Tiempo*, October 4, 2017, https://m.eltiempo.com.

58. Interview 9, political scientist, October 25, 2017.

Chapter 7

1. "Éste es el nuevo pacto político que 'salvaría' el proceso de paz," *El Tiempo*, October 3, 2016, https://www.eltiempo.com.

2. María Jimena Duzán, *Santos: Paradojas de la paz y del poder* (Bogotá: Penguin Random House, 2018), 21.

3. "'El plebiscito no tiene efecto jurídico alguno': 'Timochenko,'" *El Tiempo*, October 3, 2016, https://www.eltiempo.com.

4. "Uribismo celebra la victoria del 'No' en el plebiscito," *El Tiempo*, October 2, 2016, https://www.eltiempo.com.

5. "Éste es el nuevo pacto político que 'salvaría' el proceso de paz," *El Tiempo*, October 3, 2016, https://www.eltiempo.com.

6. Sergio Jaramillo, "Lo que hizo posible la paz con las Farc," *El Tiempo*, July 24, 2018, https://m.eltiempo.com.

7. "Éste es el nuevo pacto político que 'salvaría' el proceso de paz," *El Tiempo*, October 3, 2016.

8. "'Las FARC mantienen su voluntad de paz': 'Timochenko,'" *Semana*, October 2, 2016, https://www.semana.com.

9. Jaramillo, "Lo que hizo posible la paz con las Farc," *El Tiempo*, July 24, 2018.

10. Joint Communiqué 2, "Final Agreement, Plebiscite and Ceasefire," October 7,

2016, issued by the peace delegations of the Colombian Government and FARC-EP, http://www.altocomisionadoparalapaz.gov.co.

11. "Sistematización opciones y propuestas voceros del no y lo acordado en el nuevo acuerdo," Oficina del Alto Comisionado para la Paz, November 22, 2016, http://www.altocomisionadoparalapaz.gov.co.

12. "Las tres primeras propuestas de Uribe para seguir con proceso de paz," *El Tiempo*, October 4, 2016, https://www.eltiempo.com.

13. "Renegociar el acuerdo de paz: ¿Es posible?," *Semana*, October 3, 2016, https://www.semana.com.

14. Summary and discussion of the top-five issues for Uribe and his followers draws on "Renegociar el acuerdo de paz: ¿Es posible?," *Semana*, October 3, 2016. Quotations are also from this source.

15. "'Si dejamos la paz en manos de Uribe, al país se lo lleva el diablo': FARC," *Semana*, October 4, 2016, https://www.semana.com.

16. Interview 17a, sociologist, November 2, 2017.

17. "La sinsalida en la que entró del proceso con las FARC," *Semana*, October 8, 2016, https://www.semana.com.

18. "Triunfo del No: El poder de los cristianos," *Semana*, October 8, 2016, https://www.semana.com.

19. "¿Aceptarán las FARC las 410 propuestas del No?," *Semana*, November 5, 2016, https://www.semana.com.

20. Jaramillo, "Lo que hizo posible la paz con las Farc," *El Tiempo*, July 24, 2018.

21. Duzán, *Santos* 325.

22. "¿Aceptarán las FARC las 410 propuestas del No?," *Semana*, November 5, 2016.

23. Jaramillo, "Lo que hizo posible la paz con las Farc," *El Tiempo*, July 24, 2018.

24. Humberto de la Calle, "Como terminamos la guerra," chap. 8 in *Revelaciones al final de una guerra: Testimonio del jefe negociador del gobierno colombiano en la Habana* (Bogotá: Penguin Random House Grupo Editorial, 2019), Kindle.

25. De la Calle, "Como terminamos la guerra," chap. 8 in *Revelaciones*.

26. Las delegaciones de paz del Gobierno Colombiano y las FARC-EP, "Acuerdo final para la terminación del conflicto y la construcción de una paz estable y duradera," December 11, 2016, http://www.altocomisionadoparalapaz.gov.co.

27. The ten most important changes in the second final agreement are from the *Semana* analysis: "Los 10 cambios fundamentales que trae el nuevo acuerdo," *Semana*, November 12, 2016, https://www.semana.com. Quotations appearing in the summary and discussion of this analysis are from the second final agreement: "Acuerdo final para la terminación del conflicto y la construcción de una paz estable y duradera," Oficina del Alto Comisionado para la Paz, November 29, 2016, http://www.altocomisionadoparalapaz.gov.co.

28. Interview 4, journalist, email, October 16, 2016.

29. Eduardo Pizarro, *Cambiar el futuro: Historia de los procesos de paz en Colombia (1981–2016)* (Bogotá: Penguin Random House Grupo Editorial, 2017), 381–82.

30. "Santos decidirá mecanismo de refrendación cuando tenga nuevo acuerdo," *El Tiempo*, November 2, 2016, https://www.eltiempo.com.

31. "El nuevo acuerdo no va a satisfacer a todos," *Semana*, November 12, 2016, https://www.semana.com.

32. "El nuevo acuerdo no va a satisfacer a todos," *Semana*, November 12, 2016.

33. Rafael Nieto Loaiza, "Hedor a Maduro," *El Colombiano*, November 27, 2016, http://www.elcolombiano.com.

34. "Cristianos siguen inconformes con el acuerdo con las Farc," *El Espectador*, November 18, 2016, http://www.elespectador.com.

35. Interview 8, political scientist, October 25, 2017.

36. Interview 16a, sociologist, November 1, 2017.

37. Interview 20, leader of women's group, November 8, 2017.

Chapter 8

1. Eduardo Pizarro, *Cambiar el futuro: Historia de los procesos de paz en Colombia (1981–2016)* (Bogotá: Penguin Random House Grupo Editorial, 2017), 383.

2. Interview 15, sociologist, October 30, 2017.

3. Sergio Jaramillo, "Lo que hizo posible la paz con las Farc," *El Tiempo*, July 24, 2018, https://m.eltiempo.com.

4. Jaramillo, "Lo que hizo posible la paz con las Farc," *El Tiempo*, July 24, 2018.

5. Harvey F. Kline, *Chronicle of a Failure Foretold: The Peace Process of Colombian President Andrés Pastrana* (Tuscaloosa: University of Alabama Press, 2007), 58.

6. Unless otherwise noted, information and quotations in the paragraphs of this section are from Jaramillo, "Lo que hizo posible la paz con las Farc," *El Tiempo*, July 24, 2018.

7. Fernán E. González González, *Poder y violencia en Colombia*, 5th ed. (Bogotá: Odecofi-Cinep, 2016), 485.

8. "Santos dice que Chávez es su nuevo mejor amigo," *Semana*, November 8, 2010, https://www.semana.com.

9. Interview 15, sociologist, October 30, 2017.

10. Interview 14, historian, October 27, 2017.

11. Interview 12, historian, October 26, 2017.

12. To maintain the confidentiality of the respondent, I do not mention which interview this was.

13. Humberto de la Calle, "No es el momento de las armas," chap. 5 in *Revelaciones al final de una guerra: Testimonio del jefe negociador del gobierno colombiano en la Habana* (Bogotá: Penguin Random House Grupo Editorial, 2019), Kindle.

14. Interview 28, member of governmental negotiation team, Skype, August 16, 2018.

15. Interview 14, historian, October 27, 2017.

16. Interview 17a, sociologist, November 2, 2017.

17. Interview 12, historian, October 26, 2017.

18. Interview 16a, sociologist, November 1, 2017.

Chapter 9

1. John Leddy Phelan, *The Kingdom of Quito in the Seventeenth Century: Bureaucratic Politics in the Spanish Empire* (Madison: University of Wisconsin Press, 1967), 3.

2. "'2017 terminó con la tasa de homicidios más baja en 42 años': Santos," *El Tiempo*, January 9, 2018, https://www.eltiempo.com.

3. María Jimena Duzán, "Un nobel sin paz," *Semana*, December 2, 2017, https://www.semana.com.

4. The Central Staff of the FARC-EP, "FARC-EP separa a 5 mandos de sus filas," December 13, 2016, http://www.farc-ep.co.

5. "Implementación será difícil si políticos no actúan con grandeza," *El Tiempo*, December 30, 2016, https://www.eltiempo.com.

6. "Choque de versiones entre FARC y Gobierno por zonas veredales," *Semana*, January 25, 2017, https://www.semana.com.

7. Presidencia de la República, "Lo que parecía imposible hoy es una realidad, las Farc se están desmovilizando," February 1, 2017, http://es.presidencia.gov.co.

8. "Entrega de armas de las Farc se inicia el 1. de marzo," *El Tiempo*, February 22, 2017, https://www.eltiempo.com.

9. Álvaro Sierra Restrepo, "D+100, y jugando con candela," *El Tiempo*, March 9, 2017, https://www.eltiempo.com.

10. "Concluye entrega de armas de las Farc a la ONU," *El Heraldo*, June 27, 2017, https://www.elheraldo.co.

11. Héctor Silva Ávalos and Ángela Olaya, "Massacre in Magüí Payán, Post-Conflict Colombia's Hidden Time Bomb," InSight Crime, December 7, 2017, https://www.insightcrime.org.

12. "Fuerza Pública acelerará ocupación de territorios donde estaban las Farc," Presidencia de la República, February 23, 2017, http://es.presidencia.gov.co.

13. "Asesinados dos excombatientes de la FARC en Antioquia," FARC-EP, January 16, 2018, http://www.farc-ep.co.

14. "Cúpula militar respalda a Santos en Justicia Especial para la Paz," *El Heraldo*, March 7, 2017, https://www.elheraldo.co.

15. Summary and discussion of the Constitutional Court's ten changes to the JEP draws on "Los 10 puntos con los que la corte puede haber salvado a la JEP," *Semana*, November 15, 2017, https://www.semana.com.

16. Gabriel Ángel, "¿Y qué pasa con la amnistía y el indulto acordados?," FARC-EP, February 8, 2017, https://www.farc-ep.co.

17. "El fiscal no debería actuar como si el proceso de conversaciones siguiera abierto," *Semana*, February 14, 2017, https://www.semana.com.

18. Interview 20, leader of women's group, November 8, 2017.

19. "Consejo de Seguridad alentó a superar retos en reincorporación de Farc," *El Tiempo*, January 10, 2018, https://www.eltiempo.com.

20. Interview 11b, political scientist, email, October 29, 2017.

21. "Tras paz con las Farc, inseguridad persiste en 78 municipios," *El Tiempo*, June 6, 2018, https://www.eltiempo.com.

22. "261 asesinatos de líderes en Colombia encienden las alarmas en las Naciones Unidas," *Semana*, May 11, 2018, https://www.semana.com.

23. Quotations concerning the five issues identified in *Semana* are from "5 puntos que explican por qué la paz está al límite," *Semana*, May 13, 2018, https://www.semana.com. Summary and discussion of these issues also draws on this source.

24. "Duque Promises Steady Hand If Elected in Runoff," STL News, May 27, 2018, https://www.stl.news.

25. "Exguerrilleros de Farc condenados no podrían estar en el Congreso," *El Tiempo*, July 17, 2018, https://www.eltiempo.com.

26. "'El narcotráfico y el secuestro no van a ser delitos conexos al delito político': Duque," *Semana*, August 7, 2018, https://www.semana.com.

27. María Jimena Duzán, "Notificados," *Semana*, June 30, 2018, https://www.semana.com.

28. Fernando Cepeda Ulloa, "¿Paz desfinanciada?," *El País*, September 22, 2018, https://www.elpais.com.co.

29. Francisco Barbosa, *¿Justicia Transicional o Impunidad? La Encrucijada de la Paz en Colombia* (Bogotá: Ediciones B, 2017), 16.

30. Christine J. Wade, *Captured Peace: Elites and Peacebuilding in El Salvador* (Athens: Ohio University Press, 2016), 9, 190.

31. Wade, *Captured Peace*, 188.

32. Presidencia de la República, "'El Acuerdo de Paz no es perfecto pero es lo mejor que ha ocurrido en Colombia en los últimos 50 años': Felipe González," May 31, 2018, http://es.presidencia.gov.co.

33. María Jimena Duzán, "Por qué no sirve el acuerdo de paz," *Semana*, August 25, 2018, https://www.semana.com.

34. Harvey F. Kline, *Showing Teeth to the Dragons: State-Building by Colombian President Álvaro Uribe Vélez, 2002–2006* (Tuscaloosa: University of Alabama Press, 2009), 171–74.

Selected Bibliography

INTERVIEWS

In this book, I draw from my interviews with twenty-eight individuals between 1994 and 2018. During a trip to Bogotá in October and November 2017, I conducted twenty face-to-face interviews and one phone interview. I interviewed another individual by email shortly after the trip and another by Skype almost a year later. On a number of occasions, I had follow-up interviews over email. Five interviews predate the 2017 Bogotá trip, with the earliest three having taken place while I was working on other books. In all cases, I guaranteed confidentiality.

When approaching potential interviewees, I explained the nature of the project and promised that I would neither use their names nor describe them in such a way that would allow informed people to identify them. I then asked the interviewees whether they agreed to those conditions. All did. During the interviews, I used no recording devices. On occasion, I took notes, always asking the interviewee's permission beforehand. Immediately after the interviews, I transcribed the responses. Hence, with the exception of email, any "quotations" that appear in this book are my reconstruction of what the interviewees said.

The following interviews, all of which were conducted face-to-face unless otherwise noted, informed the research behind this book.

1. Sociologist, May 24, 1994
2. Private foundation official, June 28, 2004
3. Member of Uribe administration, September 1, 2012
4. Journalist, email, October 16, 2016
5. War college professor, email, February 12, 2017
6. Sociologist, October 23, 2017
7. Sociologist, October 23, 2017
8. Political scientist, October 25, 2017
9. Political scientist, October 25, 2017
10. Political scientist, October 25, 2017
11. (a) Political scientist, October 26, 2017; (b) email, October 29, 2017
12. Historian, October 26, 2017
13. Economist, October 27, 2017

14. Historian, October 27, 2017
15. Sociologist, October 30, 2017
16. (a) Sociologist, November 1, 2017; (b) email, November 6, 2017; (c) email, April 12, 2018
17. (a) Sociologist, November 2, 2017; (b) email, January 17, 2018
18. Political scientist, November 6, 2017
19. Historian, November 8, 2017
20. Leader of women's group, November 8, 2017
21. Psychologist, November 10, 2017
22. Political scientist, November 10, 2017
23. Feminist activist, November 10, 2017
24. Political scientist, November 14, 2017
25. Sociologist and journalist, telephone, November 15, 2017
26. Political analyst and leader of victims' group, November 17, 2017
27. Writer and journalist, email, November 20, 2017
28. Member of governmental negotiation team, Skype, August 16, 2018

BOOKS

Barbosa, Francisco. *¿Justicia transicional o impunidad? La encrucijada de la paz en Colombia*. Bogotá: Ediciones B, 2017.

De La Calle, Humberto. *Revelaciones al final de una guerra: Testimonio del jefe negociador del gobierno colombiano en la Habana*. Spanish ed. Bogotá: Penguin Random House Grupo Editorial Colombia. 2019. Kindle.

Duzán, María Jimena. *Santos: Paradojas de la paz y del poder*. Bogotá: Penguin Random House, 2018.

Fukuyama, Francis. *State-Building: Governance and World Order in the 21st Century*. Ithaca, NY: Cornell University Press, 2004.

González González, Fernán E. *Poder y violencia en Colombia*. 5th ed. Bogotá: Odecofi-Cinep, 2016.

Hartlyn, Jonathan. *The Politics of Coalition Rule in Colombia*. Cambridge: Cambridge University Press, 1988.

Jonas, Susanne. *Of Centaurs and Doves: Guatemala's Peace Process*. Boulder, CO: Westview Press, 2000.

Kline, Harvey F. *Chronicle of a Failure Foretold: The Peace Process of Colombian President Andrés Pastrana*. Tuscaloosa: University of Alabama Press, 2007.

———. *Colombia: Democracy under Assault*. Boulder, CO: Westview Press, 1995.

———. *Fighting Monsters in the Abyss: The Second Administration of Colombian President Álvaro Uribe Vélez, 2006–2010*. Tuscaloosa: University of Alabama Press, 2015.

———. *Showing Teeth to the Dragons: State-Building by Colombian President Álvaro Uribe Vélez, 2002–2006*. Tuscaloosa: University of Alabama Press, 2009.

———. *State Building and Conflict Resolution in Colombia, 1986–1994*. Tuscaloosa: University of Alabama Press, 1999.

LaRosa, Michael J., and Germán R. Mejía. *Colombia: A Concise Contemporary History*. Lanham, MD: Rowman and Littlefield, 2012.

Oficina del Alto Comisionado para la Paz. *La biblioteca del proceso de paz con las FARC-EP*. 11 vols. Bogotá: Presidencia de la República, Oficina del Alto Comisionado para la Paz, 2018. http://www.altocomisionadoparalapaz.gov.co.

Palacios, Marco. *Between Legitimacy and Violence: A History of Colombia, 1875–2002*. Durham, NC: Duke University Press, 2007.

Pizarro, Eduardo. *Cambiar el futuro: Historia de los procesos de paz en Colombia (1981–2016)*. Bogotá: Penguin Random House Grupo Editorial, 2017.

———. *Una democracia asediada: Balance y perspectivas del conflicto armado en Colombia*. Bogotá: Grupo Editorial Norma, 2004.

Reyes Posada, Alejandro. *Guerreros y campesinos: Despojo y restitución de tierras en Colombia*. Bogotá: Editorial Planeta Colombiana, 2016.

Santos Calderón, Enrique. *Así empezó todo: El primer cara a cara secreto entre el gobierno y las FARC en la Habana*. Bogotá: Intermedio Editores, 2014.

Wade, Christine J. *Captured Peace: Elites and Peace Building in El Salvador*. Athens: Ohio University Press, 2016.

ESSAYS

Bejarano, Ana María. "Estrategias de paz y apertura democrática: Un balance de las administraciones Betancur y Barco." In *Al filo del caos: Crisis política en la Colombia de los años 80*, edited by Francisco Leal Buitrago and León Zamosc, 57–124. Bogotá: Tercer Mundo Editores, 1990.

"Historia del M-19." Caracol. November 2, 2005. http://www.caracol.com.co.

Kline, Harvey F. "The National Front: Historical Perspective and Overview." In *Politics of Compromise: Coalition Government in Colombia*, edited by R. Albert Berry, Ronald G. Hellman, and Mauricio Solaún, 59–103. New Brunswick, NJ: Transaction Books, 1980.

Leal Buitrago, Francisco. "Defensa y seguridad nacional en Colombia, 1958–1993." In *Orden mundial y seguridad: Nuevos desafíos para Colombia y América Latina*, edited by Francisco Leal Buitrago, Juan Gabriel Tokatlian, and Rafael Pardo Rueda, 131–72. Bogotá: Tercer Mundo Editores, 1994.

Licklider, Roy. "How Civil Wars End: Questions and Methods." In *Stopping the Killing: How Civil Wars End*, edited by Roy Licklider, 3–19. New York: New York University Press, 1993.

Lijphart, Arend. "Consociational Democracy." *World Politics* 21 (1969): 207–25.

Mauceri, Philip. "State, Elites, and the Response to Insurgency." In *Politics in the Andes: Identity, Conflict, Reform*, edited by Jo-Marie Burt and Philip Mauceri, 146–63. Pittsburgh, PA: University of Pittsburgh Press, 2004.

Neira, Armando. "Aparece el MAS." ColombiaMania. December 2, 1981. http://www.colombiamania.com.

Pardo Rueda, Rafael. "The Prospects for Peace in Colombia: Lesson from Recent Experience." Inter-American Dialogue Working Paper, July 2002.

Pizarro, Eduardo. "Revolutionary Guerrilla Groups in Colombia." In *Violence in Colombia: The Contemporary Crisis in Historical Perspective*, edited by Charles Bergquist, Ricardo Peñaranda, and Gonzalo Sánchez, 169–94. Wilmington, DE: Scholarly Resources Books, 1992.

Rosser, Emma. "Colombian Government and FARC Rebels Announce Truth Commission in Event of Peace." Colombia Reports. June 4, 2015. http://colombiareports .com.

Summers, Nicole. "Colombia's Victims' Law: Transitional Justice in a Time of Violent Conflict?" *Harvard Human Rights Journal* 25 (2009): 219–35.

Tilly, Charles. "Reflections on the History of European State-Making." In *The Formation of National States in Western Europe*, edited by Charles Tilly, 3–83. Princeton, NJ: Princeton University Press, 1975.

Zambrano Pantoja, Fabio. "Contradicciones del sistema político colombiano." *Análisis: Conflicto social y violencia en Colombia*, no. 1 (1988): 19–26.

Zartman, I. William. "Ripeness." Beyond Intractability. August 2003. http://www .beyondintractability.org.

GOVERNMENT DOCUMENTS

Departamento Nacional de Planeación, Dirección de Justicia y Seguridad. *Cifras de violencia 1996–2002*, no. 1 (2002).

Ley 35 de 1982 (noviembre 19). "Por la cual se decreta una amnistía y se dictan normas tendientes al restablecimiento y preservación de la paz." Ministerio de Justicia y del Derecho. http://www.suin-juriscol.gov.co.

WEBSITES

As part of my research, I accessed primary source material that was made available online during the peace negotiations. The Office of the President daily issued statements about government policy and published speeches by the president and other officials (http://es.presidencia.gov.co). The Office of the High Commissioner for Peace posted new information and articles on the peace processes (http://www.altocomisionadoparalapaz.gov.co). Other government agencies also maintained an online presence, and the government dedicated a special website to the negotiations while they were ongoing (http:// equipopazgobierno.presidencia.gov.co). The FARC published regularly on its own website (http://farc-epeace.org) and also dedicated a special website to the negotiations (http://www.pazfarc-ep.org), which made material available in various languages. The Centro Democrático party also expressed its views online (http://www.centrodemocratico.com).

In addition to the *New York Times*, the *Washington Post*, and the wire services, I collected information for this book through daily reading of the following Colombian media sources: *El Colombiano* (http://www.elcolombiano .com), a Medellín newspaper; *El Espectador* (http://www.elespectador.com), a

Bogotá newspaper; InSight Crime (https://www.insightcrime.org), a nonprofit organization for the investigation and analysis of organized crime; *El País* (http://www.elpais.com.co), a Cali newspaper; *Semana* (http://www.semana .com), a magazine that posts new articles daily between its weekly issues; and *El Tiempo* (http://www.eltiempo.com), a Bogotá newspaper.

Index